LINCOLN CHRISTIAN COLLEGE

P9-CQK-828

# Memory and Forgetting in English Renaissance Drama

Engaging with current debates over the nature of subjectivity in early modern England, this fascinating and original study examines sixteenth- and seventeenth-century conceptions of memory and forgetting, and their importance to the drama and culture of early modern England. Garrett A. Sullivan, Jr. discusses memory and forgetting as categories in terms of which a variety of behaviors – from seeking salvation to pursuing vengeance to succumbing to desire – are conceptualized. Drawing upon a range of literary and non-literary discourses, represented by treatises on the passions, sermons, anti-theatrical tracts, epic poems and more, Shakespeare, Marlowe and Webster stage "self-recollection" and, more commonly, "self-forgetting," the latter of which provides a powerful model for dramatic subjectivity. Focusing on works such as *Macbeth, Hamlet, Dr. Faustus* and *The Duchess of Malfi,* Sullivan reveals memory and forgetting to be dynamic cultural forces central to early modern understandings of embodiment, selfhood and social practice.

GARRETT A. SULLIVAN, JR. is Associate Professor of English at Pennsylvania State University. A recipient of a National Endowment for the Humanities/Folger Shakespeare Library long-term fellowship, he is the author of *The Drama of Landscape: Land, Property, and Social Relations on the Early Modern Stage*, is on the editorial board for *Renaissance Drama,* and is Associate Editor of *Shakespeare Studies.* He has published articles on Shakespeare, Marlowe, Marston, Spenser and others in a number of journals including *ELH, Shakespeare Quarterly* and *Renaissance Drama*, and has contributed to *The Cambridge Companion to English Literature, 1500–1600* (1999) and *The Cambridge Companion to Christopher Marlowe* (2004).

*Cambridge Studies in Renaissance Literature and Culture*

*General Editor*
STEPHEN ORGEL
Jackson Eli Reynolds Professor of Humanities, Stanford University

*Editorial board*
Anne Barton, *University of Cambridge*
Jonathan Dollimore, *University of York*
Marjorie Garber, *Harvard University*
Jonathan Goldberg, *Johns Hopkins University*
Peter Holland, *University of Notre Dame, Indiana*
Kate McLuskie, *University of Southampton*
Nancy Vickers, *Bryn Mawr College*

Since the 1970s there has been a broad and vital reinterpretation of the nature of literary texts, a move away from formalism to a sense of literature as an aspect of social, economic, political, and cultural history. While the earliest New Historicist work was criticized for a narrow and anecdotal view of history, it also served as an important stimulus for post-structuralist, feminist, Marxist, and psycho-analytical work, which in turn has increasingly informed and redirected it. Recent writing on the nature of representation, the historical construction of gender and of the concept of identity itself, on theatre as a political and economic phenomenon and on the ideologies of art generally, reveals the breadth of the field. Cambridge Studies in Renaissance Literature and Culture is designed to offer historically oriented studies of Renaissance literature and theatre which make use of the insights afforded by theoretical perspectives. The view of history envisioned is above all a view of our history, a reading of the Renaissance for and from our own time.

Recent titles include

Valerie Traub, *The Renaissance of Lesbianism in Early Modern England*
Joseph Loewenstein, *Ben Jonson and Possessive Authorship*
William N. West, *Theatres and Encyclopedias in Early Modern Europe*
Richmond Barbour, *Before Orientalism: London's Theatre of the East, 1576–1626*
Elizabeth Spiller, *Science, Reading and Renaissance Literature: The Art of Making Knowledge, 1580–1670*
Deanne Williams, *The French Fetish from Chaucer to Shakespeare*
Douglas Trevor, *The Poetics of Melancholy in Early Modern England*

A complete list of books in the series is given at the end of the volume

# Memory and Forgetting in English Renaissance Drama

*Shakespeare, Marlowe, Webster*

Garrett A. Sullivan, Jr.

CAMBRIDGE
UNIVERSITY PRESS

CAMBRIDGE UNIVERSITY PRESS
Cambridge, New York, Melbourne, Madrid, Cape Town, Singapore, São Paulo

Cambridge University Press
The Edinburgh Building, Cambridge CB2 2RU, UK

Published in the United States of America by Cambridge University Press,
New York

www.cambridge.org
Information on this title: www.cambridge.org//9780521848428

© Garrett A. Sullivan, Jr., 2005

This publication is in copyright. Subject to statutory exception
and to the provisions of relevant collective licensing agreements,
no reproduction of any part may take place without
the written permission of Cambridge University Press.

First published 2005

Printed in the United Kingdom at the University Press, Cambridge

*A catalogue record for this publication is available from the British Library*

ISBN-13 978-0-521-84842-8 hardback
ISBN-10 0-521-84842-3 hardback

Cambridge University Press has no responsibility for the persistence or accuracy
of URLs for external or third-party internet websites referred to in this
publication, and does not guarantee that any content on such websites is, or will
remain, accurate or appropriate.

# Contents

# Acknowledgments

I am grateful to Johns Hopkins University Press and Routledge for permission to reprint revised versions of chapters 2 ("'Be this sweet Helen's knell, and now forget her': Forgetting, Memory and Identity in *All's Well That Ends Well*," *Shakespeare Quarterly* 50.1 [1999]: 51–69) and 3 ("Lethargic Corporeality On and Off the Early Modern Stage," *Forgetting in Early Modern English Literature and Culture: Lethe's Legacies*, ed. Christopher Ivic and Grant Williams [London: Routledge, 2004]: 41–52).

At Penn State, I have relied upon the expertise and fellowship of a remarkable group of early modernists: Patrick Cheney, Michael Kiernan, Laura Knoppers, John Moore, Marcy North and Linda Woodbridge. I am indebted to all of them in different ways, but special thanks go to Patrick Cheney, who has been forced to hear (and read) far too much about forgetting.

I would like to thank hosts and audiences at the following institutions for providing the opportunity to try out many of the ideas in this book: the University of Aberdeen; Harvard University; the University of Maryland; the University of Pennsylvania; and Washington and Lee University. David Riggs, Anthony Dawson and Judith Haber were organizers of three terrific Shakespeare Association of America (SAA) seminars at which portions of this book were circulated; another portion was delivered as part of an SAA panel. Thanks to seminar leaders and members, and to the SAA, which has been crucial to the development of this project.

The completion of this book was made possible by a year-long fellowship (2002–2003) at the Folger Shakespeare Library. I am indebted to Penn State's College of the Liberal Arts for sabbatical release time, and to the Folger and the National Endowment for the Humanities for their invaluable fellowship support. Working for an extended period at the Folger is a rare pleasure, and I am extremely grateful to the wonderful library staff for all of their help. Thanks also to the Folger Institute for making it possible to participate in a weekend seminar on the arts of memory, co-directed by Lina Bolzoni and Mary Carruthers, in 2000. I am also happy to acknowledge the generosity of three Penn State organizations, the Research and Graduate Studies Office of the College of Liberal Arts, the Institute for the Arts and Humanities, and the Global Fund. Thanks to both Don Bialostosky and Robert Caserio, former and present heads of the English department, for their encouragement and support.

Warm thanks to my editor at Cambridge, Sarah Stanton, for her many efforts on behalf of this book. (Thanks also to Vicki Cooper, from whom Sarah took over the project.) In the final stages of preparing the manuscript, I also received excellent help from two Penn State students, Stephanie D'Antonio and Allison Scekeres.

This book has benefited greatly from the generosity and intellectual engagement of a number of friends and colleagues. In addition to those already mentioned, I would like to thank the following: Leeds Barroll, George Bent, Bill Carroll, Tom Cartelli, Greg Colon-Semenza, William Engel, Jen Fleissner, Jonathan Goldberg, Andy Gordon, Jay Grossman, Judith Haber, Richard Helgerson, David Hillman, Chris Ivic, Rayna Kalas, Jennifer Lewin, Zack Long, Carla Mazzio, Shannon Miller, Karen Newman, Scott Newstok, Lena Cowen Orlin, Andrew Penman, Kristen Poole, Anne Lake Prescott, Tom Rist, Mary Beth Rose, Katherine Rowe, Francesca Royster, Mike Schoenfeldt, Stuart Selber, Bill Sherman, Tyler Smith, Lyn Tribble, Grant Williams and Heather Wolfe. Extra special thanks are due to the following (and I hope they can work out why): Dan Beaver, Tim Donovan, Jim Egan, Mary Floyd-Wilson, Heather Hirschfeld, Coppélia Kahn, Jeff Masten, Gail Paster, Alan Stewart, Wendy Wall, Valerie Wayne, Stephanie Wilder, Eric Wilson and Susan Zimmerman. Stephen Orgel's interest in and support for this project has meant and continues to mean a great deal to me.

I remain deeply grateful for the help and support of my family. Thanks to my parents, Cathy and Garry; my sisters, Tracy, Amy and Sheila; my half-brother, Peirce; and my step-mother, Lorry.

This book is dedicated to Marie Hojnacki, with all my love.

# Introduction: planting oblivion

In Shakespeare's "Venus and Adonis," Venus is overcome with a desire whose effects are depicted in terms of forgetting:

> And careless lust stirs up a desperate courage,
>   Planting oblivion, beating reason back,
>   Forgetting shame's pure blush and honor's wrack.[1]

By "planting oblivion," Venus abandons herself to a lust that overrides modesty and honor. Her self-abandonment is prompted by the strong passion of sexual desire, which "stirs up a desperate courage." But how precisely is Venus's giving herself over to lust an act of forgetting? Does Venus (or, more broadly, anyone driven by desire) literally fail to recollect the demands of shame and honor? It makes more sense to understand the forgetting of shame and honor as encompassing not just cognition but the entire body's operations. Shame and honor prescribe a bodily comportment; they are the end result of a disciplining process that produces a certain type of (honorable, modest) subject and helps to shape that subject's interactions with the world.[2] To "forget" shame and honor, then, is to live in the world in terms different from those specified by that process, to act in terms of a different set of desires and imperatives, to become a different person. In this example, "forgetting" modesty and honor entails less a failure of memory than a transformation of self.

These three lines from "Venus and Adonis" describe the staking of a territorial claim: lust-driven courage beats reason back and plants its standard (oblivion), thereby announcing passion's victory. Or one can read this passage as reworking the familiar metaphor of the reason-regulated body as a well-tended garden. Venus's passionate courage plants the seeds of oblivion and, in the process of doing so, beats back the weeds of reason.[3] In either case, the passage reveals something important about forgetting in early modern literature and culture, that it is frequently associated with resistance to or the retooling of normative models for behavior. The lines from the poem also introduce other major topics of this book: the conceptualization of forgetting as a fully somatic, rather

1

than a narrowly cognitive, activity; the significance of humoral physiology (gestured toward here in the discussion of the passions) for that conceptualization; the relationship of forgetting (and memory) to bodily discipline; and forgetting's importance to the representation of selfhood in the work of early modern writers, primarily Shakespeare, Marlowe and Webster. All of these topics advance a simple but crucial point: that forgetting is historical. This study's central texts are dramatic ones from the late Elizabethan and Jacobean periods, but the book also considers memory and forgetting in a range of (literary and non-literary) discourses. Its ambition is to show that forgetting both undergirds the representation of specific somatic states and modes of action, and is central to the dramatic depiction of subjectivity. Although this book recognizes that forgetting cannot be construed outside of memory – indeed, discussion of the one can quickly turn into discussion of the other – it insists that we see forgetting as more than a mere failure of memory.[4] While seeking to do justice to the place of memory in a variety of early modern texts, the book's aim is to "plant oblivion" squarely amidst ongoing critical conversations about subjectivity, embodiment and early modern drama.

This chapter, which is divided into five sections, introduces the reader to the complex relations among memory, forgetting, identity and subjectivity that are a major emphasis of this book. The first section considers the significance of memory to early modern culture. The second begins to define the terms and the terrain of the book's analysis; it takes up three components of memory labeled memoria, recollection and remembering. The third focuses on connections between forgetting and subjectivity after first distinguishing between forgetting* and forgetfulness. (I have placed an asterisk after the word forgetting whenever it is used in the narrow sense described in the taxonomy outlined below. Without the asterisk, the word describes the broader category of which the defined element is a part. I usually do not use the asterisk when discussing other writers' texts.) The fourth section gives two examples of dramatic self-forgetting, while the fifth offers an overview of the book. Throughout, early modern conceptions of memory and forgetting are considered in relation to specific moments in period texts, including Richard Mulcaster's account of Elizabeth I's royal entry, Shakespeare's *Hamlet* and *The Taming of the Shrew* and Marlowe's *Tamburlaine the Great, Pt. 1*.

### The subject of memory and the remembering subject

In recent years, memory has become a crucial category for early modern studies. Historians have examined the state's attempt to eradicate one site of collective memory through the modification of the sacred calendar of

saint's days; similarly, they have argued that the Reformation changed
the relationship between the living and the dead by altering the ways in
which the former remembered the latter.[5] Studies such as these have
impacted criticism of the early modern stage, as in the recent work of
Huston Diehl, who discusses remembrance and revenge in light of
eucharistic controversies and the reformed last supper.[6] While these
works focus on "crises" of memory, the centrality of memory to early
modern culture is easily seen. Understood as the "Renaissance," this
period experienced a rebirth predicated upon the rediscovery of ancient
texts that had putatively been forgotten in the middle ages; the recollection of classical texts was crucial not only to the humanist project
but to the intellectual self-definition of those scholars engaged in it.
Printed and circulated widely in the Renaissance, such texts (in the terms
of a classical commonplace that achieved currency in this period)
triumphed over oblivion by re-entering both memory and history.[7]

Ancient texts provided early modern readers with exemplars, and, as
George Puttenham (among others) recognized, the logic of exemplarity
depends upon the operations of memory:

no kinde of argument in all the Oratorie craft, doth better perswade and more
universally satisifie then example, which is but the representation of old
memories, and like successes happened in times past. . .No one thing in the
world with more delectation reviving our spirits then to behold as it were in a
glasse the lively image of our deare forefathers, their noble and vertuous maner of
life, with other things autentike, which because we are not able otherwise to
attaine to the knowledge of, by any of our sences, we apprehend them by
memory.[8]

These "old memories" not only ornament successful arguments, they
engender physiological effects by "reviving our spirits." They also
provoke our emulation of "a noble and vertuous maner."

In terms that will be particularly important for the third chapter's
discussion of Donne, Marlowe and spiritual self-forgetting, Lina Bolzoni
elucidates the crucial significance of memory to Christianity:

The memory question. . .has. . .a central importance in the Christian religion: it
infuses the Mass, the liturgy, and the individual life of the Christian. To
remember (and keep alive) Christ's sacrifice, to remember the awful sufferings of
Hell and the delights of Paradise, to remember one's own sins to confess, to
remember at least a few prayers and the essential contents of the faith – all this is
essential, and it is on all this that salvation or eternal damnation depends. As
formerly for the classical orator, the art of memory becomes an indispensable
technique for the Christian preacher's profession, a technique, moreover, filled
with all the importance and meaning claimed for it. When we think that for
centuries the preacher speaks to a public of which the overwhelming majority is

illiterate, we can see that there is a clear need not only to remember the things to be said, but also to cause them to be remembered, to imprint them in a lasting way on the listeners' minds.[9]

Of course, the uses and significance of memory are different for Roman Catholicism than for Protestantism. Memory informed a host of Catholic practices, such as the founding of chantries in which the dead would be remembered through prayer:

Sacred stories, prayers, and images could also be understood to remind the saints of the devotee's presence so that they would intercede for that person's soul in heaven. Faith in the efficacy of prayers for the souls of the deceased encouraged strenuous and expensive attempts by individuals to keep their memory alive in the minds of the living, who it was believed could give them spiritual aid after their death.[10]

To remember the dead was to enact a series of social performances – from funeral processions and feasts to requiem masses to daily prayer to the production of monuments for the deceased – that served both as an ongoing engagement with the dead (who were understood to be in close proximity to the world of the living in a way that Calvinism did not allow) and as intercessionary acts designed to help hasten their passage to heaven. To forget the dead was to extend their stay in purgatory – the reason why pre-Reformation wills routinely stipulated that the living continue to remember the dead through prayer. The rise of English Protestantism, then, offers one example of how the meanings and uses of memory can change; funerary rituals still commemorated the loss of loved ones, but under Protestantism, and with Henry VIII's abolition of purgatory, "the dead were forcibly alienated from the community of the living. . .and gradually forgotten."[11]

Above, Bolzoni glancingly refers to the Ciceronian tradition, which construed memory as one of the five key elements of oratory.[12] The Christianizing of that tradition, along with the Aristotelian one (with Thomas Aquinas and Albertus Magnus combining elements of both), led to increasing emphasis on memory's relation to prudence; memory becomes integral to moral judgment.[13] In early modern discussions of faculty psychology, memory is also necessary to the construction of the rational subject. As Edward Reynoldes puts it, memory is "a joynt-worker in the operations of Reason."[14] As we shall see, memory is integral to various valorized models of selfhood.

More than any other topic, it is the arts of memory that have dominated the study of individual memory in the early modern period.[15] The underlying structure of the memory arts is described by Mary Carruthers:

The fundamental principle is to "divide" the material to be remembered into pieces short enough to be recalled in single units and to key these into some sort of rigid, easily reconstructable order. This provides one with a "random-access" memory system, by means of which one can immediately and securely find a particular bit of information, rather than having to start from the beginning each time in order laboriously to reconstruct the whole system.[16]

While the arts of memory are important for chapter 2, this study attempts to correct a critical overemphasis on artificial memory evident since at least the groundbreaking work of Frances Yates.[17] That being said, there is an additional, simpler reason for this book's emphases: the plays taken up here are not terribly interested in the arts of memory.[18] What Jonas Barish says of Shakespeare holds for the texts by Marlowe and Webster discussed in this book: "Shakespeare shows no interest in pigeonholing [memory] or classifying it as a separable psychological datum, nor does he show any curiosity about the so-called *artes memorativae*, that weird melange of mnemotechnics and occultism that dazzled so many Renaissance philosophers and scientists. He is, however, keenly interested in the dynamics of memory, in how it weaves itself into the intimate texture of our lives."[19]

The interest of Shakespeare, Marlowe and Webster in memory may be partly bred of its centrality to the theatrical enterprise: actors need to memorize lines in order to perform their roles. Put differently, for playwrights to emphasize memory and forgetting is for them to reflect upon the conditions of dramatic representation. At the same time, such emphasis opens up certain kinds of possibilities. Recall Shakespeare's frequent representation of characters – most prominently, Hotspur, Polonius and Cleopatra – forgetting what they are about to say.[20] These moments are metatheatrical, as they tease us with the prospect of an actor forgetting his lines. At the same time, they are representations of a character's interiority: to see someone in the act of forgetting is also to witness the staging of a thought process. Even in brief episodes such as these, Shakespeare explores relations among memory, forgetting, dramatic subjectivity and the conditions of theatrical representation. More broadly, insofar as each of these three playwrights – along with numerous other early modern dramatists – concerns himself with subjective experience and its representation, memory and forgetting are inevitable objects of dramatic inquiry.

Of course, there are additional ways in which memory is important to the early modern theatre. In the 1960s, Yates described possible connections between the structure of early modern English playhouses, specifically the Globe, and that of the memory theatre of Robert Fludd. Since then, others have linked the theatre and memory in a variety of ways, suggesting everything from the theatre's utilization of the iconography of the art of memory to its status as a powerful locus for the formation of national memory.[21] Defenders of the theatre such as Thomas Heywood argue that plays shaped the behavior of audience members for the better by providing positive exemplars – which, as we have seen, are "old memories" that provoke physiological change.[22] However, Shakespeare, Marlowe and Webster are suspicious or even scornful of the logic of exemplarity. We see this in *Dr. Faustus*, which simultaneously develops and overturns the model of exemplarity so obviously on offer in plays like *Everyman*. In *The Duchess of Malfi*, the figure her brothers ask the Duchess to emulate is compared to a funerary sculpture, an unattainable and undesirable ideal. And *Hamlet* is the story of a prince who cannot sustain the model of vengeance promulgated by the Ghost. In these texts, possible exemplars are on offer to protagonists and audience, and memory is central to their operation. But Shakespeare, Marlowe and Webster not only stage failures of exemplarity, they stress the inadequacies, and in some cases the perniciousness, of that model. In rejecting (or at least interrogating the terms of) exemplarity, these playwrights turn from memory to forgetting (as well as its cousins, lethargy and sleep) to construe differently relations between the subject and his social world.

Finally, one must stress that if memory is important for the drama and culture of early modern England, it is also a category whose capaciousness both lends to its utility and generates specific conceptual problems. Not all of the examples of memory discussed in this section describe the same kind of (cognitive, somatic or social) operation. Different critical understandings of memory can be placed along the following continuum: at one end, "memory" is an internal, cognitive operation (as in "the art of memory"), and at the other, it describes a set of material practices with an indeterminate relationship to that operation (as in rituals that are the expression of "collective" or "social" memory).[23] This book does not attempt to consider memory in all its manifestations. Instead, both memory and forgetting are discussed as interfaces between the individual subject and the social world, as patterns of behavior as well as cognitive events. The book will account for certain key aspects of both somatic activity and social practice, but from the perspective of the individual, and not the collective, subject.

### Memoria, recollection and remembering

As just mentioned, memory and forgetting are taken up in this book at the level of the individual subject; they describe forms of engagement with the physical and social worlds. Each of these forms is best understood as fully embodied; memory and forgetting prescribe particular modes of behavior and specify kinds of action. The following taxonomies aim to map the terrain of memory and forgetting as the two categories are taken up in this book. These taxonomies create artificial but heuristically important analytic distinctions between psychic, somatic and social performances that in practice are not easily distinguishable. Certain of these definitions might seem idiosyncratic, or at least at a remove from common understandings of the two categories. Nevertheless, it is through the development of this terminology that we can isolate those aspects of memory and forgetting that are of greatest importance to this study. The terms defined here will not be rigidly adhered to and differentiated between throughout the book. Instead, precise definitions of "memoria," "recollection," and "remembering" are offered in order to suggest all that can be at issue – from cognitive act to social performance – in the representations of memory taken up in this book. In such representations, the three terms (in some or all of their meanings) inform and overlap one another, and the same is true in the cases of "forgetting*" and "forgetfulness" as components of forgetting.

*Memoria* describes not only the faculty that stores images in the brain, but also the site of that storage (often metaphorized in the period as a treasury or a wax tablet, and occupying the hindmost ventricle in the brain); the images or traces that are stored there; and the process of their inscription or storage – here "memorization" is subsumed under the term "memoria." *Recollection* refers to the process by which memory traces are retrieved and brought into consciousness. Both memory and recollection, defined in much the same way as they are in Aristotle, might be considered purely psychological, and thus "internal," operations.[24] In fact, their fully internal nature is assumed by many influential accounts of memory in the western tradition; even St. Augustine, for whom memory is a vast space that is both limitless and the location of the divine, paradoxically understands it as at the same time fundamentally internal.[25]

Reading recollection and memoria in this way, however, raises difficulties. As suggested above, memory should be thought of as a fully embodied process that presupposes involvement with the environment. Recent work in cognitive science that stresses the notion of the embodied mind – of mind understood as a set of operations not only dispersed throughout the body, but across body and environment – has brought this point into focus.[26] Andy Clark provides two relevant examples of embodied mind that encompass what are here defined as memoria and recollection, the first being the use of external symbolic media to offload memory onto the world. Here we simply use the artifactual world of texts, diaries, notebooks, and the like as a means of systematically storing large and often complex bodies of data. [Second, w]e may also use simple external manipulations (such as leaving a note on the mirror) to prompt the recall, from onboard biological memory, of appropriate information and intentions at the right time.[27]

In the first example, memoria exists as written texts; in the second, recollection is a response to an environment altered in order to provoke the act of recall. These examples do not represent the production of prompts for the internalized operations of memoria and recollection, but *are* components of memoria and recollection themselves. As Clark has it, memoria and recollection occur through exchange with the environment, an exchange that the mind helps create the conditions for through the note on the mirror or the notebook.[28] Insofar as this is the case, recollection in particular is often tied to and arises out of practice and place; the contents of our memories are recalled not merely through an act of will, but also through the effects of both physical locations and our own actions, habitual or otherwise, on the operations of our minds. In this regard, recollection is a performance that occurs across "inside" and "outside" and thus reveals the blurriness in praxis of any distinction drawn between the two. More broadly, mind itself can be thought of as something that extends beyond "skin and skull" – as an engagement with the environment in which that environment plays an "active role. . .in driving cognitive processes."[29]

Of course, the insights of cognitive science were not available to the early moderns, and memoria and recollection were usually described in the period as purposive internal faculties and/or activities, even if prescription or practice might suggest otherwise.[30] But what must be stressed is that such descriptions, appearing in texts devoted to physiology or faculty psychology, are the product of a narrowing of focus; they entail the segregation of a specific faculty from a broader somatic system. That is, while most accounts of memory isolate it (in the brain) in order to consider its operations, humoral physiology assumes that memory operates in conjunction with, and is affected by, a range of other somatic phenomena. The ability to recollect or imprint memory traces depends to a great extent upon age, gender and the humoral complexion of one's body, all of which affect relations with one's environment. In addition, the nature of the environment itself is important, as the still active discourses of climatic humoralism make plain.[31] It is variables such as these that partly necessitate the arts of memory, which theoretically offer protection "against both inordinate environmental pressures and the organic failures of memory intrinsic to humoral cognition – [which is] vulnerable to environmental impressions from the outside and unruly humors within."[32] Further, as theorists of those arts have held, the affect with which a specific memory is imbued influences its memorability. Thus, both memoria and recollection, while seemingly transpiring only in the hindmost ventricle of the brain, require and assume the full involvement of the body, including the passions. In this regard, early modern conceptions of memoria and recollection would cheer those practitioners of cognitive science who have explicitly sought to undo the legacy of the Cartesian mind-body split.[33]

The third component of memory is *remembering*, which centers not on cognitive but on social performances. There are two aspects to the term's definition: one is *the claim made on the subject that he or she remember*, while the other is *the act of remembering* performed by that subject. While in common usage "recollection" and "remembering" are largely synonymous, remembering as defined here bears no intrinsic functional relationship to recollection; it may or may not involve the recollection of specific memory traces. While supposedly working to engender recollection, the appeal to remember, which can come from without or within, actually aims to mobilize the subject to comport himself or herself in a particular way. Remembering is about praxis; it entails the arrangement of one's utterances and/or actions, even one's body as a whole, in relation to the imperatives expressed in the appeal. Remembering is the process by which the subject is urged to take up a discrete social practice or set of practices. In short, remembering, if we combine both of its aspects, is action taken in response to a call to behave in a certain (more or less precisely defined) fashion.[34] As we shall see in the case of Hamlet, however, the subject does not always respond to the appeal to remember; in order for the call to be answered, it must be experienced in conjunction with specific personal and/or societal imperatives.

"Remembering" is not a process conceptualized as such in the early modern period. In addition, the lines drawn here between "remembering," "memoria" and "recollection" are often crossed in somatic and social practice. That being said, not each of these necessitates the presence of the others; "recollection" is possible without "remembering." However, drawing distinctions as I have done brings into focus specific aspects of behavior that are not accounted for in traditional definitions of memory. An illustrative example of "remembering" is to be found in Richard Mulcaster's description of Queen Elizabeth I's royal entry into London on the eve of her coronation:

In Cheapside, Her Grace smiled; and being thereof demanded the cause, answered, "For that she had heard one say, *Remember old King HENRY VIII!*" A natural child! which at the very remembrance of her father's name took so great a joy; that all men may well think that as she rejoiced at his name whom this Realm doth hold of so worthy memory, so, in her doings, she will resemble the same.[35]

Elizabeth's smile not only marks her as a "natural child" (an interesting designation given longstanding Catholic claims of her illegitimacy), but also aligns her impulses with those of the people (as represented by the one who has called upon her to remember): she rejoices at the name of the man who "this Realm doth hold of so worthy memory." To be most closely attended to, however, is the notion that to remember Henry as approvingly as she does is to intimate that "in her doings, she will resemble the same." For Mulcaster, Elizabeth's remembering offers a premonition of her future, one in which her reign will echo if not model itself after an earlier one. To remember here is to emulate, and Elizabeth's smile marks her complicity with the shouted request that she "*Remember old King HENRY VIII!*"[36]

Arguably, Elizabeth's emulation of Henry VIII papers over what would be seen by some as her tenuous claim to the throne (as the illegitimate daughter of Henry). It also establishes her as one who will eschew the example of Mary I. Indeed, Mary is never even mentioned in Mulcaster's account, and Elizabeth's remembering of her father promises the return of England to Protestantism. Of course, the very recently deceased Mary should not be seen as literally forgotten by either Elizabeth or her subjects. She is, however, occluded from an event that is nevertheless largely structured in terms of her: her absence functions as a promise about the nature of Elizabeth's brand new reign. The demand to remember, then, aspires to define the present and prescribe the future. That is, Elizabeth's remembering of Henry entails not her recollection of the past – such recollections are not represented here beyond reference to her rejoicing – but her future adoption of a set of behaviors; she promises a pattern of action and a mode of being, one that places her in a specific relationship with her subjects. As such, the call to remember attempts to shape behavior: "to remember" often means "to behave in a certain way and with a certain end in mind." In Mulcaster, the call requires that Elizabeth (at least rhetorically and momentarily) align herself with the kind of rule supposedly summed up in and represented by Henry VIII's very name.[37] Here, remembering locates the monarch in relation to institutions (kingship) and ideologies (of right rule and of Reformation) as they are represented by one of her subjects.

In this example, the call to remember is actually the request that the queen perform certain actions; the call is designed to define and delimit her "doings." These actions are never precisely specified in Mulcaster, but they all entail her exercising authority with the good of her subjects foremost in mind.[38] The exact content of the citizen's demand is never revealed – precisely *what* about her father is Elizabeth to emulate? – but for Mulcaster that content is presumably the sum total of the royal entry's exhortations to the queen. For instance, in patterning her actions after those of Deborah, the subject of one of the entry's tableaux, Elizabeth will rely upon her male advisors: this is a kingly "doing," one insisted upon because of anxiety about the ascension to the throne of a woman. Notice that "memoria" and "recollection" are irrelevant here; we do not know what, if anything, Elizabeth (or her vocal subject) recalls about her father. Instead, we have present joy and that which it promises for the future: "in her doings, she will resemble the same." Thus, the queen's act of remembering should be considered not as the end result of an inward experience, but in terms of action, as present and projected "doings."[39] Remembering is not recollection; it is instead an action or set of actions that arises out of the subject's response to specific social circumstances and a particular imperative to remember (that is, the imperative to behave in a certain way). At the same time, both "remembering" and "recollection" can blur together in period discussions or representations of memory. It would be inaccurate, then, to read memoria and recollection as internal processes and remembering as an external one. Instead, memory is both internal and external, cerebral and bodily. In addition, it is a kind of action, one that occurs across body and environment.

We have seen that the appeal to remember both works to generate and presupposes a prescribed pattern of behaviors. However, each such appeal emerges out of a particular social context. Given a different context, what it means to remember – and what behaviors might be performed in obedience to the call to remember – could vary significantly. However, the force of any given appeal to remember lies in its taking the behaviors it prescribes to be fixed and invariable. In this regard, the appeal elevates the performance of such behaviors to the basis for a type of selfhood. For Elizabeth to behave in the manner suggested in Mulcaster's text is for her to *be* her father's daughter. The selfhood *constructed* by acceding to the appeal to remember is understood as either being *revealed* by remembering or *returned* to through it. Moreover and ironically, the precise contours of that self are differently delineated in each of the contexts or discourses from out of which the call to (self-) remembering emerges. In the Donne sermon to be taken up in chapter 2, to remember the self is to behave with one's spiritual state and inevitable demise in mind, whereas in Shakespeare's *Antony and Cleopatra*, discussed in chapter 4, it is his Roman, martial self that Antony only intermittently remembers.

## Forgetting*, forgetfulness and subjectivity

While remembering is linked to self-formation, it is not synonymous with subjectivity. Here we will adapt an important distinction drawn by Linda Charnes in her discussion of "notorious identities" in Shakespeare. For Charnes, dramatic subjectivity means "the subject's *experience* of his or her relationship to his or her 'identity.'" In the case of Mulcaster's portrayal of the queen, we have nothing to go on when it comes to locating her subjectivity. With early modern drama, however, the situation is different, for "in the Renaissance, drama is the dominant mode in which the provisional, performative, and contingent nature of subjectivity can literally be embodied." That is, it is in the theatre that a relationship between identity and subjectivity is staged. In embodying subjectivity, the dramatic texts and characters considered in this study reveal subjectivity to be "represented *only* in those moments that threaten to destabilize – or even to shatter – identity."[40] At the same time, in drama subjectivity is what makes a character distinctive, something other than a cipher or type; it is the articulation of a relationship to a prescribed (social and/or dramatic) role. Especially in tragedy, it is the shattering of an identity – say, that of Hieronimo as first and foremost a loyal subordinate to the King of Spain, an identity performed in his initial appearance in *The Spanish Tragedy*[41] – that fleshes out a character (even as, in another sense, it destroys that character).[42] In this context, then, dramatic interiority is both the product and the staging of crisis. Importantly, this crisis often goes by the name of (self-)forgetting. This is not to say that forgetting is identical to subjectivity; as we shall see, forgetting is a richer and more inclusive category than this equation would suggest. However, forgetting is a form that subjectivity – a relationship to identity that represents the shattering of identity – frequently takes on the early modern stage.[43]

But what exactly is meant by forgetting? First, we need to distinguish between its two constituent elements, forgetting* and forgetfulness. (Once again this is for heuristic purposes; the two frequently overlap in examples of "forgetting.") *Forgetting** is a specific act that refers to the unavailability of memory traces to recollection, due either to their erasure or to their being, for whatever reason, irretrievable from *memoria*. *Forgetfulness*, on the other hand, describes a mode of being and a pattern of behavior that is linked not only to forgetting* but more broadly to specific somatic phenomena – lethargy, excess sleep, inordinate sexual desire. More broadly still, forgetfulness connotes the non-normative; this mode of being is routinely understood as erosive of one's identity. In the plays discussed in subsequent chapters, forgetfulness, like subjectivity, appears at "those moments that threaten to destabilize – or even to shatter – identity." However, while "forgetfulness" can encompass subjectivity, it is also more than that. As we shall see in the first chapter, forgetfulness also mobilizes a powerful fantasy of an unregulated and undisciplined body.

An example shows some of the ways in which both "remembering" and "forgetfulness" can signify. Consider first those famous words of *Hamlet*'s Ghost, "Remember me" (1. 5. 91). It is worth pausing over the powerful opacity of that imperative. What *exactly* would it mean for Hamlet to remember the Ghost? What precisely does remembrance entail? The Ghost provides us with one answer; his appeal subsumes into itself not only his earlier call to vengeance, but also the other important demands he makes of Hamlet – that he not go mad, take action against his mother, or let the royal bed "be / A couch for luxury and damned incest" (1. 5. 82-83).[44] The imperative to revenge dominates the scene, though, and all of the demands mentioned here, including that of revenge, function as specific examples of what the Ghost believes it would mean for Hamlet to remember him. To remember is to perform a series of prescribed actions.

A few lines later we see that the Ghost's words initiate in Hamlet a fantasy of the annihilation and reformation of the self through forgetting and the subsequent inscription of a memory trace. Hamlet pledges to erase from his memory all pre-existing matter – "I'll wipe away all trivial fond records, / All saws of books, all forms, all pressures past" – and then inscribe in it the ghost's "commandment," which "all alone shall live / Within the book and volume of my brain" (1. 5. 99–103). Interestingly, the forgetting that is to precede Hamlet's inscription would destroy the contents of his memory. Hamlet understands the contents of his memoria and the Ghost's demand that Hamlet remember him as mutually exclusive. The final lines of Hamlet's speech constitute a solemn moment of oath-swearing: "Now to my word. It is 'Adieu, adieu, remember me.' / I have sworn't" (1. 5. 110–112). Here Hamlet attempts to reconstitute himself in terms of remembering the Ghost and his commands. The "I" that swears performs an act that is built upon the previous erasure of Hamlet's memory. In this speech, Hamlet's keeping his word is concomitant with his wiping away all (memory) traces of his past.

That Hamlet does not fully reconstitute himself as the Ghost's remembrancer is recognized by the Ghost himself. Two acts later, the Ghost appears in order his "tardy son to chide" (3. 4. 107): "Do not forget. This visitation / Is but to whet thy almost blunted purpose" (3. 4. 110–111). In the narrow sense of the term, Hamlet has thus far never forgotten his dead father, and he has always kept in mind the Ghost and his commands.[45] What Hamlet cannot do, though, is remember: that is, Hamlet's selfhood is not formed in untroubled accordance with the imperatives contained in the Ghost's demand that he remember, most notably the imperative to revenge. Whether he wants to or not, Hamlet cannot become identical to the self generated and presupposed through the Ghost's call to remember. Instead (and as we shall see in the next chapter), his subjectivity derives from what the Ghost understands as lethargic forgetfulness, and it is that subjectivity that also shatters the very identity that the Ghost attempts to fix. If Mulcaster's description of the queen works to reveal (and shape) a performance of her identity through the demand that she remember, in *Hamlet* forgetting is the sign under which alternatives to such an identity are staged.[46]

Relatedly, forgetting can be understood in terms of action. It is the hoariest of critical commonplaces to assert that Hamlet does not take action, but of course he does. In truth, he *never stops* taking action. The voice that utters that commonplace reveals itself as invested in the Ghost's imperatives, in a notion of revenge as defining action, in the logic of "remember me." The actions that Hamlet does take, however, are there to be observed – they constitute much of the matter of the play, encompassing everything from his most lugubrious soliloquy to his leap into Ophelia's grave – even if the Ghost would dismiss them as evidence of forgetfulness. Forgetting, then, describes a kind of action that is disparaged by the Ghost as inaction. At the same time, from the point of view of memory, forgetting connotes erasure and erosion; its perceived destructive capacity makes it a threat to memory's idealizations.

The various non-dramatic texts taken up in this book (dictionary entries, sermons, treatises on the passions, anatomies, an epic poem) would seem to confirm the view of forgetting as destructive, for forgetting is routinely cast as antithetical to everything from basic somatic self-regulation to the attainment of salvation. As diverse as these texts are, one thing that unites most of them is their emphasis, familiar from moral philosophy, on the attainment of self-knowledge (*nosce te ipsum*, "know thyself") – an emphasis that can accommodate everything from spiritual reflection to anatomical investigation. From this perspective, self-forgetting in all of its forms represents self-alienation, the failure to know oneself. Importantly, the plays discussed in this book both complicate this view of forgetting and construe the self in different terms. Shakespeare, Marlowe and Webster treat the early modern theatre as the venue for *experiments* in understanding and representing the self – experiments in which the moral philosophical view of self-knowledge is interrogated or contested. Within these plays, forgetting generates a subject who is defined in terms of desire, or lethargy, or the willful rejection of what she or he knows. In each case, forgetting is more than the antithesis to memory; it is both a condition of being and a pattern of behavior. It is to those patterns of behavior understood as modes of self-forgetting that we will turn now.

### Self-forgetting and drama

Chapters 2 through 4 each focus on a different type of self-forgetting (labeled as "erotic" self-forgetting, "religious" self-forgetting, and the forgetting of one's country, respectively). The *Oxford English Dictionary* defines what it means to forget oneself as follows: "To lose remembrance of one's own station, position, or character; to lose sight of the requirements of dignity, propriety, or decorum; to behave unbecomingly."[47] This definition may seem to suggest merely a breach of etiquette, a social gaffe. However, much more is at issue than the violation of social *mores*, for the early modern self that is forgotten is, as has often been noted, originally constituted in terms of its place in a social network. Discussion of the word "propriety," used in the *OED* definition, is illustrative here. In an account of the interconnections between property ownership and identity, James Turner asserts that "'Land' and 'place' are equivalent to 'propriety' – meaning in seventeenth-century English both *property* and *knowing one's place*."[48] "Propriety," then, requires "knowing one's place," a process connected to ownership of property; it entails the physical and social placement of the individual. (Such "individuals" are almost always male.) Propriety assumes a relational conception of identity based on the individual's location in a larger social network. In fact, the "individual" only emerges out of and in relation to that network.[49] To forget oneself by violating propriety – by no longer performing the actions inherent in occupying a specific place in a (largely land-based) social order – is to become dislodged from such a network, disengaged from that which determines your identity.[50]

This disengagement helps bring into focus interrelations of property, propriety and memory. In essays on *King Lear* and *Hamlet*, Margreta de Grazia has written of the ways in which identity and property are conceptually and materially interdependent in the period.[51] Hamlet's having been denied those "patrimonial properties that secure lineal continuity – land, title, arms, signet, royal bed" is linked by de Grazia to his forgetting of his father in the fifth act of the play. She underscores the "difficulty [of Hamlet's] remembering his father without memorabilia or 'remembrances'"[52] – without those properties (like Bertram's ring and Helena's receipt, both discussed in the chapter on *All's Well That Ends Well*) that subtend one's familial or royal identity. Etymologically, to forget means "to miss or lose one's hold" – here, to lose hold of an identity through not being able to hold on to the properties that demarcate and undergird it. To forget those properties – to miss or lose hold of them – thus already accommodates the possibility that you will forget yourself. The question remains, however, what exactly does self-forgetting look like? That is, how do we discuss the kinds of selfhood, the patterns of action, that come into being through the process of forgetting oneself?

Shakespeare frequently dramatizes self-forgetting, its relation to memory, and the implications of it for the representation of the desiring subject. Jonas Barish has astutely asserted, in relation to a range of examples from Shakespeare, that "forgetfulness of self seems to spell, or to threaten, a loss of identity, transforming the self-forgetter into something unpredictable, unrecognizable, and therefore frightening."[53] That being said, this book will trace the contours of different varieties of this seemingly unrecognizable creature. One example of self-forgetfulness is to be found in the induction to *The Taming of the Shrew*. Shortly before he "practice[s]" on the impoverished Christopher Sly, the Lord asks his companions,

> What think you, if he were convey'd to bed,
> Wrapp'd in sweet clothes, rings put upon his fingers,
> A most delicious banquet by his bed,
> And brave attendants near him when he wakes,
> Would not the beggar then forget himself?
>
> (Ind. 1. 37–41)

The answer is yes, and the means of Sly's self-forgetting include not only wealth and "brave attendants" – evidence and markers of gentlemanly status – but also the presence of his "wife." As it happens, it is only with the appearance of that wife – a page boy in disguise – that Sly adopts and adapts to his new identity:

> Am I a lord, and have I such a lady?
> Or do I dream? Or have I dream'd till now?
> I do not sleep: I see, I hear, I speak;
> I smell sweet savors, and I feel soft things.
> Upon my life, I am a lord indeed,
> And not a tinker, nor Christopher Sly.
> Well, bring our lady hither to our sight,
> And once again a pot o' th' smallest ale.
>
> (Ind. 2. 68–75)

Our lady and a pot of small ale: these are emblematic of the forces that undergird Sly's self-forgetting, both making strong appeals to pleasure and his senses. More narrowly, it is the possibility of conjugal relations with his "wife," identified immediately before this utterance as "the fairest creature in the world, / And . . .inferior to none"(66–67), that leads Sly to proclaim, "I am a lord indeed," a statement more accurate than he realizes since he is a lord *only* "in deed" and temporarily. Here, we see a gap between Sly's identity (as the tinker named Christopher Sly) and his subjectivity (as defined by thoughts and present deeds).

Were this all, we would witness a clear example of self-forgetting. However, this example goes further, as it entails a putative change in identity – from tinker to lord and husband. The pursuit of pleasures goes hand in hand with Sly's integration into the social network of the artistocratic household. His first words to the disguised page are, "Are you my wife and will not call me husband? / My men should call me 'lord'; I am your goodman." The response: "My husband and my lord, my lord and husband, / I am your wife in all obedience" (103–107). These four lines (in which the words "husband" and "lord" are uttered three times, the word "wife" twice) almost ritualistically install Sly as lord, an identity whose meaning emerges out of the hierarchy of relations within the household. "Forgetting himself" – succumbing to the temptations of the flesh offered him by the devious lord – has led to Sly's assumption of a newer, more desirable social position and to his presumably brief integration into the life of the manor. He is "lord," seemingly taking the place of the unnamed lord who deceives him.

But what of the self Sly has forgotten? Sly's statement that he is "not a tinker, nor Christopher Sly" echoes his earlier resistance to forgetting himself. "Am not I Christopher Sly," he first protests, "old Sly's son of Burton-heath, by birth a pedlar, by education a card-maker, by transmutation a bear-herd, and now by present profession a tinker?" (Ind. 2. 17–21). Sly defines himself here by name and in terms of place, family, education and profession; he delineates the contours of his identity. Indeed, he begins the scene by attesting, with unwitting comedy, to the putative pedigree of his family and their distinguished place in English history: "Look in the chronicles: we came in with Richard Conqueror" (Ind. 1. 3–4). However, that he was born a pedlar and is now a tinker marks him as the member of an itinerant laboring population often associated with vagabondage. In this light, it is worth recalling that the lord labels him a beggar, one who is commonly construed as being socially and physically unlocateable.[54] Moreover, Sly is come upon while he is asleep on a heath, seemingly placeless and devoid of property, outside of every social network other than the temporary one offered by the alehouse – and he has even been driven from there because of debt. In forgetting himself, then, Sly trades in a precarious social position for one that is characterized by stability and affluence. For him, self-forgetting leads from an unstable social identity to another, more desirable one.

One can read Sly's "transformation" in several ways, most compellingly perhaps in terms of his strategic and winking adoption of a role that he realizes will not be his forever. Of course it should also be considered in conjunction with the taming of Katherina by Petruchio that makes up the main action of the play. However, Sly's experience resonates with other examples of self-forgetting taken up in this book. The lord apparently succeeds in making Sly forget himself by appealing to his senses; the pleasures he offers and the sexual desire he incites lead to Sly's declaration, "I am a lord indeed." As the cases of Bertram, Antony and Faustus will bear out, the role of desire and the senses here is roughly the same as it is in other representations of self-forgetting, but the joke inheres in the direction Sly travels: he moves from an unstable social position to a stable one defined in terms of "propriety," of identity formation through emplacement into a social network and a world of opulent goods. Sly adopts an identity more desirable than the (unfixed) one he has "forgotten"; self-forgetting here represents less a crisis than a social opportunity.

Of course, the joke also emerges out of the fact that Sly is destined to be lord for only a short period of time. This narrative of social advancement, much like that of Bottom in *A Midsummer Night's Dream*, construes his lordship only as temporary and aberrant, thereby suggesting that the social order may bend but will eventually resume its original shape. Erotic self-forgetting in Shakespeare entails succumbing to (and being reconstituted in terms of) sexual desire; in addition, it can involve the fracturing of identity. That is, self-forgetting entails the staging of subjectivity. Here, though, Sly trades in one identity for another; his subjectivity, such as it is, can be located only in the perplexity evinced in his question, "Am not I Christopher Sly [?]" While this is an obviously elliptical representation of subjectivity, we shall see later in this book that early modern plays are sometimes constructed around the problems and opportunities generated by self-forgetting.

An intriguing, non-parodic reference to self-forgetting is to be found in Marlowe's *Tamburlaine the Great, Pt. 1*. Importantly, Zenocrate's last line of the play takes up this topic; she tells us that in order for her to want no longer to marry Tamburlaine, she would need to "forget [her] self."[55] However, this very assertion can be read as the culmination of her self-forgetting. To be Tamburlaine's lover, Zenocrate must first forget herself as an Egyptian (as well as an unmarried woman). Earlier in this scene we have witnessed both her attempts to end Tamburlaine's assault on her father's country and her identification with Damascus and its people, an identification most obvious in her lament for the city and its inhabitants after Tamburlaine's assault:

> Wretched Zenocrate, that livest to see
> Damascus's walls dy'd with Egyptian blood,
> Thy father's subjects and thy countrymen;
> Thy streets strowed with dissevered joints of men
> And wounded bodies gasping yet for life;
> But most accurs'd, to see the sun-bright troop
> Of heavenly virgins and unspotted maids,
> Whose looks might make the angry god of arms
> To break his sword and mildly treat of love,
> On horsemen's lances to be hoisted up
> And guiltlessly endure a cruel death.

(5. 1. 319–329)

By play's end, the tension between Zenocrate's status as, on the one hand, Egyptian and, on the other, Tamburlaine's lover has been resolved in favor of the latter role; her final dismissive reference to the possibility of her self-forgetting actually attests to the completion of that process, as Zenocrate, who in the above lines clearly "knows her place" as an Egyptian, reconstitutes herself entirely in terms of her new husband. Self-forgetting may be a necessary prerequisite for subsumption into marriage – and we will find analogues to Zenocrate's self-forgetting in *All's Well That Ends Well* – but this is obviously an extreme case. Zenocrate is given away by her father in a wedding ritual completely orchestrated by her husband, and the cost of the marriage lies in her severing all emotional and identificatory ties to her "countrymen."[56] This is a clear example of the reconfiguration of alliances that, as Cordelia and Desdemona so famously argue, is attendant upon marriage itself. In this case, however, the formation of new alliances goes hand in hand with the complete eradication of old ones.

The example of Zenocrate shows that not only men forget themselves. As subsequent chapters make plain, male self-forgetting often connotes emasculation, the result of succumbing to sexual desire or hedonistic pleasures; loss of identity can go hand in hand with physiological change, as the forgetful male body becomes more like the female one in its natural (cold, wet) state.[57] What, then, of the woman who forgets herself? Not surprisingly, female self-forgetting does not entail radical physiological transformation. That is, while women might forget their identities, doing so *confirms* rather than transforms female physiology. As Valerie Traub puts it, "Woman's sinfulness, inferiority, and necessary subordination were believed to originate in her body, a body generally (though not inevitably) figured as inherently weaker, naturally cooler, more vulnerable to passion, and more resistant to reason than that of man. . . women. . .continued to carry the burden of Eve's guilt: the presumption of sexual insatiability and extraordinary ability to incite male lust."[58] That being said, the plays taken up in this book stage female "inferiority," as manifested in self-forgetting, to various ends, some of which are influenced by genre. On the one hand, Helena's self-forgetting in many ways conforms with Renaissance notions of inordinate female desire, but it also leads to the consolidation of a new identity and the formation of new social relations through (the return to) marriage – much as in the case of Zenocrate.[59] On the other hand, the Duchess of Malfi responds to her brothers' exhortations not to forget herself – or, more precisely, not to give herself over to the "heavy sleeps" of strong passion – by crafting a desiring subjectivity out of the misogynist language of their opprobrium, with tragic results. If forgetting is generally devalued in early modern England – as in its association with effeminization – Renaissance dramatists nevertheless locate in it powerful representational possibilities that raise questions about the terms of Renaissance misogyny. Helena's self-forgetting is finally far less problematic than Bertram's, just as the Duchess's "heavy sleeps" are less troubling than her brothers' efforts to police her sexuality.

It is worth saying more about dramatic interest in forgetting. As we shall see in chapter 1, antitheatricalists associate the theatre with the generation of (self-) forgetting in audience members. Similarly, the protean nature of actorly transformation is assumed in the assertion that both actors and audience members "drin[k] of the wyne of forgetfulnes."[60] More broadly, as Charnes suggests, drama is well suited to the exploration of the relationship between subjectivity and identity. In this regard, theatrical texts serve as experiments in which forms of selfhood outside of the parameters and dictates of "propriety" – of "knowing one's place" – are generated, experiments conducted under the rubric of (self-) forgetting. The early modern theatre's social liminality – its status as an institution both integrated into and, literally and figuratively, on the margins of certain aspects of civic life – makes it the perfect site for such experimentation.[61] Indeed, as an entrepreneurial institution, the theatre has a financial stake in exploring and selling novel (as well as familiar) models of selfhood to its audience – some of which emerge out of the culturally available discourses of (self-) forgetting taken up in this book. Theatrical experimentation, then, engages the audience by confounding or complicating its expectations, even if the play's "promised end" delivers more or less what is expected.[62]

Finally, it should be stressed that this book's understanding of self-forgetting has been enhanced by the recognition that many early modern dramatic texts confirm a central tenet of the psychoanalytic tradition, that the subject is by definition split, internally divided.[63] And yet, this book does not offer a psychoanalytic approach to the topic of forgetting. Without claiming that current psychoanalytic work is ahistorical – a position that seems increasingly untenable[64] – this book attempts to do what psychoanalysis has not done, and that is to historicize forgetting and memory. Doing so includes, for example, construing forgetting in terms other than those of repression. Forgetting is considered not as a symptom of a foundational trauma or unconscious desire, but as a discursive presence in its own right, a presence that offers a glimpse of early modern figurations of selfhood fully legible outside of a psychoanalytic register. More specifically, the dramatic texts taken up in this book represent forgetting as productive of specific forms of subjectivity; as suggested above, forgetting is the vehicle by which experiments in the conceptualization of the self are undertaken. Such experiments, it should be stressed, are often experienced by the characters who forget themselves as *crises* of identity, and forgetting is sometimes (as when associated with lethargy) understood in terms of *pathology*. This means that while forgetting is often productive, it does not necessarily have a liberatory force. Indeed, the call to forget can function in the service of a sinister restructuring of the social order. For instance, Claudius, in urging that Hamlet forget both his grief and his father in order to become "Our chiefest courtier, cousin, and our son" (1. 2. 117), attempts to install a new set of familial, monarchical and court relations in which Hamlet will remain loving, loyal and subordinate to his father's murderer. Forgetting here goes hand in hand with the attempted consolidation of Claudius's authority. This example notwithstanding, this book tends to stress the opportunities forgetting affords over its costs.

### Overview

Throughout this study, it is assumed that memory and forgetting are inevitably social; that they are less purely cerebral processes than modes of behavior and kinds of bodily deportment; that each manifests a relationship not only with the past but with the present and the future (indeed, each aims to prescribe a future); and that each charts multiple interfaces between the subject and society: memory and forgetting are the terms through which the subject is located in relation to various social institutions and practices. As has been suggested, it is on the early modern stage in particular that forgetfulness is seen as crucial to the delineation of subjectivity. The above comments about Hamlet's forgetfulness can be understood in explicitly dramatic and generic terms: forgetfulness is the vehicle for generic experimentation. As many critics have noted, the stage avenger is one who both suffers under the burden of memory and who seeks vengeance as a form of remembering;[65] tacitly, Hamlet also carries the weight of memory in the shape of generic expectation, a burden that promises to make his identity a version of Hieronimo's (or Laertes's). Hamlet's complex negotiation of the role he inherits simultaneously from the Ghost and *The Spanish Tragedy* is constitutive of his subjectivity ("the subject's *experience* of his or her relationship to his or her 'identity'") and it goes by the Ghost's name for it, forgetfulness. In Hamlet's case, then, forgetfulness is the shape that not only subjectivity but (innovation in) dramatic character takes.

Chapter 1, entitled "Embodying oblivion," works to isolate the place of forgetting in the body and to chart a relationship between forgetting and theatre. While anatomists and psychologists offer forgetting no ventricle to call its own, it does have a somatic presence: forgetting is to be found in bodily dispositions and humoral excesses. This chapter draws on a variety of sources in order to consider some of the ways in which forgetting* and forgetfulness intersect with lethargy (etymologically linked to Lethe, the mythological river of forgetfulness) and immoderate sleep. What fundamentally connects forgetting with these two somatic phenomena is the status of the forgetful body as an idle and unregulated one. This body is defined in contrast to the body that remembers, which is constituted by discipline and regimented labor. This chapter examines the significance of lethargy and sleep, both determinants and symptoms of the forgetful body, for moments in texts such as Shakespeare's *Macbeth* and *Hamlet*, Ford's *'Tis Pity She's A Whore* and Webster's *The Duchess of Malfi*. It concludes by considering the antitheatricalist conception of theatre as generative of both forgetting and forgetful bodies.

Chapter 2, entitled "'Be this sweet Helen's knell, and now forget her': forgetting and desire in *All's Well That Ends Well*," focuses on "erotic" self-forgetting. It first considers the close connections between memory and reason in faculty psychology, then turns to an essay by Michel de Montaigne that argues for the centrality of forgetting to the proper exercise of judgment. Memory and forgetting are then shown to be attendant upon something crucial to *All's Well* in particular and Shakespearean drama in general – the representation of sexual desire and its effects, understood in terms of self-forgetting. Through the actions of both Helena and Bertram, *All's Well* offers a sustained examination of "forgetting oneself": in particular, the crisis of identity it entails and the strong desire it mobilizes. The chapter concludes by considering the

significance of forgetting for (this "problem") comedy, reading the play's
ending in terms of its failure to induce forgetting and thus to convince its
audience that all is finally well.

*Dr. Faustus* can be seen as urging audience members to remember
themselves – that is, to recall their sins and reform their behaviors.
Chapter 3, "'If he can remember': spiritual self-forgetting and *Dr.
Faustus*," begins by considering the significance of Faustus's inability,
despite his divinity training, to remember Romans 6: 23 beyond "The
reward of sin is death": even in his opening monologue Faustus forgets
the possibility of salvation offered by the rest of this scriptural text.
Faustus's incomplete recollection offers us a glimpse of early modern
conceptions of forgetting and remembering that are best represented by a
John Donne sermon that asserts "The art of *salvation*, is but the art of
*memory*." For Donne, following both Plato and Augustine, "*all Religion*
[is located] in the memory"; forgetting is not the erasure of knowledge
necessary to salvation from the memory but a performative act that
represents a particular disposition toward that knowledge. In both
Donne and Marlowe, this act is thematized and conceptualized as
spiritual self-forgetting, and it is linked in *Faustus* with everything from
sodomy to sloth. Chapter 3 pursues a reading that sees the play tracing
the disastrous effects of Faustus's spiritual self-forgetting and thus
acting as an agent of self-recollection. However, *Dr. Faustus* can also be
understood as equating the allure of self-forgetting with that of the
theatre. In the end, the significance and nature of theatre in *Dr. Faustus*
remain elusive; even as it acts in the name of self-recollection, Marlovian
theatre can serve as an agent of self-forgetting.

Chapter 4, "My oblivion is a very Antony," shows that *Antony and
Cleopatra* goes further than *All's Well* in thematizing the nature and
implications of erotic self-forgetting by linking it both to issues of cultural
identity and, relatedly, to Homeric and early modern depictions of Circe,
the mythical analogue to Cleopatra who causes men to "forget their
countries." Moreover, while numerous critics have discussed Antony's
forgetting of his Roman identity, what has remained largely unobserved
is the retroactive constitution of that identity as whole and unified.
*Antony and Cleopatra* shows (as *All's Well* does not) that self-forgetting
does the work of rendering coherent the self that has been forgotten. The
play as a whole is dominated by the retrospective characterization of
people and events; in addition, it focuses on monumentality and
commemoration as modes of knowledge production, most notably in
Caesar's and Cleopatra's eulogies for the fallen Antony. It is through
Cleopatra's commemoration of Antony that self-forgetting comes to
serve as a prerequisite for a vision of heroic masculinity.

Chapters 2 through 4 focus on different models of self-forgetting. In chapter 5, "Sleep, conscience and fame in *The Duchess of Malfi*," we return to one of forgetting's allies, immoderate sleep. Sleep is a crucial term for the representation of both the Duchess and Ferdinand; it initially describes either self-division or the dispersal of the master's subjectivity across the body (or bodies) of his servant(s). In addition to examining connections between immoderate sleep and (self-)forgetting – indeed, the Duchess's sleep combines elements of each of the three types of self-forgetting discussed above – the chapter considers sleep's significance to sixteenth- and seventeenth-century casuistical discourse. Writers such as William Perkins and Immanuel Bourne anatomize what they define as a "sleepy conscience," one in which the subject gives herself over to worldly behavior and thereby fails to remember herself or her end. While it is in terms of this conception of conscience that Ferdinand and the Cardinal castigate the Duchess, she appropriates her brothers' references to sleep – references connected to an identity they prescribe for her – in order to define for herself the subjectivity of a desiring agent. And if by the play's end sleep has come to have an entirely different meaning – one that bespeaks the Duchess's resigned acceptance of her death – it is nevertheless the case that the sleep of conscience, understood as the forgetting of one's inevitable end, remains for Webster an important locus for dramatic subjectivity.

A coda, "Wrought with things forgotten," uses a moment in *Macbeth* to ponder the relationship between forgetting and futurity. It advances and concludes the book's discussion of dramatic subjectivity by considering specific representational possibilities afforded dramatists by forgetting, as well as connections between forgetting and emergent notions of individuality.

In writing of the topics central to this analysis I have frequently been reminded of St. Augustine's assertion that memory is "a vast and infinite place" that contains "secret, and unspeakeable concavities."[66] Certainly this goes for both memory and forgetting, for this book traces the contours of only certain small portions of these "vast and infinite" subjects.[67] That being said, the ambition of this book is not entirely an immodest one, and it can be expressed in terms to be encountered in the next chapter: to hold forgetting itself up to both "good, [and] *Evill* fame," and thus to "vindicate it to Aeternitie."

# 1    Embodying oblivion

> Last scene of all,
> That ends this strange eventful history,
> Is second childishness and mere oblivion,
> Sans teeth, sans eyes, sans taste, sans everything.[1]

As suggested in the introduction, memory and forgetting are both physiological and cultural; they account not only for cognitive and somatic activity, but also for various kinds of social performance. Relatedly, memory and forgetting crop up in a wide variety of early modern discourses, with meanings not limited to (or even primarily defined by) cerebral function. This does not mean that when forgetting is described in, say, a religious tract, the "literal"/physiological gives way to the "metaphorical"/cultural. Instead, the physiological and cultural mutually inform one another (as in the association of memory with order discussed below), albeit to varying degrees at different moments. Thus, while this chapter begins with the physiology of memory and forgetting, that physiology should not be read as the materialist substrate for subsequent discussion of forgetting either here or in the rest of the book. Instead, physiological description provides specific conceptual resources through which to configure the relationship between (primarily male) "bodies and selves" in a range of discourses.[2]

We will begin with a particular depiction of oblivion *as* a male body.[3] From there, we will turn to some of the ways in which forgetfulness intersects with and shapes period understandings of lethargy and immoderate sleep. Forgetfulness, lethargy and sleep are all integral to an early modern fantasy of the body as completely unregulated and undisciplined – a fantasy enacted in a variety of texts, including antitheatrical tracts.[4] Finally, we will see that while antitheatricalists read theatre as a crucial agent in the scandalous production of forgetful bodies, the theatre, represented most notably by *Hamlet*, complicates this view by making forgetfulness and lethargy the signs under which subjectivity emerges.

The reader of early modern texts on anatomy and physiology will not have to look far to discover memory; it is housed in its own ventricle, in which "is registred and kept those things that are done and spoken with the senses."[5] Pierre de la Primaudaye's discussion of memory's role in the body resembles most others; he writes of

the *Imaginative* vertue, which is in the soule as the eye in the bodie, by beholding to receive the images that are offered unto it by the outward sences: and therefore it knoweth also the things that are absent, and is amongst the internall sences as it were the mouth of the vessell of memorie, which is the facultie and vertue that retaineth and keepeth whatsoever is committed to the custody therof by the other sences, that it may be found and brought forth when neede requireth. Therefore *Memorie* is as it were their treasurer to keepe that which they commit unto it, and to bring it foorth in due time and season.[6]

Memory is described as a treasurer, as "the facultie and vertue that retaineth and keepeth" images. What is most important about this account is the agency with which memory is imbued. Such agency is echoed in the description by Pierre Charron of memory as "Gardian and Register of all the species or kindes and images, apprehended by the sense, retired and sealed up by the imagination."[7] In both these cases, memory is metaphorized as one who not only records but also protects and preserves the images stored up in the hindmost ventricle of the brain.[8] It is not memory's status as a repository of preserved images but as the agent that maintains the integrity of those images that is most vividly conveyed in these accounts.

There are, however, depictions that represent more fully the *place* of memory. M. Andreas Laurentius describes memory as both reason's "faithfull secretarie" and as akin to

a place of greatest trustines to keepe the same the most precious treasures of the soule. . .This is that rich treasurie, which incloseth within one only inner roome all the sciences, and what else soever hath passed since the creation of the world, which lodgeth every thing in his severall place, not shufling them up disorderly together, which observeth time, circumstances and order, and which is (as *Plato* tearmeth it) a cesterne to containe the running streames of the understanding: this facultie is called remembrance, and is proper unto man alone.[9]

While memory is "faithfull secretarie," it is also a vessel, Plato's cistern.[10] Once again, the place of memory is imbued with agency. Memory is a "rich treasurie" that not only "incloseth" knowledge but crucially "lodgeth every thing in his severall place, not shufling them up disorderly together." Memory actively orders the traces that fill it. While la Primaudaye and Charron seem to have no trouble in reading memory as agent rather than treasury, Laurentius ingeniously produces a notion of memory as *both* the place of preserved images and the faculty that guarantees their continued integrity.

What is common to these representations of memory? One answer: as agent – both recorder and guardian – but especially as repository – both storehouse and inscribed text – memory is figured as vulnerable; its status as treasury or "place of greatest trustines" attests to the feared possibility of memory being ransacked or rendered disorderly. As a collection of images, memory is in need of being guarded, organized and conserved. As an agent, its job is to defend, order, and preserve. Thus, while the metaphors that we see here seem to ignore forgetting, forgetting is the unarticulated premise and ground of these representations of memory as a "rich treasurie" in need of defending. (The passages express anxiety not only about forgetting but also about the "shuffling up" of memory images. However, as we shall see, such "shuffling up" *is* a form of forgetting.) Forgetting is largely overlooked even as it defines the terms of memory's representation.

If forgetting is the conceptual ground for memory, it exists on no determinate ground. Although forgetting is *placeless* – it has neither a ventricle nor an organ – it is recognizable as a *somatic process*, one that manifests itself in diseases, bodily dispositions and humoral excesses. Moreover, this chapter's epigraph underscores that forgetting needs to be thought of in fully somatic terms ("Sans teeth, sans eyes, sans taste, sans everything"). The same is true with memory. While the examples cited above suggest that memory is all in the head, it is only such as an item in an anatomical blazon; descriptions of memory as a mental faculty should not lead us to neglect the interanimation and mutual influence of faculties, fluids, and organs within a humoral economy of the body. Indeed, descriptions of the "rich treasurie" of memory exist in synecdochic relation to accounts of the body as a whole, with fears of memory's vulnerability encapsulating a broader anxiety about the entire body turning forgetful.

With that anxiety in mind, we will turn to a visual representation of such a body found on the title page of Sir Walter Ralegh's *The History of the World* (1614; see figure 1). The poem printed opposite, which is attributed to Ben Jonson, describes the image as follows:

> From *Death* and darke *Oblivion* (neere the same)
> The *Mistresse of Mans life*, grave Historie,
> Raising the *World* to good, or *Evill* fame,
> Doth vindicate it to Aeternitie.[11]

Oblivion here represents a broadly historical forgetfulness, one aligned with death and in opposition to history. (In light of this, consider the

Figure 1. Reproduction of the title page to Sir Walter Ralegh's *The History of the World* (1614) is by permission of the Folger Shakespeare Library.

"mere *oblivion*" of the chapter's epigraph as ending the "strange eventful *history*" described by Jaques as the seven ages of man.) The association of oblivion with death is conventional; it appears, for instance, in an illustration drawn from Richard Day's *The Booke of Christian Prayers* captioned as follows: "Memorie is a treasure house," "Oblivion is as a grave."[12] In the Ralegh engraving, though, history rather than memory is set in opposition to oblivion, but the two are clearly aligned; history is the name by which various significant deeds are memorialized by either "good, or *Evill* fame."[13] As James Bednarz puts it in his description of this image, "Oblivion and Death lie sleeping under the feet of History, the teacher of life. Death and Oblivion are conquered by the power of vigilant remembrance. . .Memory triumphs over the forces that attempt to destroy it: decay and forgetfulness."[14]

Bednarz's description needs some modification. With legs loosely crossed, head pitched forward over his slumping body, an arm laying listlessly to one side, and *eyes open*, Oblivion is a figure overtaken not by sleep but by lethargy.[15] As we shall see, lethargy has connections with sleep, but most pressing here is its relationship to forgetfulness. First, etymology: lethargy owes its name to Lethe, the mythological river of forgetfulness. In *An English Expositor*, John Bullokar describes Lethe as a "Poeticall word, signifying a feyned River in hell, the water whereof being drunken, causeth forgetfulnesse of all that is past." The connection between Lethe and lethargy is rendered explicit in this example from Pierre de la Primaudaye: "And the disease called the *Lethargie* bringeth with it forgetfulnesse and want of memorie, as the name itself giveth us to understand."[16] As there is an etymological link between the two terms, so is there a physiological one. Bullokar explains that lethargy is "A disease. . .[caused by] cold Phlegmaticke humours. . .whereby [the sufferer] becommeth forgetfull, with losse (in a manner) of reason and all the senses of his body."[17] Stephen Batman goes further: "*Litargi*. . .is a postume bread in the hinder cell of the head, [and] hath that name *Litargia* of *Lethos*, that is forgetting, for it induceth forgetting. It is oft in old men [and] in winter, [and] commeth of fleme: And it cometh never it selfe, but it commeth alway of some former sicknesse: for in some sicknesse fleme is bred by working of a fever heate and boiling, is ravished up to the braine."[18] The onset of lethargy, then, occurs in the hindmost ventricle of the brain – the region of memory. Lethargy and forgetfulness here are produced by humoral imbalance, the predominance of phlegm that is cause and evidence of disease.[19] At the same time, lethargy produces a broad series of effects. Bullokar characterizes lethargy in terms of what seems to be the erosion of bodily function: the loss of reason (at least "in a manner") and of "all the senses." As both sign and agent of lethargy, oblivion is antithetical to the proper functioning of the body ("*Sans teeth, sans eyes, sans taste, sans everything*").[20]

Insofar as lethargy is associated both with the underworld and old age, it hints at a range of connections between forgetting and death. The precise nature of such connections varies: in the case of Lethe, it is the engendering of forgetfulness in the dead that is at issue, whereas "*Death* and darke *Oblivion*" are "neere the same" in Jonson's poem, which adapts Cicero, because of the threat they both pose to historical events. In the Homeric and Virgilian traditions, to be forgotten is a kind of death; memory functions as a form of immortality. One could multiply examples in which forgetfulness is shadowed by or anticipates death, at either the subjective or the social levels; moreover, connections between death and sleep, the latter of which is discussed below, will instantly suggest themselves. However, the meanings of forgetfulness, lethargy and sleep cannot be summed up by or contained in death. Just as forgetfulness should not be construed merely as memory's absence, so should it not be seen as either a subset of, or as the erasure of meaning produced by, death. Indeed, in what follows, it is the forms of *living* – the somatic patterns and modes of behavior – gathered under the headings of forgetfulness, lethargy and sleep that will most concern us.

With the above description of lethargy in mind, more can be said about the physiology of both forgetting and memory. If memory is metaphorized as both place and agent, it can also be understood as both product and process. That is, the accumulation of memory traces in the storehouse of memory, as well as the recollection of these traces, are both physiological processes requiring the operations of the animal spirits in the brain. These spirits are necessary to the performance of the faculties; they are the vehicle by which, for instance, the evidence of the senses is passed to the imagination, or from the judgment to memory.[21] From a physiological perspective, forgetting is a product of lethargy because the operations of the animal spirits in the brain are impeded by the preponderance of phlegm.[22] Relatedly, "the hinder cell of the head" refers to the ventricle within which memory is located, and so the development of a postume in that cell disables the operations of the spirits, operations that could take the form either of installing or recollecting memory images.[23] In short, not only forgetting but also the disruption of the body's operations discussed above can be attributed to the interruption of the proper functions of the animal spirits.[24]

As Bullokar states, forgetting is a symptom of lethargy; at the same time, lethargy can also be understood as the body forgetting how to perform its functions, as the disabling or the dis-integration of the body's constitutive parts and operations. This is made plain in an excerpt from

Thomas Eliot's definition of the term, in which lethargy is caused by "a moyste and verayc colde humour [i.e., phlegm], wasshyng the brayne. . . Constantinus sayeth, that where sometyme they dooe gape, they do forget to close theyr mouthes."[25] The "wasshyng" of the brain enacted by phlegm depends upon commonplace metaphors of memory as inscription: the material entered onto memory's "wax tablet" is erased when the tablet becomes so moist that it can no longer hold that inscription.[26] (Such logic lurks behind the notion that drinking water from the river Lethe leads to forgetfulness; in Erasmus's *The Prayse of Follie*, the old experience second childhood when, from Lethe, they "have drunken long forgetfulnes of things passed. . .*washing away* all the troubles & carcfulnesses of the mind."[27] In addition, one might argue that Lethe, in all its cold wetness, metaphorizes or evokes the operations of phlegm in the brain.) More importantly, lethargy not only leads its sufferers to forget what they were going to say, it also affects simple bodily performance: it leaves them with mouths agape, and this evidence of somatic slackness is understood in terms of forgetting. Another intriguing example is proffered by Walter Bruel, who tells us that the lethargic "are as forgetfull as madde men; for if they aske for a urinall to pisse in, they immediately forget for what end they did call for it."[28] Here urinating reads as an entirely willed activity, whereas lethargy suggests the forgetting of the will's command. Lethargy and forgetfulness serve a fantasy of a recalcitrant and unresponsive body, a body from which the will's purposive control has been completely evacuated. In this context, the etymology of forgetting, adduced in the introduction, takes on new force: to forget is "to miss or lose one's hold"; the lethargic subject's failure to maintain a firm grip on re-collected memory traces is matched by the broader disenabling of his bodily functions.[29]

   The examples from the last few paragraphs also suggest something else about lethargy, gender and the body's temperament. Humoral theory has it that men are by definition hot and dry, whereas women are cold and moist, their bodies naturally characterized by a predominance of phlegm. As a disease, lethargy, which both Batman and Eliot tell us arises out of that moist and cold humor, makes the male body more like a female one. Importantly, it is an increase in coldness that enables the emergence of lethargy in men; their vital heat is susceptible to diminishment either through action, such as the profligate spending of that heat in sexual intercourse, or through aging.[30] Thus, Batman has it that old men in winter are especially prone to lethargy because their vital heat has decreased over the years; as these men are already relatively cold, their bodies are increasingly likely to become phlegmatic after the ravages of fever. The larger points, though, are, first, that the recalcitrant and unresponsive body discussed above is one that, before succumbing to lethargy, is tacitly male. Second, as a result of the disease, that body is at a basic humoral level effeminized, as the condition of lethargy resembles the temperament of women in general.[31] For Eliot, effeminization also goes hand in hand with a loss of bodily integration; lethargy manifests itself through the disruption of the smooth operation of the masculine body.[32]

If lethargic forgetting can be understood as disrupting somatic functions, it can in another register also represent a more generalized inactivity. In the following example, lethargy is construed not in terms of pathology, but in terms of social performance. After hearing Hamlet pledge "with wings as swift / As meditation or the thoughts of love /. . . [to] sweep to [his] revenge," the Ghost tells him, "I find thee apt. / And duller shouldst thou be than the fat weed / That roots itself in ease on Lethe wharf, / Wouldst thou not stir in this."[33] The Ghost is pleased to recognize that Hamlet is not dull, he does not root himself in ease, he will "stir" in the matter of avenging his father; that is, Hamlet does not suffer from the effeminizations of lethargy. The connection between lethargy and forgetfulness is made explicit through the Ghost's reference to Lethe. While the river here seems to induce not literal forgetting but lethargy, the point is that in this example lethargy *is* a form of forgetfulness. It is only sixty or so lines later that the Ghost insists that Hamlet remember him, an act that the Ghost sees as entailing that Hamlet seek revenge. To forget him, the Ghost suggests, is to be idle not merely in the performance of this task but also in general – to be lethargic. Forgetfulness is here understood not simply in terms of "a moyste and veraye colde humour, wasshyng the brayne" – although the reference to the river Lethe arguably evokes the cold wetness of phlegm – but as a mode of inactivity and a reluctance toward a prescribed action or set of actions. Physiology subtends the (non-)performance of a variety of behaviors that bear no immediate relation to that physiology; the language of soma underpins the Ghost's chastising depiction of a son who "wouldst. . . not stir in this."

This account of lethargic forgetting partially explains the lassitude of the figure of Oblivion. Oblivion is phlegmatic, inactive, lethargic. The image compellingly represents a notion of forgetfulness *as inactivity*. Moreover, that inactivity is effeminizing, the male figure having fallen into an emasculated, Circean lassitude, his prone body attesting to a loss of the rectitude (both physical and ethical) that is associated with idealized masculinity. In contrast, History's is a noticeably active body; she literally steps on Death and Oblivion while "Raising the *World* to good, or *Evill* fame."[34] It must be stressed, however, that in certain contexts lethargy and lethargic forgetfulness connote not inactivity but activity that is understood as somehow improper. Again, Hamlet. While in the narrow sense of each term he is neither lethargic nor forgetful, Hamlet is in the bedroom scene exhorted by the Ghost not to forget, and this because he has seemingly grown dull in not executing his "almost blunted purpose" (3. 4. 110–111). Here, lethargy and forgetfulness bespeak not a general inactivity but the failure to perform prescribed actions. The link between lethargy and inappropriate action can also be isolated in Ford's *'Tis Pity She's A Whore*, in which the repentant Annabella asserts that "They who sleep in lethargies of lust / Hug their confusion."[35] "Lethargies of *lust*" describes active and sinful behavior – suggesting in this case Annabella's recently abandoned incestuous relationship with her brother – that will lead to the "confusion" or damnation of those who do not renounce their corrupt ways. Or, if the word confusion is taken to describe the state of the subject before death, these lethargies mark a loss of self-integration, the self as internally divided and discordant.

In *'Tis Pity*, lust is revealed to be compatible not only with lethargy but also with sleep, another of forgetfulness's allies. In *Mnemonica; or, The Art of Memory*, John Willis asserts that "*Sleep* offendeth *Memory*."[36] Sleep's offensiveness is mentioned on the same page as are the deleterious effects on memory of drunkenness and gluttony; indicted shortly thereafter are "Filthy desires, as avarice, envy, thirst of revenge, lust, love of harlots, and the ardent Passion, *Love*."[37] How are these disparate phenomena connected? Sleep, after all, seems far removed from envy or greed or "ardent Passion." As Thomas Cogan puts it, "Sleepe. . .after *Aristotle* is defined to be *an impotencie of the senses*. Because in sleepe the senses be unable to execute their office, as the eye to see, the eare to heare, the nose to smell, the mouth to tast, and all sinowy parts to feele. So that the senses for a time may seeme to be tyed or bound, and therefore sleepe is called of some *the bonde of the senses*." For Cogan, this "impotencie" of the senses has beneficial effects – it is a crucial element "in [the] preserving of health" – as long as sleep is moderate.[38] However, excessive sleep poses problems: "Wherefore they that sleepe a great part of the day. . .it is no marvell if they be both unhealthfull in their bodies, and in wit, like the horse and mule in whom there is no understanding."[39] Excess sleep suggests a degenerate, bestial corporeality attained through succumbing to morphetic pleasures.[40] Here the senses are impotent not because they are not appealed to, but because they are indulged so fully that their proper, moderate functions (in the performance of which they are regulated by reason) are not enacted.[41] For Cogan, excess sleep is also deleterious to memory; it erodes understanding, which, as numerous accounts of the brain's functioning make plain, depends upon memory for its enactment.[42] Sleep suggests a kind of subjective presentism; through the immersion of the self in the transitory pleasures of the moment, both future and past are forgotten. This subjective presentism marks the erosion of the self defined in terms of reason and memory. Also, as with lethargy, sleep is a physiological state more readily aligned with women; as Gail Kern Paster has noted, "The global implications of the contrast between male heat and female cold begin to register in direct symbolic linkages between temperature and states of consciousness. . .Waking consciousness was thought to be a hotter and drier state than sleep; rationality was less cold and clammy than irrationality."[43]

In moralizing texts, sleep is often associated with the active and sinful forgetting of God or of divine precepts; it also metaphorizes the fallen state of man. The author of *Physicke, to Cure the Most Dangerous Disease of Desperation* states that

If [Satan] espieth a man to be rich, and to have worldly blessinges through the gift of God, then will he apply him earnestly by his prosperitie to lull him asleepe *in* the forgetfulnesse of God, in world*ly* Pleasures, pleasant Vanities, and transitorie delights, comfortes, and solaces; and by trusting in his Riches to lift up himselfe arrogantly above others; to swell in pride, & to contemne his brethren, committing. . . many fonde, palpable, and grosse errours and follies, against Gods word, even as if he should say, Who is the Lord?[44]

Sleep and "forgetfulnesse of God" are associated with "transitorie delights." The end result of this appetitive sleep is a disastrous act of forgetting: so engrossed is the sleeper in "worldly Pleasures" that he finally acts as if he cannot remember who the Lord is.[45] Such extreme acts of forgetting, modes of action that encompass psychic and somatic phenomena, would also presumably constitute for this author the eradication of identity, grounded as identity is in the subject's relationship to God. To forget God – to act as if you do not know who the Lord is – is to forget yourself.[46]

Forgetfulness and sleep are routinely connected in Christian discourse with the idea of security. That is, sleep constitutes a lack of vigilance – as in the phrase "caught napping," or in the biblical injunction that the sleeper awake (e.g., Jonah 1. 6) – that is frequently linked with a false sense of security bred of over-reliance on the seductive comforts of the material world.[47] On the other hand, memory represents a call to awaken and to become vigilant. Consider the following example from a text by Benjamin Austin that announces its ambition in its subtitle, "A Watchbell to rouze up a secure Sinner out of his sleep of security":

When the *Grecians* had taken *Sardis*. . .*Xerxes* King of *Persia*, gave commandement that every day after dinner one should cry, *The Grecians had taken Sardis*: that the *Persians* thereby might be stirred up to recover it againe. The Divell hath taken thy soule by sinne, it were good to raise thee out of security in the midst of thy banquets and pleasures, to have ever sounding in thy eares, ["]The Divell hath taken thy soule["], that thou mayest be stirred up to use the meanes to recover it. Wherefore art thou sick of that spirituall Lethargy of sinne, thou must take the Physitians counsell to them which are sick of a drowsy Lethargy, to have a bell rung in their eares, that they may be kept from sleeping. Is thy soule therefore fallen into that sleepy sicknesse of security, to keepe thee from perishing in this dangerous sicknesse, thou must have the word of God ever sounding in thy eares.[48]

Austin serves as the Christian equivalent of a mnemon, the figure who in antiquity was "charged with reminding the hero of his duty to his divine mission."[49] The phrase to be repeated daily, "The Divell hath taken thy soule," acts as a *memento mori* by directing one's attention away from "banquets and pleasures" and toward last things; it stirs one to act in ways necessary to salvation. On the other hand, to slip into the "sleepy sicknesse of security" – to live for "banquets and pleasures" – is, in words we recently encountered, to fall "asleepe *in* the forgetfulnesse of God." Importantly, Christian and medical discourses intersect as the ringing bell is offered as the cure for both "a drowsy Lethargy" and the "spirituall Lethargy of sinne."

The association of sleep with forgetfulness, sensual excess and a lack of vigilance can be detected in a moment drawn from Shakespeare's *Macbeth*, a text famously concerned with sleep. Certainly most of the play's references to sleep are at least indirectly concerned with forgetting: that Macbeth has murdered sleep can be taken to suggest not merely that his conscience is asserting itself, but that he cannot forget the crimes he has committed.[50] In these instances, then, sleep is seen to have ameliorative effects and is linked to a quiet conscience. However, other associations are deployed when Lady Macbeth introduces crucial additions to the plan to kill Duncan:

> When Duncan is asleep,
> (Whereto the rather shall his day's hard journey
> Soundly invite him), his two chamberlains
> Will I with wine and wassail so convince,
> That memory, the warder of the brain,
> Shall be a fume, and the receipt of reason
> A limbeck only: when in swinish sleep
> Their drenched natures lie, as in a death,
> What cannot you and I perform upon
> Th' unguarded Duncan?[51]

Duncan sleeps the sleep of the just, which is to be denied the murderous couple. His drugged attendants, however, will fall into a "swinish sleep."

Like the horse or mule devoid of understanding, the chamberlains will have no use of their memories, the "warder[s] of the[ir] brain[s]." Arguably, their natures, as described here, are drenched not only in drink but in the (cold, moist) waters of Lethe; in overindulging in "wine and wassail," they have forgotten themselves and the roles they are to perform.[52] The "security" of which they are guilty is not registered in explicitly spiritual terms; instead, that they have let their guards down has led to their failure as guards (and, as we later see, to their deaths).[53]

While Duncan's attendants indulge in a "swinish sleep" in which memory is reduced to "a fume," the role of memory in driving the sinner from a dangerous sleep is apparent (if ironized) in Ferdinand and the Cardinal's interrogation of their sister, the title character in Webster's *The Duchess of Malfi*. Fearing that the Duchess will marry again, the two men alert her to the consequences of pursuing worldly desires by taking turns at moralizing:

FERDINAND: And those joys,
Those lustful pleasures, are like heavy sleeps
Which do forerun man's mischief.
CARDINAL: Fare you well.
Wisdom begins at the end: remember it.[54]

Ferdinand's association of sleep with "lustful pleasures" is familiar to us now. Moreover, he echoes texts like Austin's in which the sinner is exhorted to remember the final mischief that is forerun by hedonism. In the next line, the Cardinal makes an explicit appeal to the Duchess's memory, and, as in the introduction's discussion of remembering, to remember here means to behave in a prescribed and restricted fashion. Also, the "wisdom" alluded to here describes not only the advice that the brothers have just given, but also the knowledge that "begins at the end" – that emerges from remembering one's death and living accordingly. Tacit in all of this is the assumption that the Duchess needs to be reminded of such matters, that she is or easily could become a heavy sleeper. Through calling upon their sister to eschew lust, Ferdinand and the Cardinal imagine her as a forgetful woman whom they try to awaken from, in Austin's words, her "spirituall Lethargy of sinne." That each of the brothers has miscast himself in the role of reformer is made plain in the Duchess's rejoinder, which hints at their hypocrisy while also suggesting that they have recently exercised their own memories for purposes more narrowly rhetorical than spiritual: "I think this speech between you both was studied, / It came so roundly off" (248–249).

In the examples considered above, we have seen that forgetfulness is often imagined less as purely cognitive than as a bodily disposition, a mode of action, or a way of living. Thus, it is linked to a variety of phenomena, corporeal or not, that always have broadly social implications: lethargy, excess sleep, sloth, hedonism, alienation from God and the loss of identity. These linkages, which form a kind of rhizomatic chain, are not conceptualized. What ties all of these phenomena to forgetting and to one another, however, is their common emphasis on the undisciplined body. For example, forgetting God is understood as being lulled asleep by the pleasures of the flesh. Similarly, lethargy and forgetfulness are recognized as inseparable, each tied to the other by a shared and defining absence of disciplined activity. In this regard, Eliot's earlier adducement of one of lethargy's symptoms is of a piece with all of the other examples that we have encountered. Those sufferers from lethargy who "forget to close theyr mouthes" enact a (fantasmatic) vision of a body unregulated by even the most basic somatic discipline. As such, the lethargic or forgetful subject expresses the opposite of Renaissance ideals of masculinity. Insofar as these ideals are subtended by a logic that understands discipline and labor as constitutive of the masculine, lethargy's effeminizations, mentioned above in relation to feminine coldness, extend into the arenas of bodily comportment and social (in)action.

But what does this lack of discipline have to do with memory? As the forgetful body is constituted primarily in negative relation to discipline, so is there a crucial connection between memory and disciplined labor, one that to the early moderns would have been self-evident. As Norman M. Klein has recently put it, "Remembering was arduous. . . From the Romans through the Renaissance, students were trained to fight *aporia* [defined by Klein as 'an inability to know how or where to begin'] through 'memory theaters,' a spatial imaginary that kept knowledge from drifting into oblivion."[55] While Mary Carruthers has shown that the theatre was not the only mnemonic structure deployed in training the memory, the basic point is sound: shoring up memory requires labor and discipline. Above all, the properly orchestrated and functioning memory occupies and is defined as a space in which, in Laurentius's formulation, "lodgeth every thing in his severall place, not shufling them up disorderly together, which observeth time, circumstances and order."[56] It is in this regard that memory's dual status as agent and as fortified structure makes sense, for memory is vulnerable not only to outside attack from forgetting, but to inward disorder that is to be staved off through memory's agency. And such disorder can be understood *as* forgetting: not the obliteration of memory traces, certainly, but the rendering of those traces inaccessible. The fact that such traces are not marked clearly and lodged in a place from which they can be easily retrieved means that, in the context of an attempted act of recollection, they *are* forgotten.[57]

If memories are not located in their proper places, the failure belongs not merely (or even primarily) to the ordering agent that is memory, but to the undisciplined and idle subject who fails to train and exercise his memory appropriately. That memory is linked to discipline is made plain by Gulielmus Bergomatis: "An often callinge to mynde of things seene or h[e]ard, doth strength*en* and confirme the Memorie: for there is nothyng that is so soone encreased by diligence, or diminished by necgligence, as Memorie it selfe is: because except it be throughlye tylled and exercised with a continuall meditation, it is soone corrupted by sluggishenes."[58] Juan Luis Vives makes a similar argument:

We be framed and facioned by these three things, Knowledge, Wytte, and Memorie, and the dilige*n*ce, which we use to the atteyning of them, is called Studie. . .Memory [is] encreased by diligent tillyng and occuping thereof. . . Whether thou rede or here any thing, do it with attenci*on* & effectiously, let not thy mind wa*n*der, but constrayn it to be there, & to doo [the] thing which is in hand, and none other.

Paying close attention marks what one reads as memorable, but doing so is difficult; it requires that the mind remain focused on "the thing which is in hand," a focus that is described in terms of constraint. Reading "with attencion and effectiously" requires a well-regulated mind that refuses the temptation to let itself wander. Moreover, the language of "tilling" present in both of these quotations aligns the exercise of memory with arduous labor. This emphasis is also apparent later in Vives, when he insists that "Thou shalt not neglecte thy memory, nor suffre it to decay through ydelnesse: for it rejoyseth above al thing, to be set awork, & increaseth not a little therby. Exercise it therfor dayly with some worthy busines."[59] Vives's reference to idleness and Bergomatis's mention of sluggishness evoke our earlier discussion of the bodily dispositions of lethargy and sleep, both of which Bergomatis elsewhere explicitly links with forgetting.[60] In depicting the active use of the faculty of memory, Bergomatis and Vives also articulate a broader ideal for bodily deportment, one that champions and assumes a disciplined body marked by diligence and the regular exercise of its faculties. This linkage also underwrites John Willis's assertion in *Mnemonica* that a necessary precondition for keeping one's memory strong is "a prescript order of life" – a life in which one's behavior is organized so that practices as diverse as studying, combing one's hair and defecating occur in a fashion that conforms to the strict regimen mapped out by Willis.[61] To remember well, Willis tells us, one should live well.[62]

What underpins the linkage of memory and discipline is a pre-Cartesian conception of mind and body as entwined and imbricated in one another. Willis's "prescript order of life" makes most sense when we realize that there is no clear functional distinction to be drawn between "mental" and "bodily" activities. Similarly, the tilling metaphors of Bergomatis and Vives become more powerful when we recognize that the diligent tilling of memory, insofar as it is inseparable from a broader somatic disciplinary process, is a fully embodied activity. And what is true for memory is also true for forgetfulness, the association of which with lethargy and sleep makes plain that forgetfulness requires and engages the body in its entirety. Of course, in the physiological literature memory is often isolated as a mental faculty that is anatomically locatable, while forgetfulness is seen as the impedance of that faculty's operations (e.g., phlegm accumulating in the hindmost ventricle). However, the materials that I have been discussing suggest that, in early modern culture, one both remembers and forgets with one's entire body.

For Willis, then, "remembering well" connotes the maintenance of corporeal and psychic orderliness, the regulated nature of one's thinking mirrored in and maintained by the propriety of one's lifestyle; it is also assumed to be linked to, if not constitutive of, an idealized conception of masculinity. Memory in Willis is as disciplined and orderly as it is in the accounts of the art of memory famously catalogued by Frances Yates. It is worth noting, however, that this schema has no place for unbidden memories – memories the trajectories of which Proust's narrator so famously pursued and revealed as constitutive of his subjectivity. Unbidden memories have haunted at least two of the most famous and influential accounts of memory's working – they are the unclassifiable birds in Plato's aviary model of memory, the peremptory traces that assert themselves to Augustine's remembrancer – but they also in one way share conceptual space with forgetfulness in that they reveal the limits of a cognitive model built on the willed ordering of psychic materials. Put simply, both forgetfulness and non-purposive recollection exceed the limits of the model of memory I have been emphasizing and exploring here, a model whose stress on order and discipline leaves little room for somatic and cognitive practice outside "a prescript order of life."

Memory, then, is intimately linked with notions of discipline and order; forgetfulness, associated as it is with practices and physiological processes antithetical to ideals of bodily comportment, connotes idleness, sloth, lethargy, excessive sleep: all resistant to the claims made upon the body by discipline. We have seen in the above examples how the very act of training the memory requires and is associated with self-regulation, but it is important also to recognize the broader ideological and institutional implications of the somatic discipline upon which memory is built. Memory is obviously crucial to both religious and secular education. Such education entails not merely the mastering of content, but, as Richard Halpern has shown in relation to early modern grammar-school education, the internalization (through the disciplining of the subject) of protocols and bodily dispositions necessary to the performance of socially valorized behavior.[63] As the various examples adduced above show, memory is aligned with an array of social virtues – studiousness, diligence, rigor, piety – while forgetfulness and forgetting are associated, in a range of discourses, with everything from illness to alienation from God. Memory disciplines and interpellates the subject into the social order; forgetting is the vehicle by which the social order both imagines its opposite and polices its subjects through appeals for the reformation of their corporeal and spiritual deportment. In addition, forgetfulness constitutes a mode of being associated with humoral, spiritual and social disorder. In sum, oblivion has its own forms of embodiment and social practice, ones that are coded as at best passive and at worst sinful and erosive of identity.

Several times in the above I turned to dramatic texts to help illuminate the early modern logic of forgetting. While one could look at other kinds of "literary" sources to illustrate this logic, there are specific connections to be made between forgetting and the theatre – connections elucidated by those who were the stage's enemies.[64] Put simply, antitheatricalist writers routinely construed the theatre as a catalyst for forgetting and the somatic states with which forgetting was associated. An example is to be found in *A Treatise wherein Dicing, Dauncing, Vaine playes or Enterluds. . .are reproued*, in which John Northbrooke develops a debate between Youth and Age. After Youth attempts to justify his immoderate sleeping, Age replies,

And whereas you saye, by sleeping you hurt no man: That is not sufficient to hurt no man, but you must do good also. . .What good (I pray you) hath your sleepe and ydle pastimes done to you? which hath hindered you from all good and godly exercises. No good at all, but rather great hurte, for that you abused, and not used your sleepe in due time and order, by reason of your ydle nightwatching playes, and ydle wanton pastimes, to satisfie the pleasures and desires of the fleshe, and therefore you neede repentance.[65]

Youth's "ydle nightwatching playes" are both linked with sleep and seen as antithetical to "good and godly exercises" – that is, to secular and spiritual discipline. For Age, theatregoing is a form of hedonism that has, to modify a phrase we encountered earlier, lulled Youth asleep in the forgetfulness of God.

William Rankins more directly links forgetting and drama. Most probably referring to actors rather than audience members, Rankins asserts in a marginal gloss that "Playes make th*em* forgette GOD."[66] Rankins understands plays as transforming the behaviors of those who stage as well as those who view them: "Then drinking of the wyne of forgetfulnes, which seemed unto them more sweete than *Nectar*, and farre more pleasant then *Manna* from Heaven, to digest the diversitie of theyr daintie dyshes, they tempered theyr tongues, and outward gesture with such talke, that theyr action might be uniforme to the rarenes of theyr banquette."[67] Metaphorized as the wine of forgetfulness, the play induces audience members to match their actions to those which they see represented. This banquet obviously connotes hedonistic excess, as is underscored by the text's marginal assertion that "Plaiers are ministers of Idlenesse." Rankins sees plays as contaminating the audience with idleness, which is "so contagious, that as the Ryver *Laethes* maketh hym that drynketh therof, presentlie to forget his own condition & former deedes, so this damnable vice of idlenes, so besotteth the sences, and bewitcheth the myndes of menne, as they remembred not the profitable fruites of vertuous labor."[68] The theatre is an agent of forgetting that transforms the viewer's body from one marked by "vertuous labor" to one constituted by idleness. The reference to Lethe is pointed; the viewer of plays is understood as forgetting himself – "his own condition & former deedes" – as completely as if he had died and waded into that mythological river. For him to be besotted and bewitched is also for him to be reconstituted through and in terms of both idleness and theatre.

While Rankins understands the theatre as engendering (self-)forgetting, Stephen Gosson recognizes and takes advantage of the centrality of memory to theatrical practice in order to argue that the theatre offers an education in corruption.[69] Consider Gosson's mobilization of the connection between memory and discipline in the following:

If any goodnes were to bee learned at Playes it is likely that the Players them selves which committ every sillable to memory shoulde profitte most, because that as every man learneth so hee liveth; and as his study is, such are his manners; but the dayly experience of their behaviour, sheweth, that they reape no profit by the discipline them selves; how then can they put us in any good hope to be instructed thereby when wee have the sight of such lessons, but an houre or two as they study and practise everie daye, yet are never the better.[70]

While players work strenuously to memorize their lines, the usual association of memorial discipline with virtue and order is overturned, for the content of what the players learn besmirches their characters. Here, forgetfulness is not blamed for the corruption of the players; instead the discipline of memorization interpellates the actor into the debasing and debased institution of the theatre.

In a different text, Gosson makes what is by now a more familiar kind of argument. In what follows, the theatre is an integral component of the curriculum in a school of abuse, one in which the students are taught to forget themselves:

You are no soner entred but libertie looseth the reynes and geves you head, placing you with poetrie in the lowest forme, when his skill is showne too make his scholer as good as ever twangde: he preferres you to pyping, from pyping to playing, from play to pleasure, from pleasure to slouth, from slouth to sleepe, from sleepe to sinne, from sinne to death, from death too the Divel, if you take your learning apace, and passe through every forme without revolting.[71]

This is the antithesis of a proper education, to which memory would be central. Instead of discipline, the scholars/playgoers are offered liberty; the lessons they learn allow them to pass through every form, but the joke is that the longer their course of study, the more they become self-forgetful: the more inured they become to sloth, sleep, and sin (they advance "without revolting"). In addition, that they are preferred from death to the devil tells us that these students have failed to master the most important lesson of all: they do not remember who the Lord is.

The theatre, then, induces forgetting and engenders that character trait known as forgetfulness. Linked as it is with idleness, sloth and sleep, forgetting also promises to produce the kind of languid and effeminized (if not sinful) body we have seen on Ralegh's title page. At least, this is how those who denigrate the theatre see it. In the chapters that follow, we will discover the centrality of forgetting to specific dramatic texts by Shakespeare, Marlowe and Webster, but that centrality need not connote either simple condemnation of forgetting or the complete approval of the somatic logic that I have traced throughout this chapter. That is, while forgetting is routinely associated with a scandalous and enervating absence of discipline, Renaissance drama offers important qualifications to this characterization. In addition, it is arguably the productivity of forgetting – its status as a crucial determinant and marker of character – that makes it so troubling to antitheatricalists, who have in at least one way got it right: for all the rhetoric of those, like Thomas Heywood, who stress its educative virtues, the theatre is potentially a breeder of actions and behaviors that cannot be easily accommodated by disciplinary regimes. The early modern stage can be seen as occupying a conceptual space outside of the patterns of work, education and religious practice that are central to the shaping of the disciplined subject. However, it would finally be unsatisfactory to adduce a monolithic conception of theatre as either wholly transgressive of or complicit with (a homogenized notion of) social authority.[72] We can see, though, that memory and forgetting are categories in terms of which early modern debates about the theatre sometimes took place.

In the rest of this book, I will attend to forgetting and memory in the work of Shakespeare, Marlowe and Webster. These three playwrights are interested not merely in the forgetful body, but also in the (not unrelated topic of the) roles of memory and forgetting in conceptualizing selfhood. For these writers, forgetting and memory chart multiple interfaces between the subject and society. That is, they are the means by which the subject is located or locates himself in relation to various forms of desire and authority. "Forgetting" is the sign under which are collected models of subjectivity and of embodiment unsanctioned by secular and ecclesiastical authorities. Hamlet's forgetfulness, his lethargic non-performance of the Ghost's commands, charts the contours of his character, which emerges out of its relationship to the claims the Ghost makes on him.[73] What the Ghost calls forgetfulness limns the boundaries of that constellation of resistances, meditations, machinations and impulsive acts that is Hamlet; forgetfulness both has a content and traces the contours of a subjectivity. In sum, forgetfulness is generative of dramatic character; Hamlet's subjectivity is *produced* out of the forgetfulness that most of the writers we have surveyed would see as *erosive* of identity.

With this in mind, we will close with a brief return to Ralegh's title page. Oblivion's languid demeanor notwithstanding, this figure can be understood as laboring intensely, ceaselessly making claims on the viewing subject, potentially seducing him or her into modes of action and being divergent from those championed by History. At the same time, that History stands on Oblivion in order to "Rais[e] the *World* to good, or *Evill* fame" reveals forgetfulness as foundational; it is as mutely necessary here as it is to the aforementioned accounts of memory's fortified emplacedness. Literally, then, Oblivion bears much of the weight of History on his head. In this regard, I find Oblivion apt, for he carries that weight without stirring.

## 2 "Be this sweet Helen's knell, and now forget her": forgetting and desire in *All's Well That Ends Well*

"Anyway, it took a bit of forgetting, but I've forgotten now all right."
"All's well that ends well, then."[1]

Early in *All's Well That Ends Well*, Helena, upon being told that she "must [up]hold the credit of [her] father," declares that she cannot remember him:

> I think not on my father,
> And these great tears grace his remembrance more
> Than those I shed for him. What was he like?
> I have forgot him. My imagination
> Carries no favor in't but Bertram's.
> I am undone, there is no living, none,
> If Bertram be away.[2]

This is just one moment among several in the first eighty-five lines of the play that concerns the loss of fathers. Helena here reacts to the Countess's inaccurate assertion that, for Helena, "The remembrance of her father never approaches her heart but the tyranny of her sorrows takes all livelihood from her cheek" (1. 1. 49–51). What the Countess takes as evidence of sorrow for a dead father, Helena reveals to be grief over unexpressed love. The status of her tears, however, is complicated. Helena tells us both that she cries over Bertram and that the tears she spills "grace [her father's] remembrance more / Than those [she] shed for him" in the past, presumably at his funeral. She has "forgot" her father, but she also "grace[s] his remembrance": how do we explain this paradox? The answer lies in the disjunction between the public effect Helena's tears produce and the unseen longing that motivates them. The tears commemorate her father insofar as they are construed by the Countess and others as a declaration of woe at his loss. In this speech, Helena attests to the fact that her sadness is read by others in a way that locates her in terms of familial relations both disrupted by her father's death and constitutive of her identity as a grieving daughter. However, what engenders her grief – what undoes her, what threatens to eradicate "living" – is the absence or loss of Bertram. Unlike Hamlet's grief for a dead father, Helena's is (albeit unintentionally on her part) all "seems," the inky cloak of her countenance misleading those who scrutinize it. At the same time, the true nature of her grief, that which is beyond seems, attests to a subjectivity that bespeaks not her integration into a familial network (a network out of which her identity emerges[3]), but the reconstitution of herself in terms of her romantic desires. She has forgotten her father, and she thinks instead of Bertram, the pursuit of whom, as will become clear, is in certain ways inseparable from and dependent upon her act of forgetting.

In order to understand further the functions of memory and forgetting in *All's Well That Ends Well*, we must first examine their role in period psychological discourse, specifically as they pertain to reason, selfhood and the power of the passions. Next, we will turn to an essay by Michel de Montaigne which upends the psychological model by advancing a conception of forgetting as not erosive but productive of the rational subject. Finally, we will investigate the intertwined processes of forgetting and self-forgetting both in a brief episode from *Romeo and Juliet* and in *All's Well That Ends Well*. (This chapter is the first of three to deal with forms of self-forgetting; in this case, focus is on *erotic* self-forgetting.) *All's Well* offers a sustained examination of the problems and opportunities offered by "forgetting oneself": in particular, the crisis of identity that it entails and the desire it mobilizes. At the same time and more broadly, the play considers the complex relationship between memory and forgetting, enacting a conception of forgetting that is productive, and thus far more than memory's failure.

Works produced by "Renaissance psychologists" – writers who focus on psychology and the physiology of the brain – routinely stress the importance of memory to the operations of reason.[4] A more or less typical example is found in Pierre de la Primaudaye's *The Second Part of the French Academie*.[5] Reason, he states,

hath a judiciall seate. . . wherein. . . it heareth sutes and causes. Besides, it hath neare unto it *Memorie*, which is in place of a Notary and Secretary, and as it were a register booke, in which is entred whatsoever is ordained and decreed by reason. For as wee have neede of such a Judge as reason is, to conclude and determine finally in the minde, whatsoever may be called into question and doubted of, so is it requisite, that the conclusion and definitive sentence should be registred in *Memorie*, as it were in a roll or booke of accompt, that it may alwaies be ready and found when neede requireth. For what good should we get by that, which imagination, fantasie, and reason conceive and gather together, if it should all vanish away presently through forgetfulnesse, and no more memorie thereof should remaine in man, then if nothing at all had ben done?[6]

For La Primaudaye memory is both notary and "register booke," the latter metaphor suggesting a continuity between this account and classical ones depicting memory as a waxen tablet to be inscribed upon. (Mary Carruthers has identified two recurring classical metaphors for memory that are still current in the medieval period: the wax tablet and the "*thesaurus*, 'storage-room,' and later 'strong-box.'" The wax tablet is used to describe the "making [of] the memorial phantasm and storing it in a place in the memory," while the storage room model is most concerned with "the contents of such a memory and. . . its internal organization."[7] We saw in the last chapter that these classical metaphors are alive and well in the Renaissance; recall Charron's account of memory as "Gardian and Register of all the species or kindes and images," or Laurentius's view of it as a "rich treasurie."[8]) For La Primaudaye and other Renaissance psychologists, memory records the operations of reason. Memory is also a principle of subjective continuity, for we know who we are based upon who we have been, what we remember about ourselves. Given this, La Primaudaye's description of forgetting is important: forgetting is the force that threatens to make vanish that "which imagination, fantasie, and reason conceive and gather together" in the form of memory. Insofar as it derails judgment, forgetting would seem to exist as a threat to the rational subject.

How, then, to prevent forgetting? The answer La Primaudaye proffers is both simple and tautological: the information provided by the senses, once reason determines it accurate and worthy of recollection, should be written in the book of memory. The solution to forgetting is the writing of memory – a formulation that imagines that the act of inscription ensures the permanence and inalterability of that which is inscribed.[9] At the same time, memory is figured as both register and secretary because of the threat posed by forgetting, the force which threatens to erase or efface what is to be remembered, and by the forgetful body. As we saw in the last chapter, metaphors of memory as guardian or treasury or register suggest both its fortified nature and its vulnerability (to assault or erasure or a broader somatic mutability, all of which are linked to the absence or loss of discipline). That memory is configured in terms of the threat posed by forgetting reminds us that the two are conceptually inseparable.

But what of the *use* of memory here? La Primaudaye does not explicitly tell us what problems would be generated by forgetting, but the passage does hint at at least one of them. Judgment here describes the evaluation of "whatsoever may be called into question and doubted of" – especially that which has been perceived for the first time. When encountering the same phenomenon for the second time, the subject's reliance on memory allows him or her to respond to that phenomenon without again

appealing to "the Judge," reason; the presence in memory of "the conclusion and definitive sentence" makes such an appeal unnecessary. On the
one hand, then, the storehouse of memory is filled up through the operations of reason, while on the other memory makes possible, in certain
circumstances, the suspension of such operations. The subject relies first
upon reason, then upon the recollection of reason's judgments.

If forgetting should be conceptualized not simply as the erosion of
memory's plenitude but as a force against which memory produces itself,
the above passage also offers one view of what forgetting itself can help
produce. Without memory, it is as if, at least at the level of judgment,
"nothing at all had ben done." Forgetting entails not merely the loss
of memory traces, it also clears a space for and initiates a fresh act of
judgment; it is the precondition for something *new* being done. Moreover,
this act of judgment need not be construed as the simple repetition of
what forgetting has effaced, for the process of re-exercising judgment
always leaves open the possibility of a different conclusion. While construing forgetting as productive in this way goes against the grain of the
above passage, Michel de Montaigne, in a critique of accounts like La
Primaudaye's, advances such a reading by grounding an epistemology on
the benefits of forgetting.

Judgment as La Primaudaye describes it refers most immediately to
reason's evaluation of that which the subject has perceived. Montaigne
raises the stakes by having judgment encompass the scrutiny of the tenets
of social existence. He begins his essay "Of Lyers" by asserting, "There is
no man living, whom it may lesse beseeme to speak of memorie, than my
selfe, for to say truth, I have none at all."[10] After admitting this failing,
Montaigne refutes his countrymen's assertions that there is "no difference
between memorie and wit." Instead, he tells us that "excellent memories
do rather accompany weake judgements." Conversely, were his memory
stronger "I should easily lay downe and wire-draw [i.e., strain] my minde
and judgement, upon other mens traces, without exercising their proper
forces, if by the benefit of memorie, forren inventions and strange opinions were present with me."[11] Thus, a strong memory necessitates devoting "minde and judgement" to "other mens traces," ideas that are
denigrated as "forren inventions and strange opinions." Without memory
the subject can judge for himself or herself; s/he can produce a knowledge,
presumably through an unmediated and protoempirical examination of
the outside world, that is free of the taint of other men's ideas. Moreover,
forgetting is central to the production of such knowledge, fashioned as it
is through the exercise of judgment unencumbered by the (forgotten)
beliefs of others. Montaigne presents us with a fantasy of a subject who

originates a knowledge unfettered by received opinion. This subject is self-authorizing and self-generating, existing, thanks to forgetting, outside of a conception of ideology figured as "other mens traces."[12] In Montaigne's fantasy, the grounds for the subject's existence lie outside of ideology and memory, in a realm of unmediated judgment enabled by the salutary nature of forgetting.[13]

For Montaigne, then, memory positions the subject in relation to received (or "forren" and "strange") opinion. Forgetting, on the other hand, makes possible the production of a distinctive interiority, a subjectivity outside of ideology. This formulation of a subject unfettered by ideology seems both naive and familiar – this subject resembles, after all, the one simultaneously dreamed of and posited by the Enlightenment (albeit not in conjunction with a discourse of forgetting). Nevertheless, the theoretical wrongness of this formulation in no way militates against either the effects it might produce or the possibilities it might represent. Given this, we will pursue the implications of Montaigne's reworking of psychological discourse for erotic self-forgetting in Shakespeare. Montaigne inverts psychological discourse in a way that makes possible powerful refigurations of the role of forgetting. Although Shakespeare considers the role of forgetting in a different discursive arena, he shares Montaigne's insight that forgetting is a potent subjective force. While both writers assume the significance of forgetting for cognitive function, in Shakespeare erotic self-forgetting describes the production of a desiring subject who often experiences his or her subjectivity as a crisis of identity. (The productive nature of self-forgetting in no way guarantees that that which it produces is to be wished for by the characters who forget themselves.) For Shakespeare, while memory does not situate characters in terms of received belief, it is construed as a force responsible for both locating and limiting them socially.

In the Shakespearean examples taken up below, erotic self-forgetting does not represent the first eruption of desire in the subject. Instead, it describes what happens when that desire outstrips reason or regimen and becomes the central tenet of the subject's existence – so much so that his or her very identity is threatened.[14] What must obviously preexist this transformation in the subject is the possibility of being enticed by the senses. Put in different terms, ones that link up to the psychological discourse discussed above, forgetting oneself is akin to what occurs when the passions, which are supposed to be regulated by reason, so gain precedence within the subject that they undermine reason's ascendancy over desire.[15] This is not only a psychological but a physiological process, as is made clear in Thomas Wright's account:

Those actions then which are common with us, and beasts, we cal Passions, and Affections, or perturbations of the mind. . . They are called Passions (although indeed they be actes of the sensitive power, or facultie of our soule. . . ) because when these affections are stirring in our mindes, they alter the humours of our bodies, causing some passion or alteration in them. They are called perturbations, for that. . . they trouble woonderfully the soule, corrupting the judgement, & seducing the will.[16]

This physiological process, by which the rational subject is transformed by affections that corrupt judgment, finds its analogue in the process of self forgetting, a process that reconfigures the self in terms of desire. The interpenetration of the physiological and psychological – and the two cannot be easily differentiated between in the early modern period – is suggested in the term "self-forgetting." Forgetting oneself describes not a narrowly psychic process but a fully embodied one. While Shakespearean self-forgetting should not be reduced to a product of "perturbations," behind (or alongside) the metaphorics of self-forgetting lies a complex conception of the functioning of body and mind, a conception that informs but does not determine Shakespeare's representation of the production of the desiring subject through self-forgetting.

In discussing erotic self-forgetting, we are on the terrain not only of physiology but of ethics; rational control of the passions is the subject of much of moral philosophy, and is also a key element of early modern appeals to self-knowledge. Clearly accounts, such as Wright's and La Primaudaye's, of relations between reason and the passions are informed by ethical imperatives, just as early modern ethics is informed by faculty psychology. The interpenetration of the ethical and physiological is also assumed in numerous discussions of the efficacy of theatre. Debates about the nature and impact of dramatic representation, alluded to in the previous chapter, hinge upon the recognition that the theatre can generate both somatic and ethical effects upon its audience members; such is the logic of exemplarity, for instance. However, the theatre can also be understood as a site in which relations among emotions, ethics and forms of selfhood are imaginatively reconfigured. As Steven Mullaney has put it, "As a forum for the representation, solicitation, shaping, and enacting of affect in various forms, for both the reflection and, I would argue, the reformation of emotions and their economies, the popular stage of early modern England was a unique contemporaneous force."[17] Erotic self-forgetting both harnesses and redirects the energies and imperatives of a range of social discourses, including the ethical and physiological. Put differently, erotic self-forgetting describes and imagines forms of subjectivity that emerge out of the potent effects of desire on identity.

A brief example from Shakespearean tragedy suggests what can be at issue in both forgetting and self-forgetting. Consider Romeo and Juliet's exchange toward the end of the balcony scene:

JULIET: I have forgot why I did call thee back.
ROMEO: Let me stand here till thou remember it.
JULIET: I shall forget, to have thee still stand there,
Rememb'ring how I love thy company.
ROMEO: And I'll still stay, to have thee still forget,
Forgetting any other home but this.

(2. 2. 170–175)

For Romeo, this marks a *return* to the discourse of forgetting. Earlier in the play, in response to Benvolio's advice that Romeo "forget to think of [Rosaline]," the young lover moans, "O, teach me how I should forget to think" (1. 1. 225–226). His reply bitterly conceives of Rosaline, who has spurned him, as being as integral to him as thinking. This also hints at the extent to which passions, those perturbations that "trouble woonderfully the soule," have clouded his judgment, since his every thought is bent toward Rosaline. Needless to say, Rosaline and Romeo's thoughts are not so thoroughly entwined as our hero first claims. More to the point, forgetting functions differently in Romeo's exchange with Juliet than it did in his earlier (and soon forgotten) depiction of his lovelorn state. In the first four lines, the two lovers wittily play on the interpenetration of memory and forgetting. As Romeo is aware, Juliet's forgetting why she called him back has the consequence of continuing the period of their time together. Juliet's initial (and presumably feigned) forgetfulness is playfully and strategically extended, then transformed into a memory of how she loves Romeo's company. This recollection is also an affectionate declaration made under the sign of remembrance. While Romeo once found forgetting Rosaline as impossible as forgetting to think, here forgetting does not define the desire for love's (and perhaps thought's) cessation, but is the precondition for a relationship to be simultaneously advanced and consolidated through the act of remembering.

If the amorous banter of these four lines takes us away from the trope of "forgetting oneself," the last two lines return us to it, albeit obliquely. To Juliet's pledge to keep forgetting, Romeo replies "And I'll still stay, to have thee still forget, / Forgetting any other home but this." It is the last line that is important here, for it introduces into this exchange that which Romeo and Juliet have been trying so hard to bracket: the significance to their love of the feud between the Montagues and Capulets. Romeo's pledge to forget "any other home" is, of course, an articulation of his wish that he could forget not only his home but his family – more precisely, forget the fact of the deadly enmity that divides the Montagues and Capulets and that constrains his relationship with Juliet. Also, to forget home and family is to forget one's identity. Romeo's love for Juliet leads him to wish that he could forget himself, an act that describes the reformulation of the self in terms of desire. In a sense, Romeo's wish comes true, but only briefly. After secretly marrying Juliet, Romeo refuses the identity that his status as Montague provides: refuses, that is, to fight Tybalt. Moreover, he tries to re-imagine himself in terms of allegiance to both families when he calls Tybalt "good Capulet" and then refers to Juliet's surname as one "I tender / As dearly as mine own" (3. 1. 71–72). However, the feud, which has after all structured his relationship with Juliet, reinterpellates him as Montague after Mercutio's death. Romeo's killing of Tybalt not only represents the return with a vengeance of Romeo's status as Montague, it engenders all the tragic action that follows. Romeo's attempt to reconstitute himself both outside of family and feud and in terms of desire – his attempt, that is, to forget himself – in the end functions in the service of both feud and tragedy. As for remembering, at play's end we encounter it in a reified form, in the guise of the gold statues of the two lovers. Much like Juliet's "Rememb'ring how I love thy company," the projected statues function not only to commemorate but to initiate and develop, for it is under the aegis of remembrance that "glooming peace" (5. 3. 305) between the Montagues and Capulets is achieved.

*Romeo and Juliet* presents us with a paradigm for a type of Shakespearean self-forgetting – the rearticulation of the self in terms not of the social coordinates of one's existence but of one's desire – that has tragic consequences. In this case, self-forgetting constitutes the *production* of a self that is represented (and experienced by Romeo) as a *crisis* of identity. One could multiply examples: Antony's fitful and uneven abdication of his Roman identity through his pursuit of Cleopatra, a process thematized in the scene in which Antony laments that he "cannot hold this visible shape" (4. 14. 14); the erosion of Othello's identity through not simply jealousy but the inordinate desire of which it is the obverse, a desire that Othello fears will turn, in Iago's words, "Our general's wife [into] the general" (2. 3. 314–315); and, in the case of a non-dramatic text that is concerned with self-forgetting, Tarquin's pursuit and rape of Lucrece, which is explicitly defined as a reformulation of the self (in terms of desire) that cancels the self (as represented by familial and political relations): "Such hazard now must doting Tarquin make, / Pawning his honor to obtain his lust, / And for himself himself he must forsake" (155–157).[18] Again, in each of these instances, as in the case of Romeo, self-forgetting describes the production of a subjectivity (Antony as lover rather than triumvir) that is experienced by each character as a crisis of identity (he "cannot hold this visible shape").

Despite its demonstrated affinity with tragedy, self-forgetting does not always have dire consequences. Indeed, it registers quite differently in comedy. In *All's Well* we witness the production of subjectivities that are both constituted in terms of desire and are (somewhat uneasily) yoked to the integrationist imperatives of comedy. Moreover, while the above examples seem to suggest self-forgetting is undergone by male characters exclusively, *All's Well That Ends Well* makes plain how both gender and genre help shape the subjectivities produced by self-forgetting.

Alexander Leggatt has said of Helena, "Of all the sympathetic characters in the first part [of the play], she alone has forgotten the past and is launching with romantic aspirations into the future."[19] More precisely, Helena has forgotten her father, whose image has been supplanted in her mind by Bertram's. This description can be read as the culmination of the process of self-forgetting: Helena has forgotten her father, who emblematizes her identity, and has reconceived herself in terms of her desire, the object of which is Bertram. While in tragedy this is a recipe for disaster, in Helena's case self-forgetting drives the plot and eventually makes possible the play's (admittedly unsatisfactory) comic resolution. In forgetting her father, Helena sloughs off the identity that would fix her forever beneath Bertram. That is, her pursuit of Bertram necessitates she forget her father and the humble origins he represents, origins Bertram is unable to overlook.[20] (It also requires that she forget or ignore the social imperatives determining gender-based codes of behavior.) Moreover, this act of both father- and self-forgetting is a precondition not only to the pursuit of her desire but to the comedic action of the play.

If self-forgetting represents in tragedy an ontological crisis, in *All's Well* it is harnessed to the advancement of a comic plot that bridges social difference, a plot that tempers or modulates Helena's actions.[21] This is made clear in the Countess's attempt to integrate rhetorically Helena into her family. "You know, Helen," the Countess slyly states, "I am a mother to you" (1. 3. 137–138), a designation she returns to repeatedly over the next thirty-odd lines. Helena balks at this identification because she hopes to be not daughter but daughter-in-law. However, the Countess's slyness lies in the fact that she knows of and endorses Helena's hopes, and she acts here to spur Helena on to confessing her love. If Helena has only two scenes earlier abstracted herself from her identity, reconfiguring herself in terms of her desire for Bertram, it is suggested here that she is to be reintegrated into the social order at a higher rank; the potential problems inherent in her desire and self-forgetting are managed by her projected integration into the social order through marriage. Of course it is finally not quite this simple, for Bertram is yet to be convinced, but this scene foreshadows the play's resolution and makes it clear that Helena's self-forgetting is not incompatible with (and, as we shall see, actually functions in the service of) social regeneration. If Antony's pursuit of his desires means he can no longer "hold this visible shape," it is clear that Helena's desires will lead to marriage and her entrance into Bertram's family.

There are also limits placed on Helena's self-forgetting, limits exposed by the fact that in a crucial if elusive way Helena does remember her father. While Helena's "imagination / Carries no favor [i.e., contains no face] in't but Bertram's," memory of her father inheres in the form of his "good receipt" (1. 3. 244) or prescription. This textual trace of her father was his dying gift to Helena:

> On's bed of death
> Many receipts he gave me; chiefly one,
> Which as the dearest issue of his practice,
> And of his old experience th' only darling,
> He bade me store up, as a triple eye,
> Safer than mine own two, more dear.
>
> (2. 1. 104–109)

On the simplest level, the receipt is the distillation of his knowledge and "his old experience." However, the receipt is also metaphorized as an infant born "of his practice" – the "dearest issue" and "th' only darling" – which means that it is transmitted to his child both as a legacy and as a kind of birth. Not simply a prescription for a surefire cure, the receipt is a powerful trace of Helena's father figured as offspring. Her use of it, then, constitutes an act of remembrance understood in terms not of the image of her father but of his experience. Moreover, that use constitutes both the recollection and the extension of her father across generations, the child of his loins deploying the child of his experience. Thus, while Helena's forgetting of her father (and of the social coordinates of her identity) is a necessary precondition to her actions, memory of him still inheres in his "receipt" and in the actions she takes to save the king. Although Helena may not be able to recall her father's face, his memory resides in the objects and practices she inherits from him.[22] Memory and forgetting are shot through with one another, for Helena's successful enactment of her self-forgetting depends upon the memory of her father instantiated in the receipt.

That Helena simultaneously remembers and forgets (herself and her father) attests to the fact that even as she steps outside her identity she acts in accordance with it, remaining in crucial ways her father's daughter.[23] Such a juggling act is central to the project of Shakespearean comedy as defined by Mary Beth Rose, who follows Northrop Frye here: "In his comedies Shakespeare pits the world of individual imagination and sexual desire against the more tangible world of social and historical fact, causing the spectator to question the reality of both worlds and then reconciling the claims of both in a final, inclusive vision of the social and spiritual harmony symbolized in marriage."[24] Self-forgetting is a form that the struggle between desire and "social and historical fact[s]" takes at the subjective level, if such facts describe the social gulf separating Count and doctor's daughter. It is her identity as poor physician's daughter that Helena forgets even as at another level she depends upon it. Similarly, as Helena behaves in accordance with her desires, her actions are simultaneously in conflict and compatible with her identity. This is made clear by the fact that both the King and the Countess endorse the aspirations and applaud the character of the poor physician's daughter who forgets herself by pursuing and marrying the young Count Rosillion. If the passions function by "corrupting the judgement, & seducing the will," then arguably they motivate Helena to pursue Bertram against the (variably gendered) dictates of reason, modesty and decorum. At the same time, Helena's "corrupt judgment" enables the final scene's reconciliation, however troubling it may be. Self-forgetting here functions as the catalyst for the social order's self-perpetuation, injecting desire into the system in the name of that system, translating desire into marriage. Or at least it works this way in the case of Helena. Bertram is another story altogether, the problem of his subjection motivating self-forgetting of a more troubling nature.

If Helena claims to be unable to remember her father, Bertram describes his departure from Rosillion as "weep[ing] o'er [his] father's death anew" (1. 1. 3–4). Leaving for Bertram is an act of pained remembrance (while for the Countess his departure evokes the languages of birth and mourning: "In delivering my son from me, I bury a second husband" [1. 1. 1–2]), but it is also the entrance into what he calls the subjection of wardship: "I must attend his Majesty's command, to whom I am now in ward, evermore in subjection" (1. 1. 4–5). Unlike other young men in comedies who are recently bereft of their fathers, Bertram is not driven by, in Petruchio's formulation, "Such wind as scatters young men through the world / To seek their fortunes" (*Taming*, 1. 2. 50–51). Instead, he is to pass from the rule of one father to that of another, for Lafew tells the Countess and her son, "You shall find of the King a husband, madam; you, sir, a father" (1. 1. 6–7). Bertram's reference to subjection complicates Lafew's sanguine prognosis, raising questions about Lafew's belief that, in Vivian Thomas's concise formulation, "formal bonds are to be affective ties."[25]

The supposed affective ties between the King and Bertram are formed through a memory: the King's recollection of Bertram's father, whose "good remembrance," Bertram tells the King, "Lies richer in your thoughts than on his tomb" (1. 2. 48–49). The King detects the deceased Count Rosillion in Bertram's face, and hopes that Bertram may also "inherit" his father's "moral parts" (1. 2. 19–22). Shortly after both reading the father in the visage of the son and exhorting the son to live up to the example of the father, the King offers Bertram welcome, telling him that "My son's no dearer [to me than you are]" (1. 2. 76). Even if we emphasize affective ties over the formal bonds of wardship, what is most important to recognize is that Bertram's subjection is here extended, in the name not of wardship but of paternalism. Moreover, it is extended through recollection and recognition. Here memory works in the service of the King, locating Bertram in subjection to him.

The clearest evidence of Bertram's subjection is his enforced marriage to Helena. In this instance the imperatives of wardship supersede those of paternalism, and in a way that suggests the King's misuse, if not abuse, of his office. This is made clear in Margaret Loftus Ranald's precise distillation of the characteristics of wardship and their relevance to the play:

At the beginning of the play Bertram is a fatherless minor of noble birth and consequently a ward of the King. The duties of a guardian were threefold: (1) he should oversee the education, both mental and moral, of his ward; (2) he should judiciously administer the estates of his ward, taking care to prevent wastage by rapacious relatives or by the inexperienced minor himself; (3) he should arrange a suitable marriage for his ward in terms of age, rank, and wealth. When Helena chooses Bertram for her husband as her reward for curing the King, therefore, she is quite correct in stating that the young man is within his gift. But the fact that Bertram is his ward does not give the King the right to insist on his marriage to a woman of lower rank. . . This would constitute disparagement, a fate to which Bertram quite rightly objects. But the King outwits him by granting Helena a title of nobility to ratify her undoubted virtue and thus make her more than equal to her recalcitrant bridegroom. Where the King errs is in insisting on the young man's unwilling consent through reverential fear [in 2. 3. 158–165]. . . [Such coercion] could be invoked to dissolve the union, even if it were later consummated, since a key ingredient in matrimonial contracting was the free and unforced consent of the parties.[26]

The last few lines of Ranald's description, with their emphasis on both the King's errors and acts of shrewdness, suggest what critics have often noted – the crucial relationship here is not that of Helena and Bertram, but that of the King and the reluctant bridegroom. For Bertram, the enforced marriage is the means by which his subjection to the King is extended and reinforced. If Helena forgets (and reshapes) herself in forgetting her father, Bertram's wardship subjects him to the authority of a surrogate father. Of course, for Bertram to refuse Helena's hand would also set him against the wishes of his biological mother. Thus, Bertram resists not only the imperatives of wardship but those of his mother when he later flees his wife and vows never to consummate the relationship. Bertram's flight even encompasses the renunciation of his homeland: "Till I have no wife," he writes to Helena, "I have nothing in France" (3. 2. 74–75).

The above suggests that both mother and monarch work to enforce Bertram's subjection to wardship and the wishes of the King, wishes in line with those of the Countess. However, Bertram's resistance can also be construed as loyalty to a patrilineal identity that is threatened by the King's enforcement of his marriage to Helena. David Berkeley and Donald Keesee assert that "Bertram judges Helena by the stereotype of 'a poor physician's daughter,' and he is right to do so: lineally she is near baseness." Moreover, they suggest that her "social status intimated that Helena's blood was of tainted or very near tainted condition. The conception of stained or tainted blood inhered in Aristotelian and Galenic conceptions."[27] The concept of blood anchors period conceptions of patrilineage; it figures aristocratic descent in terms of the passage of blood through women from one generation of men to another, blood that can be contaminated by women but which in its purity signifies only as a marker of male identity. Whereas the Countess's wishes could be seen as articulating the imperatives of family and familial relations, Bertram appeals to an aristocratic, masculinist identity (which is emblematized by the ring "Bequeathed down from many ancestors" [4. 2. 43]) in resisting marriage to the "poor physician's daughter." Whether or not one accepts Berkeley and Keesee's apology for Bertram's actions, they correctly isolate the threat that the King's actions, here construed as a kind of coerced contamination, pose to Bertram's masculinist identity. However, the play takes a turn when Bertram, having fled the enforced marriage, himself acts against that identity. Herein begins Bertram's self-forgetting, emblematized by his giving away of his family ring.

Richard Wheeler perceptively notes the multiplicity of roles ascribed to Bertram over the course of the play:

the young count is identified at various moments as a nobleman of great promise, an object of adoration, a complete fool, a snob, an ungrateful son and subject, a whimpering adolescent, a warrior of heroic stature, a degenerate rake, a liar, a moral coward, a suspected murderer, and, perhaps, a regenerate husband.

Few characters in Shakespeare's comedies are called upon to fit so many different images, certainly none of Bertram's more compliant comic predecessors.[28]

That Wheeler labels this a catalogue of "images" that Bertram is "called upon to fit" suggests that at least some of these are identities ascribed to Bertram rather than enacted by him. Certainly it is the case that much of what we learn about Bertram comes from others; on several occasions characters offer us readings of his motivations or behavior. An illustrative example – a Lord describes Bertram's plans for Diana as follows: "He hath perverted a young gentlewoman here in Florence, of a most chaste renown, and this night he fleshes his will in the spoil of her honor. He hath given her his monumental ring, and thinks himself made in the unchaste composition" (4. 3. 14–18). For the Lord, Bertram's plans evidence the debasement of his will by his lust. Herschel Baker succinctly defines the will as "the nexus between judgment and sensation," as a faculty "whose object is what the judgment declares is good." However, "As a mediate faculty lying between sense and reason, the will. . . could, and often did, let the objects of sense rather than the objects of reason determine its conduct, and when it did, the result was disastrous."[29] In this account of Bertram's case, the will has broken free of reason's control and has been misdirected by lust. Moreover, this misdirection of the will is accompanied by and evidenced in the fact that Bertram has "given her his monumental ring," described by him as "an honor 'longing to our house, / Bequeathed down from many ancestors" (4. 2. 42–43) – a ring that symbolizes patrilineage, family memory and Bertram's identity.[30] At the same time, Bertram's act of self-*forgetting*, in which he betrays family memory and identity, is, we are told, also understood by Bertram as a form of self-*making*: he "thinks himself made in the unchaste composition." Self-forgetting is a violence done to the self that reconstitutes the self.

The Lord's summation of Bertram's motivations can be considered in terms suggested by Wheeler, as *ascribed* to Bertram. Certainly the end of the play seems to confirm the Lord's account. Bertram's description of Diana as "a common gamester to the camp" (5. 3. 188) suggests that once his lust was satisfied, he dissolved his attachment to Diana. However, it is important to draw a distinction between Bertram's retrospective characterization of Diana and the Lord's depiction of Bertram's motives, a depiction that is not confirmed by Bertram at the time of his attempted seduction. This may seem like quibbling, but the implications for the conception of Bertram's character are crucial. In fact, Bertram's relinquishment of his "monumental ring" marks a new stage in Bertram's flight from subjection. Having evaded for the time being the responsibilities of the ward, an evasion made in part in the name of blood and rank, Bertram paradoxically acts against his identity in giving over his ring. As Michael Friedman makes clear, the ring functions as a symbol of familial memory that embodies and anchors his identity:

Bertram's ring represents not only his duty to emulate his honorable forbears, but also his link in a chain of inheritance that has endured for several generations. In order to avoid "the greatest obloquy i' th' world" [4. 2. 43], Bertram must both keep the ring (the honor of his house handed down to him intact by his father) and eventually produce a "sequent issue" [5. 3. 196] to whom he may bequeath it. Thus, Bertram's responsibility extends to future generations as well as to the past; he owes it to his father *and* his son to serve as the intermediary between them.[31]

To part with the ring is for Bertram to forget himself: referring to the ring as he gives it away, Bertram says, "My house, mine honor, yea, my life, be thine" (4. 2. 52). To part with the ring is also to do a violence to the family memory that Bertram is supposed to protect. Bertram's self-forgetting, then, represents both a violence done to that memory and the reconstitution of himself in terms of his desire for Diana. If in tragedy this process leads to disaster, in *All's Well* it ends finally in recommitment to marriage, the reintegration of Bertram into an identity and order that he has rejected and fled. Before turning to Bertram's self-recollection, though, more must be said about his self-forgetting.

Above I insist on the difference between Bertram's unarticulated motivations and his retrospective account of his actions. This difference can be linked to the ideas that Bertram's self-forgetting involves a dislocation from both memory and his identity, and that his actions unfold in accordance with the logic of the passions. With this in mind, consider Charron's description of the influence of an appetite unfettered by reason – of, that is, the will unregulated by rational judgment – on the subject:

Man is a subject wonderfully divers, and wavering, upon whom it is very difficult to settle an assured judgement. . . by reason of the great contrarietie and disagreement of the parts of our life. The greatest part of our actions, are nothing else but eruptions and impulsions enforced by occasions. . . Irresolution on the one part, and afterwards inconstancy and instability, are the most common and apparent vices in the nature of man. Doubtlesse our actions doe many times so contradict one the other in so strange a maner, that it seemes impossible they should all come foorth of one and the same shop; we alter and we fele it not, we escape as it were from our selves, and we rob our selves. . . *We goe after the inclinations of our appetite, and as the wind of occasions carieth us, not according to reason.*[32]

This quotation, from a chapter entitled "Inconstancie," begins by asserting the shifting nature of all human action but ends by implying that reliance upon reason offers a corrective to inconstancy and instability.

Charron's inconstant subject is one who acts without memory, existing in a kind of eternal present generated by being in thrall to the appetites, to "the wind of occasions." At the same time, though, Charron's rhetoric assumes a subjective continuity that is being violated by inconstancy. This is made clear by his notion that when "we alter and. . . fele it not," we at the same time escape and rob ourselves. Alteration somehow fails to affect the self that, while being robbed, is not transformed. Although Charron does not say so, this continuity leaves open the possibility of self-remembering; the self scattered to the wind of occasions might in the future be re-collected. Such reintegration occurs when reason acts with the aid of memory, a form of action absent in the above limning of inconstancy's attributes. That being said, Charron's emphasis is clearly on discontinuity, on the subjectivity produced by self-forgetting.

Bertram, then, can be seen as Charron's inconstant subject, "a subject wonderfully divers, and wavering, upon whom it is very difficult to settle an assured judgement."[33] The abandonment of his ring emblematizes his dislocation, his sloughing off not only of his identity but of memory. Thus, it is imprecise to claim as one critic has that Bertram's "object. . . is not to form a lasting bond with [Diana]; rather, he means to seduce and abandon her, to achieve a conquest that will earn him recognition among his male peers."[34] To figure Bertram in this way is to see him consciously scheming to despoil Diana, but we never have direct access to Bertram's motivations; we only hear others' accounts of his motives. What does it mean to see Bertram less as schemer than as inconstant, as buffeted by desire in a manner enabled by the renunciation of his (conceptually intertwined) memory and identity? The desiring subject produced by Bertram's self-forgetting is akin to the riven subject of tragedy who "cannot hold this visible shape." This means, for instance, that when Bertram claims to Diana that "my integrity ne'er knew the crafts / That you do charge men with" (4. 2. 33–34), he is not a hypocrite – a category dependent upon subjective continuity – but one who, like Romeo with Rosaline, sincerely inhabits the position of earnest lover only for a time. Similarly, when Bertram later disparages Diana and denies their supposed affair, this betrays not the calculated nature of his earlier (attempted) seduction but the inconstancy of the subject who has forgotten himself and followed his shifting desires, first toward Diana's bed and then toward marriage with Lafew's daughter.

In terms of the "development" of Bertram's character, *All's Well* can be divided into three stages. The first describes the period of Bertram's subjection, a time during which the King creates an alliance, if not an equivalence, between wardship and affective relations. This stage is also defined by the subordination of Bertram's desires to the demands of his subjection, the uneasiness of which is manifested in Bertram's response to being chosen by Helena: "I shall beseech your Highness, / In such a business, give me leave to use / The help of mine own eyes" (2. 3. 106–108). If the first stage represents Bertram's subjection as problematically constraining, the second is characterized by Bertram's flight from subjection and by his self-forgetting – that is, his reconstitution of himself in terms of desires that both his subjection and his identity once held in thrall. Bertram's self-forgetting is a catastrophe, the dispelling of memory and reason, and the giving over of himself to appetite. Thus, if subjection is a problem posed by the play, Bertram's response – the extrication of himself from the networks constitutive of his identity – is even less satisfactory. The third stage involves a return to subjection: a return both to the King's authority and to marriage to Helena. This is subjection (at least ostensibly) made palatable through the regulation and recuperation of Bertram's desires, in the service of comedic closure and companionate marriage.

The final scene begins with recollections of the supposedly dead Helena: "We lost a jewel of her," the King says, "and our esteem / Was made much poorer by it" (5. 3. 1–2). Nevertheless, the King is willing to give Bertram, the cause of Helena's death, another chance: "I have forgiven and forgotten all" (5. 3. 9), he says, adding later, "The nature of his great offense is dead, / And deeper than oblivion we do bury / Th' incensing relics of it. Let him approach / A stranger, no offender" (5. 3. 23–26). While Bertram's offenses have been buried "deeper than oblivion," so in a sense has his identity; he approaches as a stranger. At the same time, his appearance before the King involves his reinstallation in relations of subjection. Two lines after the reference to Bertram as a stranger there appears the following exchange:

KING: What says he to your daughter? Have you spoke?
LAFEW: All that he is hath reference to your Highness.
KING: Then shall we have a match. I have letters sent me
That set him high in fame.

(5. 3. 28–31)

Here there is the strong echo of two earlier moments in the play. First, Bertram's merits are set forth in letters, as if he were indeed a stranger being introduced to King and court for the first time. The affective bond between the King and Bertram, established earlier through the memory of Bertram's father, has been forgotten, but forgetting is necessary to the formation of this new relationship. Second, Bertram is on the brink of another arranged marriage, one that will again attest to the King's authority over him: "All that [Bertram] is hath reference to your Highness."

This brief exchange constitutes the quasi-ritualistic reinstallation of relations of subjection, a reinstallation made possible through the forgetting of the past. And yet, the scene both echoes the forgotten past and transfigures it in the present. While forgetting is a precondition of these reconfigured relationships, the relationships themselves are haunted by that which must be forgotten in order for them to come into being.

The forgetting discussed here is obviously not self-forgetting. It is instead the forgetting necessary for the formation of a new set of social relations, a kind of forgetting the role of which is made clear in two lines uttered by the King to Bertram: "Be this sweet Helen's knell, and now forget her. / Send forth your amorous token for fair Maudlin" (5. 3. 67–68). And while the new set of relations echoes the old, involving both the return to and the reinstallation of Bertram's subjection, there is no equivalent to Bertram's reluctance to marry Helena to be found in his willingness to wed Lafew's daughter, Maudlin. While in response to Helena Bertram pleaded with the King to "give me leave to use / The help of mine own eyes," we discover here that he had earlier "stuck [his] choice upon [Maudlin]" (5. 3. 45). In fact, Bertram describes his admiration of her as the reason for his earlier denigration of Helena. Through wedlock, then, Bertram's desires will be yoked to his subjection to the King. Also, the anarchic potential of sexuality is to be contained in marriage.

Of course the projected marriage to Maudlin does not take place, in part because of the appearance of Helena's ring. This ring, one that Helena received from the King and as Diana passed on to Bertram, ruptures the relations I have just chronicled the emergence of and undoes the acts of forgetting upon which those relations were hastily built; it accomplishes this by leading the King to believe that Bertram has by "rough enforcement" taken the ring from Helena (5. 3. 107). While the King once claimed that he had forgiven and forgotten Bertram's actions, and had even encouraged Bertram to forget Helena, the ring forces the King to remember her. In fact, the ring functions as evidence of her death as powerful as the presence of her body: "And she is dead, which nothing but to close / Her eyes myself could win me to believe, / More than to see this ring" (5. 3. 118–120). Whereas Bertram's ring signifies and commemorates his family's patrilineage, Helena's functions to force recollection of her after she has been forgotten, and in doing so the ring unravels the social relations knit together by forgetting.

If the memory of Helena in the form of a ring disrupts Bertram's projected marriage to Maudlin, a marriage built upon forgetting, the appearance of the ring also marks the first step in the shaming of Bertram that makes up much of the rest of the play. Bertram's intended marriage seemed to promise the channeling of Bertram's erotic energies, but there was obviously a problem here: this, the audience knows, is the wrong marriage, and consequently Bertram's expression of interest in Maudlin is troubling. Throughout the rest of the scene, a public mortification of Bertram is enacted; evidence of his disruptive erotic escapade with "Diana" is paraded before him, in ways that both summon up his past actions and transmogrify them. That is, Bertram is provided with evidence of what he has done, evidence which he both recognizes and disingenuously denies, but which in some cases is also false: Bertram thinks that he has slept with Diana, and her appearance would seem to confirm that, but he has not actually done so. Bertram's ring functions as a pivotal piece of evidence here. Owned by "six preceding ancestors [and] / Conferr'd by testament to th' sequent issue" (5. 3. 196–197), the ring produced by Diana is read as proof positive of her claim that Bertram has promised to marry "a common gamester." The trajectory of the ring emblematizes Bertram's self-forgetting, his renunciation of his identity through the pursuit of his shifting desires, directed first to Diana and then, in accordance with the King's plans, to Maudlin. It is through his shaming, the reformation of his character through the public revelation of his inconstancy bred of self-forgetting, that Bertram's sexual desires are (arguably) finally channeled in the direction of Helena.

Shaming here is a series of acts of recollection. Additionally, remembering in this scene is a creative act, not in that it involves the construction and public promulgation of false memories (such as Bertram's memory of sleeping with Diana), but in that it is productive of the terms necessary for Bertram and Helena's renewed relationship. In describing the putatively dead Helena to the King, Bertram calls her "she whom all men prais'd, and whom myself, / Since I have lost, have lov'd" (5. 3. 53–54). Even though they appear at the end of a speech in praise of Maudlin, these lines articulate a precondition for the revivification of Bertram's relationship with Helena and offer a sign of his transformation to come. Bertram's memory of Helena, along with the ritualistic chastening and channeling of his desires, recasts her in terms that allow for his final assertion that "I'll love her dearly, ever, ever, dearly" (5. 3. 316).

And yet, there are notorious problems with the ending of this play. That the comedic closure offered by *All's Well* is so unsatisfying attests to, among other things, the ongoing problem of subjection. The ending is marked not, as in most comedies, by the promise of a wedding, but by a return to an enforced marriage. More importantly, as Wheeler puts it, "Instead of dramatizing conditions that facilitate a completed union between Bertram and Helena, the last scene. . . emphasizes Bertram's place in the social and moral world of the king."[35] Even Bertram's last

line, incompletely rendered at the end of the previous paragraph, is
equivocal; not only does it establish conditions for his affection, it also
turns a response to a question posed by Helena – "Will you be mine now
you are doubly won?" (5. 3. 314) – into a pledge directed toward the
King: "If she, my liege, can make me know this [that is, that she is with
child and wearing the ring he gave to Diana] clearly, / I'll love her dearly,
ever, ever, dearly" (5. 3. 315–316). Once again, Bertram's marriage to
Helena seems the latest in a series of negotiations between guardian and
ward, even his attenuated protestation of love made not to her but to the
King. Crucially, this ending fails to represent as most comedies do the
ascendance of the young over the old, for it is still the King's authority
that structures the scene. A happy ending? Even the King, whose authority has been reaffirmed here, acknowledges only that "All yet *seems* well"
(5. 3. 333, italics added). David Scott Kastan shrewdly notes that "If the
ending fails to satisfy it is because it is so willful, so desperate to claim
what may be 'won,' which is always less, as even Helena knows, than what
may be given."[36] The victor at the play's end is the King, but the reinstallation of his subjection over Bertram troubles the ending, suggesting
as it does the possibility that Bertram's love has been coercively won
rather than given.

The problems with *All's Well*'s ending are obviously not exhausted by
this discussion of subjection. In fact, the dissatisfactions of that ending
can be linked to a larger problem that governs *All's Well*'s reception: the
play's apparent reluctance to induce forgetting. As shown above, the
opening of the play's final scene functions as both commemoration and
invitation to forgetting ("Be this sweet Helen's knell, and now forget her")
while also making clear that the creation of a new set of social relations,
manifested in the projected marriage of Bertram and Maudlin, depends
upon forgetting. Similarly, the ending of *All's Well*, however unconvin-
cingly, calls upon both the play's audience and its characters to forget. Put
simply, to believe in a happy ending, in all being well that ends well, much
must be forgotten. This is the condition not only of this play but of all
comedies, driven as they are by conflicts that are often erased from the
minds of audience and characters by an ending that strives to make all
well.[37] Or so the theory goes. As has been ably demonstrated by critics of
Shakespeare over the last twenty-five years or so, comic resolution is
not the tidy business it purports to be, and traces of the supposedly
forgettable preconditions of that resolution linger. (Just think of feminist
accounts of "Kate's" final speech in relation to her taming.) In *All's Well*,
though, we encounter a much more radical disjunction between the social
relations (re)formed at play's end and the conditions of their emergence
than is usual in Shakespeare. Barbara Hardy notes this disjunction when

she argues that "this end doesn't simplify memory of the past for charac-ter or audience."[38] Instead, the ending does not simplify forgetting, does not allow for the troubling preconditions of the ending – the mortification of Bertram, for instance, or his reinforced subjection to the King – to be forgotten. In refusing such simplification, the play offers us an explor-ation of the meanings and effects of forgetting, one that goes on not only at the level of theme or content – through the representation of acts of forgetting and of the process of forgetting oneself – but also at the level of structure. What this exploration makes explicit is that forgetting is not merely erosive of memory but is a productive force in its own right.

Perhaps most important, however, is *All's Well*'s emphasis on erotic self-forgetting. As we saw in the previous two chapters, defenders and assailants of the theatre read both memory and forgetting along the axis of exemplarity. Self-forgetting's significance lies elsewhere. In *All's Well*, erotic self-forgetting registers the effects of strong desire and, especially in the case of Bertram's bad behavior, provokes the audience to ethical judgment. But the response of the audience is not limited to judgment, for self-forgetting also harnesses the theatregoer's own desires. Cynthia Marshall has analyzed "the considerable pleasure afforded to early modern audiences by experiences of shattering or dissolution."[39] Both a figure for and a product of the dissolution of identity, erotic self-forgetting is a source of such pleasure for the audience (if not necessarily for *All's Well*'s characters). However, pleasure lies not only in the shat-tering of identity, but also in the imaginative gains self-forgetting has to offer. If, as Mullaney suggests, the theatre is a site for reconfiguring relations between passions and modes of being, then *All's Well* can be understood as staging different possibilities for such relations. While by the end of the play both Helena and Bertram have resumed identities they had earlier lost or abandoned, they have also renegotiated relations between their desires and those identities. One would be hard pressed to see either character as an exemplar, except in the most imprecise and least convincing of ways. Instead, our interest in Helena and Bertram lies finally in their self-forgetting – in, that is, *All's Well*'s dramatic exploration of the effects of desire on identity.

# 3    "If he can remember": spiritual self-forgetting and *Dr. Faustus*

In the opening monologue in which he urges himself to "Settle [his] studies . . . and begin / To sound the depth of that [he will] profess," Dr. Faustus skims across the surfaces of logic, medicine, and law before asserting that "divinity is best."[1] Soon, however, Faustus rejects religious study, shaken by his reading in Romans 6: 23 that "The reward of sin is death," then in 1 John 1: 8 that all humans are sinners. These readings precede and catalyze his embrace of the "metaphysics of magicians" (1. 1. 49), for, rather than sin and death, necromantic texts offer him "a world of profit and delight, / Of power, of honour, and omnipotence" (53–54). Critics have long pointed out what would have been obvious to an early modern audience, that in his scrutiny of Jerome's Bible Faustus stops short. His hasty summation and rejection of various forms of study are mirrored at the level of the scriptural text by his premature repudiation of Christianity, an action predicated upon an incomplete reading of Romans 6: 23 that effaces the possibility of salvation. This repudiation marks Faustus as a "learned fool," one for whom "Simple, plain truths" are precisely the ones he "can neither see nor hear."[2] In relation to Faustus's incomplete reading of Romans, Judith Weil asks a crucial question: "How should we regard a 'divine in show' who . . . seems to be reading St Paul for the first time?"[3] How indeed. This chapter suggests that Faustus is not encountering this text for the first time, but is instead forgetting where it leads, forgetting the passage's full meaning and significance. In fact, insofar as reading scripture is an exercise designed to *remind* readers, to bring them to knowledge they already have, Faustus can be understood as forgetting what is never erased from his mind. This view of Faustus's reading is confirmed by Mephistopheles' later revelation: "When thou took'st the book / To view the Scriptures, then I turned the leaves / And led thine eye" (5. 2. 99–101). Mephistopheles' power lies not merely in his turning of the pages but in his ability to suppress the passage's mnemonic function by "leading Faustus's eye." Indeed, this moment echoes several others in which Mephistopheles lures Faustus to abandon what he knows in favor of visual, even theatrical, pleasures that do the work of inducing self-forgetting.[4]

Faustus's incomplete recollection of the passage from Romans hints at early modern conceptions of forgetting and remembering that are intimately connected with Marlowe's play. In these conceptions, which are extensively developed in a sermon by John Donne discussed below, forgetting is understood not as the erasure of knowledge necessary to salvation from the memory, but as an action or series of actions that represents a particular disposition toward that knowledge. *Dr. Faustus* traces the disastrous effects of Faustus's spiritual self-forgetting, a process that can be described in terms of what Richard Waswo has called the "mystery of choice against knowledge and conscience."[5] However, *Faustus* can also be read as equating the allure of self-forgetting with that of the theatre itself. The significance and nature of theatre in *Dr. Faustus* remain elusive; even as it acts in the service of self-recollection, Marlovian theatre threatens to engender self-forgetting. At the same time, the play should be accounted for less in terms of either its heterodoxy or orthodoxy than as a text in which categories for moral valuation are revealed to be inadequate to the drama of Faustus's self-forgetting.

Whereas *All's Well*'s representation of erotic self-forgetting stems from its engagement with the physiology and ethics of reason, memory and the passions, in *Dr. Faustus* we encounter a model of self-forgetting to which issues of salvation and damnation are central. (As will become plain, this is not to say that the erotic plays no part in Faustus's self-forgetting.) The language of spiritual self-forgetting and self-remembering appears in a variety of early modern British works written by both "hot" and "cold" Protestants, usually in conjunction with exhortations against worldly and sinful behavior. For instance, the Puritan divine Paul Baynes asks, "What makes men sweare, bowze, give place to their lusts, goe on in hardnesse of heart?" then answers, "it is forgetting themselves, and never once considering what they doe, and how they goe on."[6] In an example particularly resonant for *Dr. Faustus*, one writer, while discussing devil-inspired misreadings of the Bible, asserts that the true purpose of Scripture is not "to drive men into despaire, but rather hereby to exhort, perswade, and to give caveats, and warning peeces unto all men that run at randome after the world, to remember them selves, and their dangers, and tickle states."[7] A sermon delivered by John Donne defines and develops the logic of spiritual self-recollection and self-forgetting.[8] This work also offers the interpretive key necessary to unlock Faustus's forgetting.

In a sermon preached at Lincoln's Inn in 1618, Donne famously states that "The art of *salvation*, is but the art of *memory*."[9] Strategies for memory training emerged in antiquity, and their influence was still felt in the Renaissance.[10] Mary Carruthers offers a succinct definition of the logic and practice of memory training:

The fundamental principle is to "divide" the material to be remembered into pieces short enough to be recalled in single units and to key these into some sort of rigid, easily reconstructable order. This provides one with a "random-access" memory system, by means of which one can immediately and securely find a particular bit of information, rather than having to start from the beginning each time in order laboriously to reconstruct the whole system.[11]

The memory architecture of the "rigid, easily reconstructable order" – the order upon which artificial memory is built – provides both storage and an organizational principle for the placement and retrieval of information. One prominent memory structure is that of the *thesaurus sapientiae*, which metaphorizes memory as a storage room or strong box. Of the *thesaurus,* Carruthers says, "For whatever memory holds occupies a *topos* or place, by the very nature of what it is, and these *topica*, like bins in a storehouse, have both contents and structure. Every topic is in this sense a mnemonic, a structure of memory and recollection."[12] Thus, the rememberer imaginatively travels to one of these *topica* to gather up not only a specific piece of information, but also other pieces on the same "topic." The retrieval of information should not be construed as a simple mechanical process, however.

Because it recalls signs, reminiscence is an act of interpretation, inference, investigation, and reconstruction, an act like reading. . . . The task of the recollector who is composing (and . . . recollection is commonly described as an act of composition, a gathering-up into a place) is to select the most fitting and adequate words to adapt what is in his memory-store to the present occasion.[13]

This formulation helps us understand why memory was understood as a crucial element of rhetorical performance, which entailed the composing of recollected matter in accordance with the exigencies of a specific rhetorical situation.[14] It also shows that recollection is interpretive, a central component of a creative process.

Importantly, the book itself could serve less as a source of novel information than as an aid to memory.[15] While print eventually spelled the death of memory training, early modern manuscripts and printed texts could still operate as medieval books often did, as reminders of things already known. The books of the Bible provided the raw material for a memory structure, their very titles lending themselves to the construction of a "rigid, easily reconstructable order" in terms of which scriptural matter is first organized in, and then retrieved from, the subject's memory. Moreover, as Donne's sermon will make plain, the early modern church sermon constitutes such an order.[16] Donne renders explicit the connection between the logic of the sermon and the processes of memory; he also defines what it means to remember yourself in ways that help to illuminate the nature and implications of Faustus's act of forgetting.

In light of the above, two main implications emerge from Donne's assertion that "The art of *salvation*, is but the art of *memory*." These implications imply slightly different effects generated by the sermon. First, we can understand the "art of salvation" as describing the disposition of material in a way that makes it available to the remembering subject. The sermon functions to provide information necessary to salvation, information to be planted in and retrieved from the memory under specific mnemonics. The second point focuses not on the disposition of material but on the recollection of it. Read in terms of retrieval, Donne suggests that knowledge necessary to salvation is already available to his audience, and that his sermon, which details that knowledge, only serves as a reminder. The sermon answers to the imperative to "know yourself"; it is the vehicle by which the auditor is reminded of salvational knowledge and brought to the realization of his own sinfulness. As we shall see, at different points in the sermon Donne mobilizes both of these meanings, each expressive of different facets of the art of memory.

Devoting his exegesis to Psalm 38. 3, Donne argues that this line ("There is no soundnesse in my flesh, because of thine anger, neither is there any rest in my bones, because of my sinne") functions as a "key" to remembrance and that "The faculty that is awakened here, is our *Memory*."[17] How this key works is made explicit in the following passage. After discussing in the preceding sentence the effects on David of a different "*Psalm for Remembrance*," Donne explicates the line from Psalm 38:

Being lock'd up in a close prison, of multiplied calamities, this [line] turns the key, this opens the door, this restores him to liberty, if he can *remember*. *Non est sanitas, there is no soundnesse, no health in my flesh*; Doest thou wonder at *that*? Remember thy selfe, and thou wilt see, that thy case is worse then so; *That there is no rest in thy bones*. That's true too; But doest thou wonder at *that*? Remember thy self, and thou wilt see the cause of all that, *The Lord is angry with thee*; Find'st thou *that* true, and wondrest *why* the Lord should be angry with thee? Remember thy self well, and thou wilt see, it is *because of thy sins, There is no soundnesse in my flesh, because of thine anger, neither is there any rest in my bones, because of my sinne*. So have I let you in, into the whole Psalm, by this key, by awaking your memory.[18]

Donne forms a logical chain that leads the sinner from "multiplied calamities" to the recollection that the frailness of the flesh owes itself to God's anger at his sinful state; each phrase in the line from Psalm 38 is designed to prompt self-recollection. Here, to remember yourself is to remember the unsoundness of your body and the righteousness of God's wrath; Donne's reading also leads to the memory of the possibility of salvation, that which will open the door and restore the listener to liberty through his becoming susceptible to the operations of grace. Remembering is performative, the shaping or reconstituting of the self in terms of knowledge already acquired but not necessarily lived in terms of. The sermon concludes with Christ's sacrifice and the medicine it offers to the sinner's aching body and soul: "Gods physick, and Gods Physician [are] welcome unto you, if you be come to a remorsefull sense, and to an humble, and penitent acknowledgement, that you are sick."[19] Salvation is the medicine that cures those ailments the penitent realizes he suffers from only as a result of remembering himself.

Crucial to the logic of performative remembering in this or any other sermon is repetition. As we have seen, the sermon is designed to remind the auditor of what he or she knows. The anonymous author of *The Doctrine of the Bible: Or, Rules of Discipline* states that a central function of the preacher is "To remember the hearers of the word, what they have heard: & to be serious with them, not to forget that which they have learned, but to bring forth fruits of good life."[20] The fruits of good life are available to those who do not forget, who keep constantly in front of them "what they have heard." Knowledge conveyed by a preacher is salvational not if it is merely recognized or understood, but if it is integrated into the fabric of the auditor's being and thus translated into action. How does the sermon attempt to turn what is known – what can be recollected – into what is lived? Echoing the disciplinary procedures of the grammar school, sermons (both individually and in a series) strive through repetition to turn matter worth remembering into salvational knowledge in terms of which the auditor lives. Such sermons are designed to prompt meditation in each auditor, and it is thanks to meditation – upon one's sins, perhaps, or one's mortality – that the subject is shaped through religious doctrine; meditation is one vehicle by which that doctrine is internalized. Moreover, while not identical to recollection, meditation can be hard to distinguish from it.[21] Remembering mortality without proper spiritual reflection could lead to despair or damnation (as in Faustus's case). It is meditation and repetition that give the sermon's appeal to memory its potential efficacy.[22]

The function of meditation and repetition is important for thinking about both Donne and *Dr. Faustus*. Self-forgetting is not incompatible with the recollection of knowledge that could save you. However, having that knowledge and living in terms of it – meditating upon it, remembering it, acting upon it – are two different affairs. Living in terms of that knowledge requires its translation into behavior and into specific bodily comportments; remembering the future is a fully somatic practice. Faustus's initial act of forgetting – his failure to complete the sentence from Romans 6: 23 – describes his willful refusal to live in accordance with what he knows. In choosing at this same moment necromancy over divinity, Faustus emblematically turns his back on the process by which scriptural knowledge could, through his self-subjection to the discipline of further study of divinity, "bring forth fruits of good life."

For Donne, self-remembering can involve accessing a knowledge that exists independently of, but which finds its analogy in, holy writ – a knowledge that emerges out of the subject's remembering of spiritual wisdom attained through communication with God. Donne reworks Plato, who argues in the *Meno* that memory is the soul's recollection of knowledge that it had before its incarnation. As Donne himself puts it, "*Plato* plac'd *all learning* in the memory; wee may place *all Religion* in the memory too: All knowledge, that seems new to day, says *Plato*, is but a remembring of *that*, which your soul knew before."[23] Interestingly, both here and in Plato's schema embodiment is conjoined with the initial forgetting of knowledge, whereas education entails the (usually partial) recollection of the world of the forms. As Mircea Eliade describes it, "For Plato, living intelligently, that is, learning to know and knowing the true, the beautiful, and the good, is above all remembering a disincarnate, purely spiritual existence. 'Forgetting' this pleromatic condition is not necessarily a 'sin' but is a consequence of the process of reincarnation."[24] In Donne's syncretic reworking of Plato, though, the forgetting of spiritual knowledge is the forgetting of the self, and both describe the condition of being in sin.[25]

In addition to advancing the notion of self-remembering as the recollection of wisdom communicated by God, Donne's sermon strives to engender in its auditors a simpler kind of self-remembering. This kind requires drawing upon a spiritual and scriptural education, the traces and foundations of which are organized in terms of the mnemonics of biblical book titles. Both kinds of self-remembering are evident in the following passage:

Nay, he that hears no Sermons, he that reads no Scriptures, hath the Bible without book; He hath a *Genesis* in his *memory*; he cannot forget his *Creation*; he hath an *Exodus* in his memory; he cannot forget that God hath delivered him, from some kind of *Egypt*, from some oppression; He hath a *Leviticus* in his memory; hee cannot forget, that God hath proposed to him some Law, some rules to be observed. He hath *all* in his memory, even to the *Revelation*; God hath *revealed* to him, *even at midnight alone*, what shall be his portion, in the next world; And if he dare but remember that nights communication between God and him, he is well-near learned enough. There may be enough in *remembring our selves*; but sometimes, that's the hardest of all; many times we are farthest off from our selves; most forgetfull of our selves.[26]

The thrust of this passage is plain: the knowledge and wisdom contained in the Bible, first, can be accessed in ways that do not require familiarity with scripture and, second, can be collected under the term "self-remembering." Self-remembering for those not versed in Scripture consists of both the individual subject's recollection of deliverance from a personal oppression and his "remember[ing] that nights communication between God and him."

Self-remembering, then, would seem to entail divine illumination not necessarily mediated by scriptural texts. However, Donne's sermon asserts the primacy of the events (and book titles) that structure the Bible's contents: Genesis, Exodus, Revelation. Those who do not attend sermons or read the Bible are still to process their experience through categories laid down in that text, categories that take on a universal authority. For Donne's auditors, these headings function as mnemonics; they are asked first to recall the contents of each book of the Bible and then to find analogues in their pasts for the material they encounter there. Such a process arguably occurs through the location of a set of correspondences between Scripture and subject. According to A. M. Guite, Donne shows in this sermon that "the pattern of the whole Bible has an interior correspondence and reflection in our own memories, and if we can only return to our memories and discern the pattern we will discover the meaning of the experience which leads us to God."[27] Perhaps, but the practical effect of Donne's sermon is to contribute to the broader shaping of the auditor's past in terms of the contents of these books. Donne works to ensure that future mention of Exodus evokes in his auditors not only the passage of the Jews from Egypt, but also the personal deliverances they have been invited to frame in terms of biblical precedent. That is, while Donne allows for the retrieval of memory units present in the subject's mind "without book," he also works to ensure that the listener's experience is organized in terms of the biblical mnemonic. It is through use of this "rigid, easily reconstructable order" that a consolidation of scriptural and personal memories is effected.[28] Donne's sermon aspires to engender in its audience a kind of self-remembering predicated upon the yoking of biblical content, retrieved from under the mnemonic of the book title, and individual experience, planted in the mind under the sign of that mnemonic. Not only is the auditor to internalize scripture, he is to reorganize his interior life and his history in terms of it.[29] More broadly, in recalling individual experiences, the auditor is to situate them in relation to biblical imperatives and the values they are believed to underwrite.

While Donne is obviously invested in educating his auditors, he at the same time posits a pre-existing and coherent Christian self to be remembered or forgotten, an identity for the subject to act in the service of or against. Put differently, he imagines the self-forgetting subject as one who is divided from his true self and thus from his proper relationship to God. Judith Butler's influential discussion of gender as imitation can be usefully appropriated to describe spiritual self-remembering in different terms. Like gender, the remembered self "*is a kind of imitation for which there is no original*; in fact, it is a kind of imitation that produces the very notion of the original as an *effect* and consequence of the imitation itself."[30] In other words, the remembered self is the "true self" constituted as it is seemingly returned to. On the other hand, self-forgetting is the *fashioning* of a self understood by Donne as a *deviation* from self. That is, *contra* Donne, self-forgetting defines its own form of selfhood. But exactly what is described when Donne refers either to remembering or forgetting the self?

Donne presents us with multiple but related models for self-remembering: as awareness of bodily infirmity, divine wrath, sin and the possibility of salvation; as reliance on a knowledge that is both innate and emerges out of a "nights communication" with God; as a scriptural education that precedes and is recalled, extended and personalized by the sermon itself; and as a pattern of behaviors that arises out of and alongside all of these. Donne sees self-remembering as action in the service of a known future. As suggested in the introduction, self-forgetting routinely connotes dislodgement from one's proper "place." Self-recollection implies the resumption of that place, with "place" understood here less in social than in cosmological terms. To remember oneself is to live in accordance with the imperatives of one's position in the divine order, and evidence of such self-recollection is found in renouncing the worldly and focusing on death. As if confronted with a *memento mori*, each person in Donne's audience is tacitly asked to remember his sin and thus his fate, to recall what is to come and to consider the state of his soul.[31] Self-remembering activates knowledge contained in memory that renders the self susceptible to the workings of grace, and the "psalm for remembrance" can aid the reader in accessing that knowledge: "this turns the key, this opens the door, this restores him to liberty." The difficulty of this operation is made plain, however, in the phrase that finishes the sentence just quoted: "if he can *remember*." Donne recognizes how difficult self-remembering can be: "There may be enough in *remembring our selves*;

but sometimes, that's the hardest of all; many times we are farthest off from our selves; most forgetfull of our selves." What does self-forgetting mean here? To forget oneself is to give oneself over to the pleasures of this world and to live without a ready awareness of sin, to be "farthest off from" and to act against the self that emerges out of spiritual and/or scriptural knowledge, a self that is recalled (and constituted) through the intertwined arts of salvation and memory. At the same time, self-forgetting also describes and defines a selfhood: that of the unrepentant sinner who acts against what he knows. In addition, self-forgetting for Donne all too frequently limns the early modern subject's spiritual condition.

"This turns the key, this opens the door, this restores him to liberty, if he can *remember*": Donne's account of the ideal functioning of the Psalm also serves as a description of what Romans 6: 23 offers to Faustus, the possibility of salvation if he can both recollect the end of the passage and remember himself. However, Faustus is Donne's self-forgetting subject, as is made plain by his forgetting in his first monologue both Christian doctrine and what he already knows. Following Donne, we can see that this act of forgetting does not represent the erasure of knowledge from the memory; instead, it represents the failure to live in accordance with that knowledge, to structure one's life in terms of it. Thus, Faustus's forgetting of the possibility held out by Romans – his failure to recognize the phrase from Romans as a mnemonic for the entire verse and the doctrine of salvation it articulates – is performative; it both stages and stands in for the type of selfhood that emerges when we are "most forgetfull of our selves."

Faustus's forgetting of the rest of Romans 6: 23 reveals to the audience at the very outset of the play that his memory has been clouded by sin and worldly ambition. The process of mortification offered Donne's auditors (which begins with their acknowledging their sins and thereby "remembering themselves") is rejected by Faustus, along with the study of divinity, in favor of "a world of profit and delight" (1. 1. 53).[32] Faustus refuses to recognize the purpose of Scripture, which, as we have seen, was not "to drive men into despaire, but . . . to [prompt them to] remember them selves, and their dangers, and tickle states." The important point is that Faustus's self-forgetting represents, in Waswo's phrase, "choice against knowledge and conscience." That Faustus reads or remembers no further than "the reward of sin is death" does not represent merely a failure to remember but also a will to forget. Such a will is not to be confused with an anachronistic conception of repression predicated on the submergence of disagreeable psychic matter; instead, the will to forget suggests a form of selfhood grounded in worldly affairs. This selfhood is constituted in direct contradiction to matter that, as long as it is remembered only intermittently, remains external to the subject's sinful self-formation – a self-formation described by Donne as a failure to remember the self. That such matter can be remembered without permanently shaping the subject is critically important. This possibility is suggested by Paul Baynes, whose emphasis on repetition attests to the necessity of *continual* recollection for the formation of the pious subject: "therefore as you will have the latter end peace, so remember your wayes, sinnes, declinings; the more you remember them, the more God will forget them (protionably [sic] to that, If we condemne our selves, God will not condemne us), and we had need hold our hearts to the remembrance of them."[33] Repeatedly remembering our sins increases the chance that God will forget (and/or forgive) them; in addition, the discipline of frequent recollection might save us by shaping our behavior (as our hearts act in accordance with the remembrance of our sins) in ways that make us susceptible to the workings of grace. For Baynes, Faustus's initial act of forgetting would immediately reveal how far he is from having his sins forgiven by God.

Repeatedly Faustus takes the first step toward salvation as delineated in Donne's sermon by (fleetingly) remembering his sins, only to return to performing them.[34] In at least one instance, memory is made central to the possibility of Faustus's attainment of redemption. After Mephistopheles refuses to tell Faustus who made the world, the following exchange occurs:

FAUSTUS:  Villain, have not I bound thee to tell me anything?
MEPHISTOPHELES:   Ay, that is not against our kingdom.
This is. Thou art damned. Think thou of hell.
FAUSTUS:  Think, Faustus, upon God, that made the world.
MEPHISTOPHELES:   Remember this.

(2. 2. 170–175)

Mephistopheles then exits, only to return shortly thereafter with other demons. What Mephistopheles means when he demands that Faustus "Remember this" is not immediately clear,[35] but a compelling reading that intersects with my argument can be offered. While Faustus thinks "upon God, that made the world," Mephistopheles with his utterance (and perhaps the sweep of his arm) gestures toward the world itself and urges Faustus to remember it. Certainly Marlowe's "world" is not always clearly distinct from the hell which Mephistopheles asks Faustus to think of; as Mephistopheles famously uttered a few scenes earlier, "this is hell, nor am I out of it" (1. 3. 75). More significantly, in this instance remembering the world is distinct from remembering the God who made it. Remembering the world – being worldly, "run[ning] at randome after the world" – involves forgetting yourself, whereas to think upon God is to remember both the state of your soul and your inevitable end. That Faustus remembers this world is made plain about thirty lines later, when we witness him, after quickly quelling self-doubts articulated by the Good Angel, eagerly awaiting the parade of the seven deadly sins: "That sight will be as pleasant to me as paradise was to Adam the first day of his creation" (2. 3. 104–105). Faustus's thinking "upon God" is answered by Mephistopheles' appeal to his memory: remember this world (by committing the sins associated with it) and forget its creator. This appeal stands as an example of Mephistopheles' strategy of "leading Faustus's eye" away from the spiritual and toward the pleasures of this world.[36] To accede to Mephistopheles' appeal, Faustus must forget himself, as he does by revelling in the spectacle of the seven deadly sins, which, we are told, "doth delight [his] soul" (163). Moreover, in forgetting himself he is forgetting God – that is, forgetting the precepts that both constitute obedience to the divine and mark one's susceptibility to the operations of grace.[37]

The penultimate sin to parade before Faustus is Sloth, who describes himself as "begotten on a sunny bank," and follows up on that revelation by saying that "I'll not speak a word more for a king's ransom" (2. 3. 155–156). (In the A-Text, Sloth has slightly more to say for himself: "I am Sloth. I was begotten on a sunny bank, where I have lain ever since, and you have done me great injury to bring me from thence. Let me be carried thither again by Gluttony and Lechery. I'll not speak another word for a king's ransom" [2. 3. 155–159].) Joseph T. McMullen discusses the ways in which sloth is conceptualized in relation to, in his words, "inadequate knowledge and ultimate despair." He offers as evidence this excerpt from *Two Guides to a Good Life*, published in 1604 and sometimes attributed to Bishop Hall:

Omission is a kinde of sloth, whereby we let slippe the knowledge of such thinges as we ought to knowe, or the prosecution of such thinges as we ought to doe, and this is the faulte of those that being c[om]maunded to watch and pray, overpasse that duety by the means of being imploied about worldly vanities, or of such as know that god is the gracious giver of all those benefites which they enjoy, and yet forget to give him thanks for the same, or resolving upon some good worke to the advauncement of gods glory and the profite of the common wealth, are carried away through the streame of their owne affections and so leave it unfinished.[38]

While this passage begins with things we ought to know, it soon turns to what we know but do not acknowledge. This account of omission as a kind of sloth intersects with the depiction of Faustus as self-forgetting subject; in his exchange with Mephistopheles, Faustus reveals himself as one who "know[s] that god is the gracious giver of all those benefites which they enjoy, and yet forget[s] to give him thanks for the same." Despite what one might expect, sloth, like self-forgetting, is not incompatible with activity; both entail behaving in a way that is contrary to one's own spiritual knowledge.[39]

A crucial episode of self-forgetting occurs in act four, scene one, and, interestingly, Faustus is not the one who forgets himself. For the entertainment of Emperor Charles of Germany, Faustus, with Mephistopheles' aid, "present[s] the royal shapes / Of Alexander and his paramour" (4. 1. 93–94). Faustus warns Charles that he must "in dumb silence let them come and go" (96). The stage directions tell us that, after Alexander kills Darius in this spirits' dumb show, "He embraceth [his paramour] and sets Darius's crown upon her head; and, coming back, both salute the [German] Emperor, who, leaving his state, offers to embrace them, which Faustus seeing suddenly stays him." To the emperor, Faustus then says, "My gracious lord, you do forget yourself. / These are but shadows, not substantial" (103–104). Charles's (self-)forgetting has numerous valences. First, Charles forgets that Faustus insists he must let the spirits "come and go"; in a parody of Faustus's pursuit of forbidden knowledge, Charles disobeys the edict of the creator of this tableau. Second, Charles forgets his identity as emperor. He "leav[es] his state," a phrase that suggests both the physical movement from his throne and those who attend upon him there and the metaphorical departure from his proper role as ruler. (The fact of this departure comes more clearly into focus once we recall that in period theories of the body politic, the head of state ideally functions as the force that regulates the potentially unruly passions of the other members of the commonwealth; here Charles gives himself over to those passions as they manifest themselves in the would-be diabolic embrace.) Third, he is ravished by this spectacle much as Faustus was by the earlier pageant of the seven deadly sins, which we have already linked to the latter's self-forgetting; connecting the two events helps us see that both examples of diabolic magic distract their viewers from thinking upon God by "leading their eyes" to theatrical spectacles.

A fourth point emerges when we consider Charles's attempted embrace as having both sexual and spiritual connotations. Here the emperor's forgetting of himself entails acting upon his desires and against his identity as both emperor and one who is "substantial"; it implies an unholy union with "shadows" that is interrupted by Faustus. The emperor fuses two forms of self-forgetting, the spiritual and the erotic. If Faustus's earlier self-forgetting involved his acting against knowledge that he possessed, the emperor's connotes something approaching a diabolic union.

The sexual nature of this attempted embrace is glanced at in the comment made by Benvolio immediately before the appearance of the spirits: "An thou bring Alexander and his paramour before the Emperor, I'll be Actaeon and turn myself to a stag" (98–100). Actaeon's metamorphosis into a stag, which was in turn torn apart by Actaeon's own hounds, was prompted by his witnessing the spectacle of Diana bathing naked; his forbidden desire for the chaste goddess led to a transformation that metaphorizes the subject's giving himself over to his passions, a process echoed here in the emperor's "leaving his state." By succumbing to his desires, that is, the self-forgetting Charles could be torn apart, disarticulated much as Actaeon is.[40] With this in mind, it is worth pausing further over the allegorical significance of Actaeon. In his *A Choice of Emblemes*, Geffrey Whitney tells us that Actaeon stands for "those whoe do pursue / Theire fancies fonde, and thinges unlawfull crave," while his hounds represent "theire affections base, [which] / Shall them devowre, and all their deedes deface."[41] Torn apart by his own devouring desires, the self-forgetter is also destined to be forgotten, for his previous deeds are defaced by his own corrupt actions. Self-remembering, on the other hand, promises reintegration and the restoration of a lost wholeness – the re-collection of the self.

The implications of the emperor's sexual and spiritual transgressions can be pursued even further. In his groundbreaking *Homosexuality in Renaissance England*, Alan Bray has discussed the linkages between sodomy, sorcery and heresy.[42] Sodomy, Bray argues, cannot be reduced to homosexual desire or activity; it is instead both a "disorder in sexual relations that, in principle at least, could break out anywhere," and, more broadly, "a universal potential for disorder which lay alongside an equally universal order."[43] The emperor's attempted embrace of the incubus and succubus who take the shape of Alexander and his paramour not only evokes the sodomitical (through the desire for demons gendered male and female), but also reveals a connection between discourses of self-forgetting and a conception of sodomy as corrosive of both social and cosmic order. In the diabolic union, the two forms of self-forgetting coalesce, for that union not only mobilizes a desire erosive of traditional identity and of order – again, the Emperor emblematically abandons his role and responsibilities by "leaving his state" – but, relatedly, represents an aggressive action taken against one's knowledge of self and God. In this instance, however, Charles's self-forgetting is disrupted by the intercession of Faustus. This is ironic, for Faustus later enacts what he here prevents the emperor from doing; his kissing of the succubus Helen of Troy marks the culmination of Faustus's self-forgetting.

Just as Faustus turned quickly from thinking upon God to revelling in the spectacle of the seven deadly sins, he later quells his anxieties about his fate by calling for Mephistopheles to "glut the longing of [his] heart's desire" (5. 1. 86) by conjuring up Helen of Troy to be his paramour.[44] That this is an instance of self-forgetting is made obvious in Faustus's assertion that Helen's "sweet embraces may extinguish clear / Those thoughts that do dissuade me from my vow, / And keep my vow I made to Lucifer" (89–91). This scene echoes the one that we have just been examining; in fact, Charles's attempted embrace can be seen as establishing limits that are transgressed in this scene.[45] Faustus takes precisely those steps he has forbidden the emperor to take, thereby committing the act of diabolic union. Moreover, the "thoughts that do dissuade" Faustus are those described by Donne as evidence of self-remembering, thoughts summed up in Faustus's stated intention of less than thirty lines earlier to "ponder on my sins" (62). Immediately before this pledge to ponder, the Old Man makes reference to the possibility of grace offered to Faustus: "I see an angel hover o'er thy head, / And with a vial full of precious grace / Offers to pour the same into thy soul" (57–59). Despite this possibility and in response to Mephistopheles' badgering, Faustus renews his vow "with [his] blood again" (75) and confirms it through his union with the demon Helen. At the same time, this confirmation of his vow also constitutes Faustus's attempt to forget the state of his sin by "glut[ting] the longing of [his] heart's desire."[46]

As we have seen, episodes like the one above, in which Faustus momentarily seems to remember himself – he ponders his sins and thinks upon God – only next to forget himself, recur throughout the text.[47] However, Faustus's vacillations between recalling salvational knowledge and then forgetting himself anew take on greater significance toward the end of the play. Moreover, memory and forgetting in general are pointedly thematized in act four, scene six. After having performed at their expense several acts of low conjuration, Faustus is confronted by Robin, Dick, the Carter and the Horse-Courser. Those once duped by Faustus appeal to his memory through a series of questions. After Faustus assures them that he has no wooden leg (which the group believes he must have, since the Horse-Courser has earlier torn Faustus's "real" leg from its socket), the Carter states, "Good Lord, that flesh and blood should be so frail with your worship! Do you not remember a horse-courser you sold a horse to?"

FAUSTUS: Yes, I remember I sold one a horse.
CARTER: And do you remember you bid he should not ride into the water?
FAUSTUS: Yes, I do very well remember that.

CARTER: And do you remember nothing of your leg?
FAUSTUS: No, in good sooth.
CARTER: Then, I pray, remember your curtsy.
FAUSTUS: [Making a curtsy.] I thank you, sir.

(4. 6. 82–92)

According to Bevington and Rasmussen, the Carter's mention of the frailty of Faustus's flesh and blood refers to the imperfect nature of the latter's memory, and the interrogation that follows constitutes a test of that memory. At the same time, the references to memory contain a punning joke, for Faustus through his curtsy reveals himself as re-membered, his new leg attesting to the *regenerative* nature of Faustus's flesh and blood. At issue here is the relationship between recollection and embodiment. From at least the above-mentioned reference to Actaeon onward, the play concerns itself with bodily dis-integration, a theme that culminates in the Scholars' discovery of "Faustus' limbs, / All torn asunder by the hand of death" (5. 3. 6–7). However, memory here is aligned with re-membering, the cohesiveness of selfhood promised by re-collection reinforced at the corporeal level by the restoration of wholeness to the once-maimed Faustus.

This episode prompts further consideration of memory's function. The above interrogation manifests a relationship between bodily integrity and subjective integrity that is accomplished through recollection. For the Carter, Faustus's ability to remember what has happened to him must be coincident with the loss of his leg, but the joke is that Faustus's account of events is seemingly mirrored in and proven true by his corporeal wholeness. (Although Faustus lies about not remembering the loss of his leg, even the lie is reinforced by this wholeness.) Of course, Faustus does not, in Donne's sense of the term, remember himself. The frailty of his flesh and blood has in fact driven all of Faustus's actions and engendered his spiritual self-forgetting. The questions posed by the Carter function as a kind of catechism, or a partial itemization of Faustus's misdeeds. Faustus remembers those misdeeds at the moment he is revealed as being re-membered, but while his wholeness is corporeal, it is not spiritual. The restoration of Faustus's flesh provides a temporary "soundness" whose fleetingness and insecurity are manifested in his final dismemberment. This scene has an allegorical force, as it highlights Faustus's continued faith in things of the flesh – a reliance reinforced through the false advantages accorded him through his deal with the devil – even as it prefigures his being torn limb from limb.

The appeal to Faustus's memory that we just witnessed is extended in subsequent lines, and in a way that becomes more threatening to him. Less than twenty lines later, the catechism proceeds as follows:

CARTER: Do you remember, sir, how you cozened me and eat up my load of –
    [*Faustus charms him dumb.*]
DICK: Do you remember how you made me wear an ape's – [*Faustus charms him dumb.*]
HORSE-COURSER: You whoreson conjuring scab, do you remember how you cozened me with a ho – [*Faustus charms him dumb.*]
ROBIN: Ha' you forgotten me? You think to carry it away with 'hey-pass' and 'repass'. Do you remember the dog's fa – [*Faustus charms him dumb.*]
    *Exeunt* CLOWNS.
HOSTESS: Who pays for the ale? . . . I pray, who shall pay me for my a –
    [*Faustus charms her dumb.*]

(4. 6. 110–120; brackets in text)

The Hostess's query reveals the logic of this scene, which is about, both literally and metaphorically, the payment of the reckoning.[48] Each of the "Clowns" seeks retribution through an appeal to Faustus's memory. Moreover, their utterances prefigure and parody the "bill" that is to be delivered to Faustus once his twenty-four years are up.[49] That is, this scene functions much as the Old Man does, to prompt Faustus to reflect upon his sins and turn his thoughts heavenward. That Faustus silences those who itemize his sins is significant. It might seem to represent his attempt to banish from his thoughts that information which he does not want to confront. However, the silencing of the Carter and his companions is not equivalent to a literal act of forgetting, or suggestive of repression; indeed, in this exchange Faustus's past misdeeds so inexorably close in on him that forgetting them would be impossible. This scene reveals Faustus's will to forget, described by the Duke as his "artful sport which drives all sad thoughts away" (4. 6. 125); it exemplifies the "choice against knowledge and conscience" that is constitutive of the self-forgetting subject.

This exchange between Faustus and the "clowns" can be read as a variation on the psychomachia most often associated with Faustus's encounters with the devils and the Old Man. That is, Faustus's rendering mute of these characters could be seen as the representation on stage of the internal operations of Faustus's will to forget, the quelling of dissenting voices inside his head. However, the exchange between the Carter and Faustus, which occurred earlier in this same scene, shows how memory is conceptualized in fully somatic terms. Indeed, the *psychomachia* of this play would be best understood as a *somamachia*, a contest in which memory and forgetting operate within the realm of action and are made manifest in the representation of the body. Memory here is also a transaction among subjects; it is an intersubjective relationship of which Faustus refuses to acknowledge the terms. Indeed, this is how self-forgetting and self-recollection usually function, not as evidence of a subjective organicism but as forms of selfhood that emerge out of and describe relations to others.

Act five opens with Faustus vacillating between self-recollection and self-forgetting. On the one hand, Faustus is described as preparing for death, which might suggest he has finally taken to heart spiritual accountings like the one we have just seen (somewhat parodically) represented. Faustus's preparations entail allocating his possessions to others: "he has made his will and given me his wealth," Wagner tells us (5. 1. 2). But, "I wonder what he means. If death were nigh, / He would not frolic thus" (5–6). (There is a recognizable irony in this situation, for wills routinely stipulate that the testator is "of perfite minde and memorie."⁵⁰) Faustus's frivolousness in the face of death sums up his self-forgetting throughout the text. To remember yourself, after all, is to be constantly cognizant of not only your sinfulness but your mortality, to live with death always in mind. As a self-forgetting subject, Faustus is aware of his impending death, but he does not translate that awareness into repentance; as in the first scene, the wages of sin do not recall Faustus to salvation. Through much of the final act he vacillates between preparation for death and frolicking in the face of it, a vacillation made most apparent in the incident discussed above: Faustus's flight from the words of the Old Man and into the arms of the succubus Helen of Troy. By now, however, Faustus's self-forgetting is motivated not merely by sensual desire but by despair, for he believes that "Faustus' offence can ne'er be pardoned" (5. 2. 44). The extent to which *Dr. Faustus* enacts an orthodox Calvinist view of individual predestination has been the subject of much critical debate; most plausible to me seems Alan Sinfield's view of the play as "amenable at every point" to a theologically orthodox reading while also offering (especially in the B-text) "a more genial alternative."⁵¹ This alternative would include the possibility of Faustus accepting the "vial full of precious grace" mentioned earlier by the Old Man. However, whether or not we read him as damned from the start, Faustus cannot bring himself to imagine his sins as pardonable. Moreover, he remains true to his initial act of forgetting, convinced in his despair that the reward for his sins is to "die eternally" (5. 2. 30).

As suggested above, the theme of bodily disintegration culminates in Faustus's dismemberment. In his final speech, however, Faustus wishes for a less violent sort of corporeal dissolution:

> You stars that reigned at my nativity,
> Whose influence hath allotted death and hell,
> Now draw up Faustus like a foggy mist
> Into the entrails of yon labouring cloud,
> That when you vomit forth into the air,

My limbs may issue from your smoky mouths,
But let my soul mount and ascend to heaven.

(5. 2. 160–166)

In a fantasy describing his soul travelling to heaven, Faustus imagines his body melting away as he becomes a mist drawn into a cloud. Even in this fantasy, however (at least rhetorical) traces of Faustus's corporeality remain: his limbs would later issue from that cloud. Moreover, while Faustus's body dissolves, the cloud is embodied: it has a mouth and entrails, and it vomits. Faustus's imagined ascension is described as a disgorgement in which his own corporeality is projected onto, if not exchanged with, the intangibility of a cloud. Even his vision of bodily transcendence is formed in terms of a grotesque corporeality of entrails and mouths and vomited limbs. While we earlier saw that the intactness of Faustus's body could symbolize subjective coherence manifested in and produced out of remembering, corporeal disintegration here goes hand in hand with subjective disintegration. Just as this passage simultaneously registers and effaces the body, it describes both a desire to ascend to heaven and a longing for dissolution. Such dissolution would entail Faustus's loss of memory and, more importantly, the erasure of his sin (and identity) from the memory rolls of God.

Faustus's fantasy of disinterment from his soon-to-be-dismembered body is followed shortly thereafter by his wish that Pythagorean metempsychosis were

true [so that]
This soul should fly from me and I be changed
Into some brutish beast.
All beasts are happy, for, when they die,
Their souls are soon dissolved in elements.

(175–179)

In desiring his soul to pass from his body and into that of an animal, Faustus again longs for disintegration, the eventual decay of his soul into the elements. One could add further that the "brutish beast" is happy because it does not remember; it is, in Nietzsche's words, "fettered to the moment and its pleasure or displeasure, and thus [is] neither melancholy nor bored . . . the man says 'I remember' and envies the animal, who at once forgets and for whom every moment really dies, sinks back into night and fog and is extinguished for ever."[52] At stake for Faustus is more than boredom or melancholy, of course. In the minutes preceding his death and damnation, the self-forgetting subject wishes he had no identity, no memory, no sin. Such a longing is expressed in a sermon by Henry King, Bishop of Chichester and a friend of Donne's:

How well were it for Man-kinde, if we might glorie in that infirmitie which beasts may doe: they cannot be sayd to have lost what they never had, nor to forget what they never had organs to remember. We had a great deale lesse sin to answer for, could we say so too. Man once had what he now hath lost, and for default of a little memorie at the first, hath taught us to forget wee might have beene happie.[53]

In wishing to become a "brutish beast," Faustus also longs for his humanness, a category routinely constructed in this period through opposition to beastliness, to dissolve, and along with it his sin.[54]

It is worth contrasting Faustus's fantasy of dismemberment with the promise of memory – that is, of re-membering and re-collecting. As pointed out in the introduction, to forget is, etymologically, "to miss or lose one's hold," a relaxing of one's cognitive grip that is, in this fantasy, extended to a total loss of bodily integrity. Faustus desires here a complete dispersal of the self, a dispersal simultaneously physical and mental. This desire for self-erasure through corporeal dissolution stands in stark contrast to the fame that Faustus seeks and acquires earlier in the play. The Virgilian tradition has it that fame constitutes the only consolation for mortality[55], and one can read Faustus's actions in the face of damnation as the search for consolation in this world for his fate in the next. In pursuing the acquisition of worldly fame – which Faustus gains, as is made most explicit in the A-text Chorus's assertion that his "fame spread forth in every land" (4. Chorus. 12) Faustus attains a kind of sublunary immortality, which by play's end seems to him to be no consolation at all.[56] Faustus's desire for dissolution, expressed on the eve of his death and damnation, attests both to the hollowness of his earlier pursuit of fame and to his near-death desire to forget and be forgotten.[57]

I mention above that *Dr. Faustus* as a whole can be compellingly read as either religiously orthodox or heterodox. Similarly, the play can be seen as either radical in its celebration of Faustus's worldly pursuits or conservative in its condemnation of his transgressive actions. The epilogue, which marks the culmination of the play's interest in memory and forgetting, lends itself to a socially and religiously conservative reading. If Faustus greets his impending death with fantasies of forgetting and being forgotten, the last words of the play demand that we remember him as a negative exemplar: "Faustus is gone. Regard his hellish fall / Whose fiendful fortune may exhort the wise / Only to wonder at unlawful things [rather than] . . . / To practise more than heavenly power permits" (Epilogue, 4–8). The story of Faustus becomes for the play's audience a cautionary tale, or an allegorical tableau to be regarded.[58] To regard means not only "to look at, gaze upon, or observe" (*OED* 1. a), but also "to look to, have a care of or for (oneself, one's own interest, health, etc.)" (*OED* 3. a). In this final scene, to regard Faustus's fall is also to have a care for the state of one's *own* soul. If at the outset Faustus forgot the possibility of salvation, in these final lines Marlowe's audience members are called upon to recall their own sinfulness. Moreover, as with self-remembering in Donne's sermon, this is recollection in the service of the future, as the audience is enjoined to recall, and act in relation to, what is to come: death and the afterlife. The play as a whole traces the effects of self-forgetting, delineating the contours of a spiritual state in which a subjectivity emerges not merely out of sin, but out of actions taken against knowledge and conscience – and it is knowledge and conscience that are reaffirmed in the Epilogue's demand that we "Regard [Faustus's] hellish fall." Faustus is a kind of inverted Everyman whose fate functions as an exhortation to audience members to reform their behavior through self-remembrance.[59]

Read along one axis, then, *Dr. Faustus* is representative of what Huston Diehl has described as "the kind of art approved by Protestant theologians. Although they condemn as idolatrous images and plays that seduce, dazzle, and trick the beholder, the English reformers routinely defend art . . . that enables its viewers [in words drawn from Foxe's *Actes and Monuments*] 'to remember themselves, and to lament their sins.'"[60] Certainly the epilogue seems to function in this way, as do other moments in the play. In fact, the play sometimes resembles a kind of religious "memory theatre" in which, as in Donne's sermon, scriptural mnemonics are deployed in the service of the audience's salvation. This is the way the fragment of Romans works, as a mnemonic recognizable and interpretable to the audience but opaque to the willfully forgetful Faustus. One could also consider the play's numerous biblical echoes, such as Faustus's notorious "*Consummatum est*" [2. 1. 74], in this light.[61] Moreover, as "Genesis" can function as a mnemonic for both biblical content and personal experience, Faustus's fall becomes the sign under which can be (re)collected not only the actions of the hubristic doctor, but also those actions imagined or performed by audience members who have been tempted to "practise more than heavenly power permits." From this perspective, play and sermon work upon their audiences in similar ways, both deploying and reinforcing mnemonic systems in the name of salvation. Herein would seem to lie a major reason for Marlowe's engagement with spiritual self-forgetting as it is theorized in Donne's sermon.

And yet, this engagement is of a complex nature, for mnemonic systems either break down or are in some way compromised in *Dr. Faustus*. Faustus's eyes are drawn away from the Bible and he forgets both the rest of Romans and himself; the attempt by the horse-courser and others to make him remember fails; even the effect of scriptural mnemonics

(*"Consummatum est"*) on the audience is complicated by the scandalous nature of their deployment. Re-membering competes for prominence with the powerful poetry of "losing one's hold," and it is seduction and dazzle that are offered to both Marlowe's characters and his audience by events that are notable for their theatricality: the procession of the seven deadlies, or the dumb show in which Alexander subdues Darius. Arguably Marlowe's drama is always potentially seductive, offering a kind of ravishment akin to that which drives his characters[62]; any member of *Faustus*'s audience might act as Charles does by (metaphorically) moving to embrace the triumphant Alexander and his lover. Moreover, the supposed exemplarity of many of the scenes in this play is complicated by Marlowe's rhetoric, which can be read as undercutting or ironizing scenes of seemingly high orthodoxy. In his final speech, which is the prelude to his long-anticipated demise, Faustus echoes Ovid's *Amores* by uttering *"O lente, lente currite noctis equi!"* (5. 2. 147); a lover's plea that the night pass slowly injects a hint of sensuality into Faustus's final desperate moments. Certainly this utterance could underscore Faustus's intransigent and fatal addiction to the pleasures of the flesh. On the other hand, it may constitute an ironic deflation of the seemingly repentant moralism of this speech, a deflation that celebrates rather than repudiates the erotic.

Most significant for considering the effect of the play on its audience is Faustus's character. To read *Dr. Faustus* as a simple didactic drama designed to prompt self-remembering – to see it as no different from, say, *Everyman* – does not do justice to the ways in which the story and actions of Faustus engage and captivate the audience. Stephen Greenblatt is one among many critics who have read Marlowe's characters as harnessing the energies of "the period in which European man embarked on his extraordinary career of consumption, his eager pursuit of knowledge, with one intellectual model after another seized, squeezed dry, and discarded."[63] In light of this, Faustus's self-forgetting can be registered as heroic if transgressive aspiration, as constitutive of Faustus's status as "overreacher."[64] This status has a significance that need not be summed up by Donne's pejorative understanding of what it means to forget oneself (although it is worth taking seriously the notion that the triumphal heroism of Greenblatt's "European man" can also be read as the self-forgetter's "run[ning] at randome after the world"). This is the case not merely because Faustus's self-forgetting can be seen as describing the fashioning rather than the loss of a self. In addition, the drama of Faustus's self-forgetting generates theatrical pleasure that emerges not merely out of his condemnation, but also out of the ways in which his actions capture, refract and crystallize the desires and ambitions of an audience living in an age of extraordinary exploration and consumption.[65] In this light, then, spiritual self-forgetting signifies the deployment of aspirations and desires that since at least Burckhardt have been seen as concomitant with the emergence of "Renaissance man."

What I have been suggesting over the last few paragraphs is that while *Dr. Faustus* can be read as championing self-remembering, it can also be seen as recognizing, if not depending upon the fact, that the allure of the theatre and the energies it mobilizes make it an agent, and perhaps an advocate, of self-forgetting. This view resonates with claims made about the stage by early modern antitheatricalists. Compare Mephistopheles luring Faustus's eyes away from holy texts and toward theatrical display with Phillip Stubbes's account of competition between the playhouse and the church: "Doe [plays] not drawe the people from hearing the word of God, from godly Lectures, and Sermons? For you shall have them flocke thither thicke and threefolde, when the Churche of God shall be bare & emptie."[66] In this view, plays, unlike the sermons that they seduce audiences away from, do not condemn but rather catalyze self-forgetting.[67] That Marlowe recognized this possibility is made plain in *Edward II*, in which Gaveston aims to use "Italian masques" and the works of "wanton poets" to "draw the pliant king which way [he] please[s]."[68] However, *Faustus* functions in a more complicated fashion than Gaveston imagines his masques will do. Indeed, it prompts questions such as these: does the play condemn the actions of Faustus even as, for its theatrical success, it depends upon them? Or does it embrace those transgressive actions, even if only as good theatre? Answering these questions is less important than merely posing them, for they remind us of the necessity to Marlovian theatre of the representation of transgression. Moreover, even if *Faustus* is designed to function in the service of self-remembering, it always threatens to engender in its audience the forgetting of self that has been the play's subject. While at times *Dr. Faustus* seems the kind of text of which it can be said, "this turns the key, this opens the door, this restores him to liberty," it also enacts, reveals and revels in the conditionality of Donne's final phrase: "if he can *remember*." Indeed, that very conditionality exists as the ground for Faustus's representation.

In a fundamental way, Faustus is throughout the play caught between forgetting and remembering, always threatening to "backslide" into self-recollection. And while it is Mephistopheles' theatrical displays that finally ensure that Faustus does not remember himself, it is the drama of Faustus's self-forgetting that is the subject of Marlowe's play. Moreover, just as Marlowe's play both inherits and subverts the morality structure of plays like *Everyman*, his representation of self-forgetting both harnesses and deviates from the moralism of Donne's sermon. One might (somewhat simplistically) assert that the play suggests the antitheatrical-ists are right and that theatre is a debased institution. However, it seems more accurate to say that just as Marlowe's play invites such manichean moralism, it also confounds it. Indeed, self-forgetting in *Dr. Faustus* finally works to reveal the limits of moral valuation – as in its failure to accommodate those aspects of Faustus's self-forgetting that for Greenblatt make him akin to "European man." Moreover, *Dr. Faustus* combines a critique of self-forgetting with the shrewd recognition of the theatre's reliance upon it; religious self-forgetting functions less as a scandal than as an opportunity, for it provides the conceptual resources through which Marlowe generates the character of his fallen "divine in show."

# 4    "My oblivion is a very Antony"

> [M]emory has the orderliness and the teleological drive of narrative. Its
> relation to the past is not that of truth but of desire.[1]

Critics of Shakespeare's *Antony and Cleopatra* have routinely focused on
Antony's loss of his Roman identity. In doing so, they have assumed that
Antony once had a unified identity to lose – assumed that he is "un-
identical to himself and *what he has been* in the past."[2] This is true even
of psychoanalytic criticism, which presupposes a subject who is not
"stable and completely integrated" but is made up of "shifting and
contradictory impulses."[3] Put simply, critics have attended closely to the
non-self-identicality of Antony in the *present* of the play but have for
the most part simply accepted his putative self-sameness in the *past*.[4]
In addition, given that Antony's Romanness is inseparable from his lost
self-identicality, the category of *Romanness itself* is read as stable rather
than fluid, contested and appropriable.[5] Such views ignore *Antony and
Cleopatra*'s sustained interest in the *constructedness* of the past, an interest
extended through the play's examination of the interrelations of memory,
forgetting and desire.

Partly through analysis of the Circe episode in *The Odyssey*, this
chapter argues for the supposed decay of Antony's identity as an example
of erotic self-forgetting understood also as the forgetting of his country.
(It must be pointed out that identity is meant differently here than in
previous chapters. While identity has heretofore been discussed in terms
of the physical and social placement of the subject within a given culture,
Roman identity in *Antony and Cleopatra* is the expression of the putative
singularity of a cultural identity within the context of a cross-cultural
encounter.[6]) In addition, what separates *Antony and Cleopatra* from the
texts analyzed in previous chapters is that the play not only represents but
reflects upon the operations of self-forgetting. It does so by offering
two almost contradictory views of self-forgetting. On the one hand, self-
forgetting understood *as the condition of identity loss* both renders coherent the self that has been forgotten and marks the triumph of a specific

version of Romanness. On the other hand, self-forgetting understood *as a form of selfhood* emerges, through Cleopatra's commemoration of Antony, as a distinctive type of heroic masculinity. This second view shows that to describe Antony's oft-noted self-*division* as a form of self-*forgetting* is not merely to substitute one term for another; self-forgetting marks a specific kind of discursive presence and introduces into the play a range of particular meanings that link up with the play's broader interest in commemoration and oblivion.

Antony and Cleopatra is, as has been recognized, a play dominated by the retrospective characterization of people and events.[7] The text also considers commemoration as a mode of knowledge production, most apparently in Caesar's and Cleopatra's eulogies for the fallen Antony. *Antony and Cleopatra* lays bare the mechanisms of the retrospective consolidation of identity, which occurs through both memory and self-forgetting. This consolidation also reveals the centrality of desire to individual acts of recollection – in particular, those of Caesar, Cleopatra and Antony himself. These eulogies help us to see that *Antony and Cleopatra* underscores and represents the construction and the construct-edness of identity in terms of memory and forgetting. It is through Cleopatra, though, that we learn that the putative erosion of identity can be understood as the revelation of identity's basic condition.

In *All's Well That Ends Well*, the coordinates of Bertram's and Helena's forgotten identities are primarily familial; even the King casts himself in the role of surrogate father. In *Antony and Cleopatra*, Antony's identity is configured in terms of his "country"; Antony is constituted first and foremost as a Roman, and the self he forgets in his love affair with Cleopatra is emphatically a Roman one. Apposite for Shakespeare's play is Samuel Daniel's description of Antony's behavior after he abandons Octavia for Cleopatra: "For *Antonius* falling into the relaps of his former disease, watching his oportunity got over againe into *Egypt*, where he so forgot himselfe, that he quite put off his own nature, and wholly became a pray to his pleasures, as if hee had wound himselfe out of the respect of Country, bloud and alliance."[8] Country, blood and alliance, all integral to "his own nature" and all sacrificed to his pleasures, are intertwined both here and in Shakespeare. However, in *Antony and Cleopatra* the two final terms are subordinated to the first. "Country" evokes (Antony's relation-ship to) both the rulers of Rome and the kinds of ideals and behaviors – most importantly here, military prowess and valor – that are associated with the empire over which Antony has shared control.[9] In Shakespeare, Antony's self forgetting is primarily a forgetting of his "country."

Antony's self-forgetting is adduced in the opening lines of the play, which narrate the degeneration of the martial hero, whose "goodly eyes, / . . . o'er the files and musters of the war / Have glowed like plated Mars . . ." (1. 1. 2–4), into "the bellows and the fan / [That] cool a gipsy's lust" (9–10).[10] Very shortly thereafter, Antony boldly, if temporarily, transforms his self-forgetting into a virtue: what Philo referred to as "this dotage of our general's" becomes in Antony's view "the nobleness of life" (1. 1. 1, 37). For Antony, such celebrations of self-forgetting are in constant conflict with an understanding of it as a form of emasculation, and the play charts the slow erosion of Antony's Roman identity, which culminates in the scene in which Antony finds a corollary to his own mutability in the shifting clouds: "Here I am Antony, / Yet cannot hold this visible shape" (4. 14. 13–14).

References to Antony's self-forgetting recur throughout the play. Caesar scornfully compares Antony to boys "who, being mature in knowledge, / Pawn their experience to their present pleasure / And so rebel to judgement" (1. 4. 31–33). This rebellion against judgment is also a rebellion against memory, for, as we saw in chapter 2, memory houses the results of judgment; it is the repository for a series of judgments that together constitute the wisdom against which Antony reacts.[11] Antony later indirectly casts Cleopatra in the role of the agent of his forgetting, for she is one who "bound me up / From mine own knowledge" (2. 2. 96–97).[12] In both instances, Antony is represented as one who would know better were he able to remember, one who, in Daniel's words, "so forgot himselfe, that he quite put off his own nature." Antony refers to the period of his bondage as "poisoned hours," a characterization that is echoed in Pompey's depiction of Antony as one he hopes will continue to pursue pleasure and avoid combat:

> Let witchcraft join with beauty, lust with both;
> Tie up the libertine in a field of feasts;
> Keep his brain fuming. Epicurean cooks
> Sharpen with cloyless sauce his appetite
> That sleep and feeding may prorogue his honour
> Even till a Lethe'd dullness–
>
> (2. 1. 22–27)[13]

For Antony's brain to be kept fuming is for his memory to be disabled. Henry King, in describing the "many Pick-lockes which oft times wrench [the memory] open," says of wine that its "subtile fumes unrivet each joint of it, and loosen the cement which held it fast; for you shall note that deepe drinkers have but shallow memories."[14] Antony, of course, is the consummate deep drinker – elsewhere he asserts that "the conquering wine hath steeped our sense / In soft and delicate Lethe" (2. 7. 107–108), explicitly conjoining alcohol and forgetting – but in this passage it is not wine alone that disables memory. "Witchcraft," sexual desire and epicurean feasts "keep the brain fuming" as Antony gives himself over to the pleasures of self-forgetting.[15]

The passage's emphasis on Antony's self-forgetting is underscored by references to sleep and "a Lethe'd dullness" that should be familiar from chapter 1; Antony is depicted as the forgetful, undisciplined subject whose hedonism is of a piece with a lethargic dullness. In addition, the yoking of sleep and appetite evokes classical conceptions of fame. An early seventeenth-century translation of Sallust, for instance, alludes to the men "whose mind is their belly; their delight sleep" as ones who, because they failed to achieve honor, ensure that "with their bodies their remembraunce is buried."[16] That is, sleep and appetite are antithetical not only to the achievement of greatness, but also to the attainment of the immortality acquired by performing memorable actions.[17] Pompey here represents an Antony who is not merely forgetting himself, but who, in seeking the oblivion of libertinism, decreases the chances of his being remembered.

The reference to "sleep and feeding" also necessarily evokes the classical association of these two practices, when they define one's behavior, with the loss of "visible shape" that comes with the degeneration of men into beasts.[18] Sallust begins *The Conspiracie of Cateline* by stating that "Nature hath created *Man* the worthiest of all living Creatures, by so much, the rather ought he by Vertuous exercises to Dedicate to eternity, some *Record* of his proficiency, and not to die in Scilence [sic] or Oblivion, like the *Beasts* of the field, whom God hath fashioned onely of a Servile condition, fit for no project, but to feede the belly."[19] Men strive in order to ensure that they leave "some *Record*" – that they will be remembered – whereas the grovelling beast, slave to its belly, is entirely forgettable. To see that these associations resonate in this period, one need only consider Hamlet's late soliloquy announcing the "Bestial oblivion" of men who merely "sleep and feed."[20] In *Antony and Cleopatra*, though, witchcraft, susceptibility to beauty and lust are all aligned with "sleep and feeding."[21] While the linkage of the other terms is explained by the hedonism that underwrites all of them, the reference to witchcraft is telling. For Pompey, it is Cleopatra who is the witch – he refers to her "charms of love" (2. 1. 20) – who takes Antony from the field of battle and ties him up, like an animal, in a "field of feasts." To deploy the same pun that the phrase suggests (thanks to the word "field"), Antony is rendered a beast by the feasts put on by Cleopatra, who is read here as an agent of his self-forgetting. Thought of this way, we can see that Cleopatra resembles

Circe, whose transformation of Ulysses's men into swine is also linked to self-forgetting.[22]

It is usual to understand Circe in terms such as those advanced by Abraham Fraunce, who notes that she emblematizes lust, and states that "If she over rule us, she transformeth us into the shapes of severall beasts, according to the sundry beastly pleasures wherein we delight."[23] What is crucial to this play, however, is the role of forgetting one's country in this story of bestial transformation. In Book 10 of George Chapman's translation, entitled *Homer's Odysses*, Circe's treatment of Ulysses's sailors is depicted as follows:

> They enterd, she made sit; and her deceit
> She cloakt with Thrones; and goodly chaires of State;
> Set hearby honey, and the delicate
> Wine brought from *Smyrna*, to them; meale and cheese;
> But harmefull venoms, she commixt with these;
> That made their Countrey vanish from their thought.
> Which, eate; she toucht them, with a rod that wrought
> Their transformation, farre past humane wunts;
> Swines snowts, swines bodies, tooke they, bristles, grunts;
> But still retaind the soules they had before;
> Which made them mourne their bodies change the more.[24]

This passage intriguingly raises questions about what Ulysses's sailors remember and forget. We see that they are given "harmefull venoms" that make them forget their country. Such forgetting is depicted as a necessary first stage of their transformation into beasts, which only occurs in a second step, through the agency of Circe's rod. However, while forgetting "their Countrey" may be a precondition for the sailors' becoming swine, their status as beasts does not completely obliterate their memories; they "retained the soules they had before" and thus "mourne[d] their bodies change." Once changed back, however, these men, along with Ulysses and the rest of his crew, linger with Circe for a year. If forgetting their country preceded their corporeal transformations, the restoration of the men to their bodies seems to precede their recollection of and return to home. In fact, it is Ulysses's "friends [who] rememberd [him] of home; and said, / If ever Fate would signe [his] passe; delaid / It should be now no more."[25]

That Ulysses needs to be reminded of his country is ironic, for earlier in the Circe episode he serves for others as a mnemonic for home. Upon Ulysses's return to his ship, those in the crew that he had left behind

> Circl'd [him]
> With all their welcomes, and as cheerfully
> Disposde their rapt minds, as if there they saw
> Their naturall Countrie, cliffie *Ithaca*;

And even the roofes where they were bred and borne.
And vowd as much, with teares: O your returne
As much delights us; as in you had come
Our Countrie to us, and our naturall home.[26]

We witness in this episode examples of self-forgetting understood in terms of forgetting one's country. While Ulysses does not fall under Circe's spell, he does come close to forgetting himself; he must finally be reminded of his country to ensure that he not give in to what he terms "refreshing sweetnesse" in the attainment of which "Men sometimes, may be something delicate"[27] – a sweetness associated with Circe and, from an early modern perspective, the threat of emasculation.[28] Antony's self-forgetting, then, has its Homeric analogue, one that casts Antony less as Ulysses than as one of his shipmates who succumbs to beastly pleasures and the effeminization they connote. Antony's suicide can be understood as metaphorically suggesting his escape from Cleopatra/Circe and the threat of emasculation she poses, as well as his return to Rome, his Ithaca.[29] Instead of suggesting the final stage in the dissolution of his identity, suicide here connotes self-affirmation, an attempt to recuperate and assert his lost martial Romanness: by falling on his sword, Antony defines himself as "a Roman by a Roman / Valiantly vanquished" (4. 15. 59–60).[30] In this figuration of himself as both slayer and slain, Antony is Roman twice over.

Or at least this is how Antony hopes his suicide will signify; that he bungles his attempt at an heroic death arguably complicates this salutary formulation of a Roman end. For the moment, though, it is enough to notice the desire expressed in Antony's suicide, a desire that Antony might remember himself – that is, recover his identity as a Roman. (As in chapter 3, "remembering oneself" here describes not a psychic process but a mode of action or a pattern of behavior out of which an identity is both enacted and recovered.) Significantly, this is also the desire to be recalled in a certain way by others; Antony's suicide marks his attempt to achieve a memorable fate as a Roman, to regain the honor and fame that he has lost and to become (again) a martial exemplar. At least, this is what Antony at certain moments hopes to make of his death, through the attempt to control how he is to be recollected.[31] His status as a Roman valiantly vanquished by a Roman is of a piece with his appeal that Cleopatra "please [her] thoughts / . . . with those my former fortunes / Wherein I lived the greatest prince o'th' world" (4. 15. 54–56). Antony's final act of self-remembering is coincident with, and emerges directly out of, this attempt to shape the way in which he will be recalled, as "the greatest prince o'th' world" and as a Roman.[32]

That Antony seems to have been successful in his endeavors both to remember himself and to be remembered in a certain way is suggested by the rhetoric of emulation Caesar deploys in his commemoration of Antony.[33] In response to the announcement of his rival's death, Caesar states that

> The breaking of so great a thing should make
> A greater crack. The round world
> Should have shook lions into civil streets
> And citizens to their dens. The death of Antony
> Is not a single doom; in the name lay
> A moiety of the world.
>
> (5. 1. 14–19)

Shortly thereafter Caesar continues:

> But yet let me lament
> With tears as sovereign as the blood of hearts
> That thou, my brother, my competitor,
> In top of all design, my mate in empire,
> Friend and companion in the front of war,
> The arm of mine own body, and the heart
> Where mine his thoughts did kindle, that our stars,
> Unreconciliable, should divide
> Our equalness to this.
>
> (40–48)

Antony's status as a "moiety" of the world (rather than as "bellows and fan") is secured not only through his death but also, and perhaps more significantly, through Caesar's lamenting characterization of his former companion in rule. Certainly this characterization is somewhat equivocal in that it is designed to assert Caesar's supremacy over his rival – the "greater crack" was not produced, and Antony is figured as only the arm to Caesar's body. That being said, the terms of Caesar's epideictic oratory assume and reinstall Antony's martial Romanness.

In sum, then, Antony can be read as the self-forgetting subject who both finally remembers himself and is remembered as he would (more or less) want to be.[34] While Bertram's self-recollection takes the form of both acceptance of marriage and subjection to the king's authority, Antony's depends upon his death; his self-cancellation constitutes an attempt at self-recovery, the success of which is made plain through the way that he is remembered by Caesar. And yet, insofar as this success emerges through another's commemoration of him, our attention is drawn to the disjunction between self-recollection as a *subjective* process (culminating here in Antony's self-identified Romanness) and as a *social* process requiring the validation of others. Put differently, Antony's rehabilitation as a Roman necessitates not merely that he embrace the values and relations that he has earlier abandoned, but that he be recognized to do so. Caesar's eulogy offers such recognition. What does it mean, then, that Caesar's granting of this recognition jars with his earlier descriptions of the dissolute Antony?

Caesar's first and most famous characterization of Antony occurs in act one, scene four. Like most characterization in the play, this is retrospective. Here we encounter Caesar recounting the fall of Antony, lost not to his sword but to his pleasures. That is, Antony's self as described here is one that he has forgotten through his alliance with Cleopatra:

> Antony,
> Leave thy lascivious wassails! When thou once
> Was beaten from Modena, where thou slew'st
> Hirtius and Pansa, consuls, at thy heel
> Did famine follow, whom thou fought'st against,
> Though daintily brought up, with patience more
> Than savages could suffer. Thou didst drink
> The stale of horses and the gilded puddle
> Which beasts would cough at. Thy palate then did deign
> The roughest berry on the rudest hedge.
> Yea, like the stag when snow the pasture sheets,
> The barks of trees thou browsed. On the Alps,
> It is reported, thou didst eat strange flesh
> Which some did die to look on. And all this –
> It wounds thine honour that I speak it now –
> Was borne so like a soldier that thy cheek
> So much as lanked not.
>
> (1. 4. 56–72)

While it attests to his former greatness, this passage serves primarily to denigrate an Antony consumed by "lascivious wassails," one seemingly at odds with Caesar's later depiction of his "mate in empire." Moreover, it represents a kind of heroic parody of those wassails; this Antony drinks not wine but the "stale of horses," eats not grapes but "the roughest berry." As scornful as the sentiment that animates this passage is, we should attend to the fact that, as with Caesar's eulogy, it valorizes the actions of Antony before he forgot himself. One could explain Caesar's praise in the 5. 1 speech in terms of an unexpected upwelling of sentiment for the Antony of old, or as a final act of (probably qualified and self-serving) graciousness on the part of the victor; or one could also point out that in the Roman plays the logic of emulation extends to the lionization of one's dead rival, as in Antony's final description of Brutus in *Julius Caesar*. However, there is something else at issue here, for Caesar's needs and desires are mobilized in significant ways through his depiction of

Antony. While Antony's self-recollection is recognized as such by Caesar, so is a specific and fantasmic conception of Romanness forwarded and reinforced, a conception that aids in the ongoing mystification of Caesar's authority.

As it was once standard critical practice to understand *Antony and Cleopatra* as organizing a whole host of strong oppositions around the difference between Rome (masculinity, martial discipline, self-abnegation, borders and boundaries, etc.) and Egypt (femininity, indolence, hedonism, "o'erflowing," etc.), it has become customary to question the stability of such oppositions.[35] Thus, if desire once seemed the exclusive property of Egypt, recent critics have attended to the forms of desire that structure Roman action as well as Rome's representation of itself and its Others. This critical emphasis makes it possible to identify the self-interestedness of crucial Roman depictions of the city's representatives and its enemies; even more, it allows us to recognize the mystifications necessary to any formulation of "Rome" (or "Romanness"), and, again, the limitations of oppositions understood as absolute and/or as foundational of Roman identity. At the same time, and in ways enabled by the opacity of its content, "Romanness" is open to appropriation and reconstitution by those in positions of power. It is in this context we should situate Caesar's depictions of Antony, as moments in which Caesar appropriates Romanness (and Antony) in the service of a mystified martial ideal conducive to his authority. That is, Caesar's depictions of Antony install Romanness as stable – as a set of behaviors which Antony once performed but has since fallen away from – in the face of actions performed by Antony that render transparent Romanness's very instability. Put differently, that the great Roman Marc Antony could behave in ways discontinuous with "Rome's" cherished conception of "itself" – that is, the view of Rome valorized by Caesar – troubles that very conception. How is this problem managed? By insisting simultaneously on Antony's one-time adherence to Roman ideals and on his falling off from the same, a falling off associated with Cleopatra and Egypt. In doing so, Caesar works to preserve the integrity of Romanness, a conceptual category upon which the cultural and martial superiority of the empire is built.[36]

To a great extent, Shakespeare's play seems complicit in the construction and maintenance of Caesar's view of Romanness, just as it at least partly underwrites the idea that Antony's "lascivious wassails" are erosive of his sense of self. This complicity manifests itself in the pathos with which Antony experiences his own self-forgetting.[37] It also confirms Janet Adelman's point that "Longing for [Antony's] heroic masculinity is . . . at the center of the play."[38] In short, *Antony himself* has internalized the view of Romanness represented by and through Caesar's actions and utterances, even though his own past provides evidence of this view's inadequacy. Shortly after Caesar urges the absent Antony to "leave [his] lascivious wassails," he refers to the fact that the fallen hero was "daintily brought up." This passing remark, placed in parentheses in many modern editions of the play, glances toward a version of Antony's past not wholly constituted by heroic self-abnegation; Antony's drinking of "the gilded puddle" is discontinuous with the "dainty" behavior that characterized his upbringing. This reference to Antony's daintiness is important in that it hints at the provisionality of his lost Romanness. For Caesar's Antony, Romanness is attained through the transcendence of his upbringing, which Caesar here denigrates. Antony's past, then, is characterized not by the effortless enactment of Romanness, but by the seeming division of his "Roman" self from his upbringing.

To read such division here, however, is perhaps still to assume a stable Roman identity predicated upon heroic sacrifice and self-denial in the service of the empire, an identity that Antony aspired to and finally attained. While this view reveals that one is not merely "born Roman," it nevertheless lines up with Caesar's values in an unproblematic way: bad "daintiness" gives way to good Romanness. A more complex view of both Antony's seemingly forgotten Romanness and the place of desire and hedonism vis-à-vis martial heroism is offered in Shakespeare's primary source, Plutarch's *The Lives of the Noble Grecians and Romanes*.[39] Plutarch's chapter devoted to "The life of Marcus Antonius" offers the delineation of a character whose actions were always characterized by both hedonism and military valor.

The early history of Plutarch's Antony is one in which our hero repeatedly succumbs to bad influences:

Now *Antonius* being a faire young man, and in the prime of his youth: he fell acquainted with *Curio*, whose friendship and acquaintance (as it is reported) was a plague unto him. For he was a dissolute man, given over to all lust and insolencie, who to have *Antonius* the better at his commandement, trained him on into great follies, and vaine expences upon women, in rioting and banqueting. So that in short time, he brought *Antonius* into a marvellous great debt, and too great for one of his yeares.[40]

After his father intervened to secure him from Curio's malign influence, Antony for a time fell under the sway of Clodius, a wicked tribune. Shortly thereafter Antony went to Greece, where he studied rhetoric and served in the military. Here we might expect to see Antony repudiate his decadent past, but he remains at least intermittently dissolute. After describing Antony's success in Julius Caesar's army, Plutarch tells us that the noble men (as *Cicero* saith) did not only mislike him, but also hate him for his naughtie life: for they did abhor his banquets and drunken feasts he made at unseasonable times, & his extreame wastfull expences upon vaine light huswives, & then in the day time he would sleepe or walke out his drunkennesse, thinking to weare away the fume of the aboundance of wine which he had taken over night. In his house they did nothing but feast, dance, and maske: and himselfe passed away the time in hearing of foolish playes, or in marrying these plaiers, tumblers, jeasters, & such sort of people.[41]

Antony's hedonism here sounds "Egyptian," and this before he has met Cleopatra. Moreover, we encounter here one of several precursors to Cleopatra in a female player "whom he loved dearly: he caried her up and downe in a litter unto all the townes he went; and had as many men waiting upon her litter, she being but a plaier, as were attending upon his own mother."[42]

Caesar's narrative of Antony's heroic self-abnegation also finds its origins in Plutarch. We are told of the occasion on which "it was a wonderfull example to the souldiers, to see *Antonius* that was brought up in all finenesse and superfluity, so easily to drinke puddle water, and to eate wild frutes and rootes: and moreover it is reported, that even as they passed the Alpes, they did eate the barkes of trees, and such beasts, as never man tasted of their flesh before."[43] However, Antony soon "gave him selfe againe to his former riot and excesse, when he left to deale in the affairs of the c[om]mon wealth."[44] This sentence could be seen as demarcating the sphere of Antony's hedonism: when not engaged in warfare, Antony repeatedly neglects the good of the state. Such a reading of Antony's behavior is potentially continuous with Shakespeare's depiction of him, but with one crucial difference: while Antony's vacillations between heroism and hedonism represent for Shakespeare's Romans the erosion of Antony's Roman identity through his relationship with Cleopatra, in Plutarch such vacillations have always marked Antony's actions. In light of Plutarch, then, what we encounter in Shakespeare is an Antony whose self-forgetting marks the extension rather than the repudiation of a "Romanness" constituted in terms quite different from those of "absolute self-consistency and singleness of being."[45] This Antony is one for whom the wistful *recollection* of an identity is actually the *generation* of that identity as unified; Antony's acts of self-commemoration are designed to efface his lifelong history of self-forgetting. That history should not be understood only as Antony's failure to live up to the terms of a specific, stable conception of Romanness, however. If self-forgetting connotes for Caesar a failure to be Roman, it also from another perspective gives the lie to Caesar's model of Romanness.

Thus, while both Caesar and Antony are invested in the nostalgic recasting of Antony's past as an unequivocally heroic one – the former so as to shore up a notion of Romanness that ideologically undergirds both his rule and his dominance over Antony, and the latter in order to fantasize a stability of identity to be reclaimed through suicide – Caesar's own reference to Antony's upbringing undoes both of their attempts at generating singleness of being and a stable conception of Romanness. Referring to Plutarch makes this particularly obvious, but one does not have to go so far afield. As Michael Neill has shown, the first lines of the play gesture at the complexities of the nostalgic construction of Antony's Romanness. In Philo's characterization of Antony, "the evocation of the martial firmness and restraint which characterized Anthony's soldierly past is compromised by suggestions of heroic excess ('His captain's heart . . . hath burst / The buckles on his breast') quite incompatible with the stoical 'measure' and 'temper' (temperance) that Philo professes to admire [1. 1. 1–8]."[46] Here even the seeming opposition between Antony's hedonism and his martial self-abnegation is complicated, as excess is seen to lie at the heart of Antony's "soldierly past." Philo ascribes a lost "singleness of being" to Antony even as his language suggests otherwise; the multiple, non-self-identical nature of Antony (and of Romanness itself) is revealed but not recognized as such. In the opening lines of the play we are introduced to a self-divided conception of Roman martial heroism by a character who promulgates that conception without perceiving fully its nature. This encapsulates the play's broader examination of the workings of retrospection, most evident in the multiple depictions of Antony: even as Antony is remembered in ways that ascribe to him a lost "absolute self-consistency," the constructedness of this consistency is betrayed by the very ones who mourn its passing.

In at least one instance, however, this constructedness is less betrayed than openly acknowledged. Late in the play, Caesar, as part of his attempt to lure Cleopatra to Rome, tells Egypt's queen that "The record of what injuries you did us, / Though written in our flesh, we shall remember / As things but done by chance" (5. 2. 117–119). Caesar's comment plays upon the Aristotelian distinction between memory and recollection. On the one hand, he evokes the classical notion of memory as being like "a book, a written page or a wax tablet upon which something is written,"[47] with the tablet here being the body itself. On the other, in pledging to recall the material inscribed on his flesh as "things but done by chance," Caesar describes a process of recollection that exists in willful relation to the contents of memory. This utterance speaks to the always interpretive and selective nature of recollection, gestured toward in Mary

Carruthers's description of memory as "a process most like reading written characters."[48] More immediately, Caesar here reveals himself as one for whom recollection is constituted in ways dictated by political expedience. Recollection becomes a tool of specific ambitions and agendas, and this act of recollection is contingent upon Cleopatra's complicity. Just as Caesar's commemoration of Antony is driven, consciously or not, by the necessity of maintaining the (false) integrity of Romanness, so is his offer to "remember" Cleopatra's actions in a specific fashion subsidiary to the achievement of his political goals. Moreover, Caesar's willful recollection contains within it a tacit pledge to Cleopatra; it promises a future in which Cleopatra will be forgiven. For Caesar to remember in this fashion would be for him to adopt a specific pattern of action toward Cleopatra. As we saw in the introduction, "to remember" can mean to behave in accordance with a prescribed future.

Although I have emphasized Caesar's eulogies for Antony, it is Cleopatra who most famously characterizes her fallen lover. Moreover, while the dying Antony desires to remember himself and to be remembered, and while Caesar recuperates Antony's character in the service of Romanness, Cleopatra recasts what is from a Roman perspective[49] the dissolution of Antony's identity into the basis of it. But to say that is not to go quite far enough. Cleopatra transforms the discontinuous and multiple nature of identity into a principle of selfhood that on at least one occasion goes by the name of oblivion.

A complex articulation of this transformation occurs early in the play as Antony prepares to return to Rome. Cleopatra reads Antony's resolve upon leaving as "excellent dissembling" designed to "look / Like perfect honour" (1. 3. 80–81). She states that he only plays the "Herculean Roman," then requests "one word" before the now-exasperated Antony leaves (85, 88):

> Sir, you and I must part, but that's not it;
> Sir, you and I have loved, but there's not it;
> That you know well. Something it is I would, –
> O, my oblivion is a very Antony,
> And I am all forgotten!
>
> (89–93)[13]

In saying matter of factly that Antony knows well that they have loved and must part, Cleopatra here projects emotional detachment; their impending separation is handled, in a pair of self-evident propositions, as fully recognized by them both. In the last three lines, however, the emphasis changes from what each of them has no trouble recalling to what each forgets. The basic accusation is clear enough: Cleopatra is "all forgotten" by Antony. However, these lines are more complex than such a simple statement allows. Antony's forgetting of Cleopatra is mentioned only after we witness a Cleopatra whose loss of composure is manifested in the fact that she cannot remember the "one word" she was going to say.[50] Moreover, in the last two lines Cleopatra describes a relationship between the act of forgetting and her self-constitution. First she asserts that her "oblivion is a very Antony," thereby identifying her bout of forgetfulness *as* (a version of) the lover she accuses of forgetting her. In the subsequent line, she moves from a single act of forgetfulness to an assertion of self: "I" refers not only to the person abandoned by her lover, but also to the self that was to be voiced through the final "word" that she was to speak, the self that she has forgotten. Here, then, we see "a very Antony" constituted by oblivion – he even *is* her oblivion – while Cleopatra exists as the disjunction between the voice that accuses her lover of forgetfulness and the "I" that is forgotten. At the same time, insofar as this Antony is her oblivion, his selfhood emerges out of her forgetfulness. In these few lines Cleopatra assumes not only that the two lovers are constitutive of one another, but also that each of the linked identities she gestures toward arises out of its relationship to forgetting. At the same time and ironically, this delineation of the interpenetration of identities appears at the precise moment that the two are parting. While her oblivion is "a very Antony," it is described as such as Antony turns his back on her and his own self-forgetting.[51]

Through the disjunctions between the Antony that leaves her and "a very Antony," or the Cleopatras that speak, forget or are forgotten, Cleopatra's conception of identity is revealed as multiple and discontinuous. This is not to make gender- or culture-specific claims about Cleopatra's "infinite variety"; Jonathan Gil Harris has persuasively suggested that that variety is as much a projection of Antony's and Rome's instability onto Cleopatra as it is an accurate descriptor of her.[52] I would argue, however, that such projection involves the intensification or distortion of a multiplicity that is evident in Cleopatra's character; she is a suitable screen for the projection of Roman desires and anxieties because, while multiplicity is arguably the condition of identity, Cleopatra foregrounds what others suppress. Thus, it is possible to see both Egypt and Rome as characterized by such variety. The difference between Antony and Cleopatra lies in each character's relationship to his or her own discontinuity (a formulation that in and of itself manifests discontinuity). In leaving Cleopatra, Antony makes the first of several attempts to break free from this Circe-like figure[53] and to remember himself (as a Roman). Cleopatra's response is to reveal the foundationality of forgetting to each of their intertwined identities. This view is rejected by Antony, who states immediately after the above lines, "But that your royalty / Holds idleness your subject, I should take you / For idleness itself" (1. 3. 93–95). Antony is dismissive here of what he takes to be Cleopatra's frivolous grand-standing, but he also responds to her reference to oblivion by playing upon the association of forgetting and idleness, discussed in the first two chapters of this book. Most importantly, he indirectly rebuts Cleopatra's assertion that she is "all forgotten" by stating that she is not constituted in terms of idleness, but that idleness is subject to her royalty. This is the voice of a man in denial of his own self-rivenness, asserting not that idleness (or, for that matter, forgetting) makes Cleopatra what she is, but that idleness is a practice performed by a sovereign subject. For Antony here, forgetting and idleness are what a unified subject *does*; for Cleopatra, they are what the subject *does* and *is*.[54]

It is in the last act, after Antony has died, that Cleopatra is most actively engaged in representing Antony, and in ways that have much to do with memory. Janet Adelman has written powerfully of the difference between Caesar's commemoration of Antony and Cleopatra's:

*Antony and Cleopatra* is ostentatiously framed by its two memorializing portraits of Antony, Caesar's in act 1 and Cleopatra's in act 5. Caesar's locates Antony in the Timonesque landscape of absolute deprivation, where he must browse on the bark of trees and eat strange flesh to survive; and it figures his heroic masculinity as his capacity to survive in this wintry landscape. Cleopatra locates him in a landscape of immense abundance with no winter in it; and it figures his heroic masculinity as his capacity to participate in the bounty of its self-renewing autumn.[55]

Cleopatra's depiction of Antony constitutes "the relocation and recon-struction of heroic masculinity": "Claiming the right to Antony's memory, [Cleopatra] in effect reinserts herself into the story from which she has just been occluded; furthermore, she makes herself – and not Caesar – the repository of his heroic masculinity."[56] In addition, as critics have pointed out, Cleopatra's depiction of Antony diverges drastically from the audience's experience of his character on stage. As Brian Cheadle says in relation to Cleopatra's account of Antony as one whose "legs bestrid the ocean" (5. 2. 82), "Th[e] peculiar undertow of irony in the speech is such as to make us aware of the gulf that there inevitably is between a man and how he would be seen"[57] – or, more precisely, how others see him. Certainly the presence of such a gulf could be read as deflating Cleopatra's commemorative rhetoric: for all the nobility and generosity he does evince, the Antony that we have seen falls far short of the figure who boasted a "bounty" with "no winter in't," and whose "reared arm / Crested the world" (5. 2. 81–86). Indeed, Cleopatra's recollection of Antony is an unabashedly creative act, as is suggested when her question to Dollabella, "Think you there was or might be such a man / As this I dreamt of?" is greeted by the answer, "Gentle madam, no" (5. 2. 92–93).[58] At the same time, this rhetoric can be seen less as self-deceptive than as fecund, as composing "the great generative act of the play."[59] The poetic force of Cleopatra's dreaming is undeniable, and it offers another view of Antony's character. Whereas both Caesar and Antony paper over the non-self-identical nature of the latter's identity in the name of a unified conception of Romanness, Cleopatra remembers Antony in ways that explicitly foreground the gap between the hero of her dreaming and the character we have encountered throughout the play; discontinuity becomes central to Cleopatra's conception of heroic masculinity and, through her remembering, to our view of Antony's character.

Not only is the Antony of Cleopatra's eulogy discontinuous with the Antony we see elsewhere in the play, the speech itself represents him as, from the Roman perspective, conflicted and non-self-identical. Cleopatra refers at one moment to his military valor – "when he meant to quail and shake the orb, / He was as rattling thunder" (5. 2. 84–85) – and at the next makes bawdy reference to "His delights / [Which w]ere dolphin-like: they showed his back above / The element they lived in" (87–89). This double-ness seems of a piece with Plutarch's characterization of Antony, but what Plutarch sententiously condemns here comprises Antony's majesty.[60] While the Antony of these lines may not be able, from a "Roman" perspective, to "hold this visible shape," Cleopatra reads such shapeless-ness as foundational. Put differently, what Caesar would construe as Antony's self-forgetting is for Cleopatra integral to his selfhood.

Cleopatra's construction of Antony should be understood in terms of the emphasis on death and commemoration that is predominant at the end of the play. As many have noted, act four marks the end of Antony's tragedy, whereas act five is devoted to Cleopatra's. In fact, at the end of the fourth act, Cleopatra briefly casts herself in the familiar role of the loyal Roman woman who kills herself immediately after her lover's death: "We'll bury him, and then what's brave, what's noble, / Let's do't after the high Roman fashion / And make death proud to take us. Come, away. / . . . we have no friend / But resolution and the briefest end" (4. 15. 90–95). These lines promise the twin conclusions of Cleopatra's "Roman" suicide and the end of the play, but there is a good deal more to come: the majority of act five unfolds in a period defined here as the deferral of a promised end, as the time between this utterance and the suicide that Cleopatra pledges soon to perform.[61] Thus, the space of the final act not only belongs to Cleopatra, it exists as and thanks to this deferral. At the same time, much of the act is devoted to considerations of how Cleopatra and Antony are to be remembered.

Act five offers crucial examples of the phenomenon C. C. Barfoot has identified as characteristic of the play: "Characters are prompted to become their own memorialists and historians, and the memorialists of others, both for their own benefit and for ours."[62] How is Cleopatra's memorializing of Antony to her benefit? The answer is simple: it does the work of elevating the status of their affair; it is part of Cleopatra's (and arguably the play's) effort to transform herself and Antony into great lovers, a transformation that is finally secured only with Cleopatra's suicide.[63] There are various obstacles to this transformation, most notably the one posed by Caesar's ambition to parade Cleopatra before "the shouting varletry / Of censuring Rome" (5. 2. 55–56).[64] Even if she is tempted to remain alive by placating her conqueror, Cleopatra harbors no illusions about the effects of being turned into a spectacle: to be paraded thus would mark her as one of the emperor's "scutcheons and . . . signs of conquest" (5. 2. 134). That is, she would function to advance and emblematize Caesar's power and fame. As he puts it, "For her life in Rome / Would be eternal in our triumph" (5. 1. 65–66). Caesar claims that his triumph would be eternal were he able to ensure Cleopatra's life in Rome, but the line also suggests that Cleopatra's "life in Rome" would be eternal in his triumph; he is offering her immortality through fame, but as a vanquished foe of Caesar. Concomitant with this fame would be the denigration of Cleopatra's relationship to Antony, for Cleopatra recognizes that her immortality as great lover is incompatible with the immortality attained by becoming an emblem of Roman conquest.

If act four ends, then, with Cleopatra's pledge to commit suicide in "the high Roman fashion," act five witnesses Cleopatra's resistance to becoming a trophy of Rome. Moreover, her suicide is preceded by the advancement of her conception of heroic masculinity, a conception that can accommodate what Caesar would consider Antony's self-forgetting. The foregrounding of this conception, generated in the time between Cleopatra's pledge to die and her actual end, helps change the circumstances of Cleopatra's suicide, contributing to its transformation from the dramatically ancillary act of a bereaved lover to the culmination of a tragedy of heroic passion. In killing herself Cleopatra states that she will become "from head to foot / . . . marble-constant" (5. 2. 238–239), seemingly becoming self-identical in ways that eluded Antony in his protracted suicide.[65] Moreover, the comic bathos of Antony's death finds no equivalent in the moving and carefully orchestrated suicide of

Cleopatra. It seems, then, that Cleopatra has in fact achieved a Roman death, her self-sovereignty mirrored even in the donning of her robe and crown (5. 2. 279). And yet, this achievement of "marble-constancy" is complicated by the undeniable eroticism of Cleopatra's suicide, which Cleopatra describes as, among other things, entrance into marriage with Antony – "Husband, I come!" (5. 2. 286) – and the pursuit of sexual relations – "The stroke of death is as a lover's pinch / Which hurts and is desired" (5. 2. 294–295).[66] Whereas this eroticism might seem to parody her claims of marble-constancy, it instead reveals yet again her non-self-identical nature, even at the moment of suicide. Moreover, this scene brings into sharper focus the eroticism attendant upon Antony's attempt at a Roman death, as in his reference to being taught by Eros (4. 14. 97–98), or his plan to act like "A bridegroom in my death and run into't / As to a lover's bed" (101–102). Even this act of identity consolidation – "a Roman by a Roman / Valiantly vanquished" – betrays a mystified conception of Romanness while also gesturing toward a selfhood characterized by multiplicity rather than "absolute self-consistency and singleness of being." Both of these suicides reveal multiplicity as the fundamental condition of identity. In Antony's case, this multiplicity is alternately misrecognized by him and experienced as the failure to attain the stability promised by a Roman death. For Cleopatra, the non-singleness of being is seen as being's very condition, and it is foregrounded in her masterfully theatrical suicide.

Above I discuss the classical formulation of fame as antithetical to a "beastly" life characterized solely by sleep and feeding. It is worth pointing out that while sleep, which we saw in chapter 1 is frequently linked with forgetting, is a recurring theme of the play, the majority of references to it appear in the last act.[67] Most of these references at least indirectly associate sleep with death, but sleep is also integral to Cleopatra's memory of Antony. Her "his legs bestrid the ocean" speech, which Adelman reads as generative of her vision of heroic masculinity, is Cleopatra's dream of "an emperor Antony. / O, such another sleep, that I might see / But such another man!" (5. 2. 75–77). But if Cleopatra's sleep is here productive of a dream that helps generate Antony's fame as a great lover, the play's final reference to sleep glances toward her Circe-like ability to engender Antony's self-forgetting. The words describing the dead Cleopatra are Caesar's: "she looks like sleep, / As she would catch another Antony / In her strong toil of grace" (5. 2. 345–347). Cleopatra appears to be asleep, and this seems to Caesar a provocation and a lure to "another Antony."[68] Or is that Cleopatra "looks *like* [or is a figure *for*] Sleep"? If so, it is *sleep* that seduced Antony – sleep, which represents both a respite from the pursuit of fame and the embracing of oblivion and self-forgetting.[69]

Certainly this is the promise of sleep in the Circean tradition. Tasso's Circe figure, Armida, lures Rinaldo to sleep with the following words, uttered by a spirit in her charge:

> Vertue it selfe is but an idle name,
> Priz'd by the world bove reason all and measure,
> And honour, glorie, praise, renowme and fame,
> That mens proud harts bewitch with tickling pleasure,
> An Eccho is, a shade, a dreame, a flowre. . .
> ***
> But let your happie soules in joy possesse
> The Ivorie castels of your bodies faire,
> Your passed harmes salve with forgetfulnesse,
> Haste not your comming evils with thought and caire.[70]

Caesar's lines reveal his recognition that the promise of sleep could be seductive to others, luring them to salve their "passed harms" with forgetfulness. Even in death, Cleopatra as Sleep evinces the power to "catch *another* Antony": perhaps even Caesar himself? Caesar's description of the dead Cleopatra attests to the tremendous allure of sleep and oblivion, both of which mark the suspension of the pursuit of "honour, glorie, praise, renowme and fame."

The play ends with orders for the funeral and burial of the two lovers, with Caesar stating that "No grave upon the earth shall clip in it / A pair so famous" (5. 2. 358–359). Much of the final act of the play has, for Cleopatra, been given over to the elevation of the status of her love for Antony. At the same time, this elevation is dependent upon Caesar and the way in which he remembers the couple; it is his voice that not only ends the play but that becomes the voice of history. Why does Caesar, who earlier emphasized Antony's self-forgetting, choose to commemorate and to bury Antony and Cleopatra as "a pair so famous"? An answer lies with "another Antony," the next Roman in danger of being seduced by Sleep. To read Antony as a famous lover is to paper over the problems posed by the non-self-identical nature of the Roman subject. Caesar transforms what he perceives as the emasculating desire for oblivion into a principle of fame, not to champion that desire but to contain it by recasting it as that which he sees as its opposite. Antony and Cleopatra are understood at play's end as lovers; Antony in particular is granted by Caesar an identity that is positive, a form of selfhood that is not defined as the forgetting of the self. In this scene, Caesar recognizes that memorializing heroic love is preferable to acknowledging that which "another Antony" might be implicated in, the desire for oblivion. Moreover, that

Antony has been, in Maecenas's words, "a spacious mirro[r] set before [Cacsar]" (5. 1. 34) arguably animates the emperor's eulogizing, rendering it legible as an effort to deny any possible identification of his own desires with those of the man who has been seduced by sleep.[71] At the same time, that the love of Antony and Cleopatra renders them famous means that Cleopatra has succeeded in redefining identity in terms other than those aligned with narrow Roman conceptions of masculine heroism. While Caesar denies the non-self-identical nature of the subject, he nevertheless introduces a form of fame that ensures that the "infinite variety" of Antony and Cleopatra is not completely effaced.

If Caesar's final words constitute the voice of history, it is the queen of Egypt who has throughout stressed the conditions of identity as they are represented in this play. Both Antony and Caesar engage in mystification and denial; it is only Cleopatra who recognizes the non-self-identical nature of the subject, whether Roman or Egyptian. Self-forgetting is revealed as a Roman construct, one that both renders monolithic the self that has been forgotten and masks the discontinuous nature of identity. Acts of remembering can perform a similar masking function, but it is Cleopatra's account of an Antony whose "legs bestrid the ocean" that offers an alternative form of remembering. Recognizing that Antony's character emerges out of the contradiction between his longing to be remembered and his eager pursuit of oblivion, Cleopatra transforms the discontinuities generative of self-forgetting into a prerequisite for heroic masculinity, and thus into an alternative to Rome's (or Caesar's) conception of fame.

It is worth considering *Antony and Cleopatra* as the expression of a cultural memory of the classical past. We have encountered some of the raw materials out of which Shakespeare constructed his play: Homer, Plutarch, Sallust. It is easy to see that *Antony and Cleopatra* functions as a dramatic re-collection both of Greek and (especially) Roman texts and of the ancient world.[72] And yet, as with Caesar's retrospective accounting of Antony, the economy of memory here is not one of reproduction or repetition; as a representation of the past, Shakespeare's play confirms John Frow's point that "rather than having a meaning and a truth determined once and for all by its status as event, [the past's] meaning and . . . truth are constituted retroactively."[73] This is a view of memory not necessarily antithetical to the common early modern practice of "read[ing] histories . . . of Rome . . . as a source of ethical and political lessons."[74] However, such lessons *are* antithetical to the model of masculinity promulgated by Cleopatra. In this model, memory has as its object of investment a character who forgets himself.

The Circean narrative is one in which the female object of male desire represents the threat of oblivion – of his forgetting his country, or his quest, or his duty. In *Antony and Cleopatra*, we encounter a transvaluation of the logic of the Circe myth, for the forgetting of self and country becomes the basis for rather than the abdication of heroic masculinity. This act of transvaluation is in and of itself a form of memory – memory understood not as reproduction or repetition, but as appropriation and recontextualization. Put differently, this transvaluation describes one of the operations of that form of memory known as intertextuality. In both Shakespeare's reworking of classical texts and Caesar's and Cleopatra's distinct commemorations of Antony, memory is a kind of making, performed with received cultural materials and in the service of present desires and future needs. What is striking about *Antony and Cleopatra*, though, is that oblivion both challenges and underwrites these operations of memory.

# 5 Sleep, conscience and fame in *The Duchess of Malfi*

[S]lumb'ring is a common worldly wile.[1]

In the last chapter, we saw that Cleopatra's commemoration of Antony is inseparable from the construction of a specific conception of heroic masculinity. John Webster's *The Duchess of Malfi* similarly concerns itself with retrospective representation. The final lines of the play, which are usually taken as having the Duchess as their subject, assert that "*Integrity of life is fame's best friend, / Which nobly, beyond death, shall crown the end.*"[2] The word "integrity" refers to "The condition of having no part or element taken away or wanting; undivided or unbroken state" (*OED* 1); fame is awarded to those whose deaths reveal the undivided nature of their lives. From the perspective of the ending, then, the Duchess is understood as being both self-identical and fame-worthy. However, throughout the early portions of the play a radically different view is proffered. Both the Duchess herself and her brothers describe her in terms of immoderate sleep, which we have seen is both a threat to the attainment of fame and is conceptually linked with lethargy and forgetfulness; as John Willis puts it, "*Sleep* offendeth *Memory*."[3] In *The Duchess of Malfi* such associations are operative, and the Duchess can be understood as having forgotten herself. Indeed, the representation of the Duchess draws upon all three of the types of self-forgetting that we have encountered in previous chapters. However, forgetting is subordinated to sleep when it comes to Webster's depiction of the Duchess as desiring subject.

While sleep signifies in a number of different ways in Webster's play, three main patterns emerge in (more or less) the following order. First, sleep is central both to Ferdinand and the Cardinal's efforts to regulate their sister's behavior and to the Duchess's crafting of a subjectivity out of the refusal of those efforts. Second, sleep comes to describe a particular way of representing Ferdinand in relation to those who act in his service; it figures the *intersubjective* relations out of which Ferdinand's *subjectivity* is formed. Finally, as the Duchess approaches death, sleep connotes resignation and spiritual peace. What impinges upon all of these

109

conceptions of sleep is conscience: in particular, the idea of the sleeping conscience advanced in casuistical discourse of the late sixteenth and seventeenth centuries. Also at issue in discussions of sleep and the sleeping conscience are complex relations among identity, subjectivity and agency. If initially sleep describes the division or dispersal of the self, the Duchess's death is compared to a sleep that connotes her "integrity of life." However, such integrity is revealed as imbricated in (and concomitantly undermined by) a fantasy of the future adduced in the play's final scene, while the sleep of conscience remains an important locus for dramatic subjectivity.

# I

Act one, scene two of *The Duchess of Malfi* stages two crucial events: the castigation and attempted correction of the Duchess by her brothers, and, immediately following, the Duchess's wooing and winning of Antonio. These two events are tightly connected, as the terms imposed upon the Duchess in the first are transvalued by her in the second. As for the first event, what we putatively witness is an attempt made by secular and religious authority figures to rouse from a deep sleep one they deem a sinner.[4] In the supposed pursuit of the desires which her brothers ascribe to her, the Duchess, they claim, can be compared to a heavy sleeper: as Ferdinand puts it, "those joys, / Those lustful pleasures, are like heavy sleeps / Which do forerun man's mischief" (1. 2. 244–246). A sleep that "forerun[s] man's mischief" is a prelude to damnation, and it is ostensibly the prospect of her damnation that leads the Cardinal to urge the Duchess to consider her mortality: "Wisdom begins at the end: remember it" (1. 2. 247). The Cardinal gestures toward a form of self-knowledge that arises from the confrontation with death; this is a kind of wisdom familiar from the *ars moriendi* tradition: "Well the perfection of our knowledge is to know God, & our selves: our selves wee best know, when we acknowledge our mortall being."[5]

Her brothers link the Duchess's desires to "heavy sleeps," and they are right in doing so: the Duchess's first important action in the play is performed while, according to her own account, she is sleeping. At the end of a speech describing her pursuit of a second marriage as a "dangerous venture," the Duchess declares, "Let old wives report / I winked, and chose a husband" (1. 2. 267–268). Critics have seldom discussed what is meant by the Duchess's winking. Most would presumably follow Elizabeth M. Brennan in glossing the word as the "clos[ing of one's] eyes to something wrong" and, presumably, to its consequences.[6] In this reading, the Duchess's winking is like Macbeth's when he describes the projected murder of Duncan in terms of "The eye wink[ing] at the hand."[7] However, a reading more responsive to the Duchess's actions in this scene, and to the play's recurrent emphasis on sleep, reveals her to be both retooling and scoffing at her brothers' scornful reference to heavy sleeps. As the *OED* tells us, to wink can mean "To have the eyes closed in sleep; to sleep; sometimes, to doze, slumber" (*OED* 3).[8] That the word often connotes a light sleep (as a noun, it means "A closing of the eyes for sleep, a (short) spell of sleep, a nap" [*OED* 1]; think of "taking forty winks") shows how the Duchess mocks her brothers' exhortations, which she has rightly recognized as hypocritical and self-interested. In setting out to marry again, the Duchess performs the very action her brothers fear most; by closing her eyes to what *her brothers* believe to be wrong, she is also, from their perspective, falling into a kind of moral slumber. More importantly, their speech provides her with the vocabulary necessary to her behavior. "If all my royal kindred / Lay in my way unto this marriage," the Duchess says just after her brothers exit, "I'll'd make them my low foot-steps [i.e., stepping stones]" (1. 2. 260–262). Similarly, it is the language of sleep provided by her "royal kindred" that the Duchess transforms from obstacles into "foot-steps."

The Duchess further appropriates the terms of her brothers' admonitions to woo Antonio. She echoes the Cardinal's emphasis on "the end" when she asserts that "It's fit...[to] inquire / What's laid up for tomorrow" (1. 2. 285–286). After Antonio responds as her steward – he takes her to mean that she wants to inspect "The particulars of [her] revenue and expense" (290) – the Duchess clarifies her emphasis: what's laid up for tomorrow, she explains, means "What's laid up yonder for me" (294). It is concern about her fate, she claims, that has led her to make her will; both her spiritual and worldly houses are to be put in order. However, it is soon revealed that the Duchess uses the device of the will to advance her own willful designs. Webster deploys the pun deliberately; we move from the will made "In perfect memory" (296) to Antonio's flirtatious assertion, uttered in response to hints from the Duchess, that it would be strange "If there were no will in [the Duchess] to marry again" (310). It is her willful desire, described in terms of "violent passions" that require that she "leave the path / Of simple virtue" (361–363), that is stressed in the wooing scene.[9]

If the Duchess is willful, the terms of her willfulness emerge out of her brothers' attempts to constrain her actions and limit her will.[10] The limits she encounters have a definitional force. The Duchess greets Antonio's anxiety about her brothers' response to their marriage by asserting that "All discord, without this circumference, / Is only to be pitied, and not fear'd" (1. 2. 384–385). Here the Duchess crafts out of the couple's enforced secrecy a charmed circle. While her brothers seek to reform both her behavior and her "privat'st thoughts" (235), the Duchess responds by expelling not only their influence but also "all discord" – meaning their dissent and interference – from the space generated by both her marriage and the willfulness that brought it into being.[11] This circle was also rhetorically cleared for the Duchess and Antonio by sleep and the actions it enables – by her winking and choosing.

Critical evaluations of the Duchess and her actions hinge upon the perceived significance of the charmed circle and what it connotes, a sphere of activity marked by the pursuit of desire and removed from both the baleful influence of the Duchess's brothers and the world of public responsibility. Some scholars read the Duchess negatively in terms of her "willful obsession with private happiness, her lack of sexual self-discipline, her violation of degree in marrying below her rank, her irresponsibility in abandoning her subjects, her secrecy and deceptiveness, her trifling with religious pilgrimage, and even her questionable piety in remarrying at all."[12] Other critics see her as "clearly represent[ing] elements missing from public life and opposite to the depravity her brothers charge her with: normal sexuality, nurturance, independence, recognition of value not associated with class and status."[13] In the former view, the circle is the site of sleep as it is defined by the Duchess's brothers, a site characterized by immorality and the abdication of responsibility, by "willful obsession" and the pursuit of pleasure; in the latter, sleep demarcates an arena of "normal sexuality, nurturance, independence." In either case, sleep is discursively generative – it helps produce the arena within which the Duchess enacts her will. It is generative in a more corporeal sense, also; the circle represents the space not only of a putatively "normal" sexuality but also of sexual reproduction, as the birth of the three children of Antonio and the Duchess make plain. Later in the play, in response to a proposal made by Antonio, the Duchess asks, "Alas, what pleasure can two lovers find in sleep?" (3. 2. 10). We might answer that it is in "heavy sleeps" that the Duchess and Antonio have found "lustful pleasures" as well as nurturance and independence.

That the Duchess's sleep connotes both violent passion and a valorized mutuality tells us that her character answers to aspects of both negative and positive evaluations of her. In this regard, Webster's play deviates markedly from its major source. In *The Second Tome of the Palace of Pleasure*, William Painter depicts the Duchess in wholly pejorative terms, as one who "forget[s] the Noble bloud of *Aragon* whereof she was descended, to couple hir self almost with the simplest person of all the trimmest Gentlemen of *Naples*."[14] Painter repeatedly construes both Antonio and the Duchess in terms of an immoral forgetting; for instance, the Duchess is one who "become[s] amorous by forgetting & straying from the limittes of honest life."[15] While the Duchess is disparaged throughout Painter, Webster goes out of his way to render her character in a fashion that disrupts any simplistic moral evaluation. While Lori Schroeder Haslem is persuasive in her suggestion that the Duchess's voracious consumption of the apricots proffered by Bosola bespeaks a disparaging (and misogynist) representation of her sexual desire,[16] the playful scene between the Duchess, Antonio and Cariola which Ferdinand interrupts is arguably the most convincing and touching re-presentation of affective relations in all of Jacobean tragedy. Moreover, the Duchess's response to Ferdinand's opprobrium rings true: "Why might not I marry? / I have not gone about, in this, to create / Any new world, or custom" (3. 2. 110–112).[17] In short, the behavior that Painter describes as the Duchess's forgetting of both blood and honesty is in Webster complexly rendered and resistant to any kind of manichean moralism.

There are two additional points to be made about her brothers' chas-tisement of the Duchess and her subsequent pursuit of Antonio. One might read this pursuit merely as her stubborn performance of forbidden actions, but that does not go far enough. First, we must consider the gender dynamics of the Duchess's brothers' words to her. In urging their sister to remain unmarried, Ferdinand and the Cardinal mobilize the cultural association of women with both "lustful pleasures" and the cold wetness of "heavy sleeps."[18] As we have begun to see, however, the Duchess turns the terms of their misogyny into the basis of a desiring, resistant subjectivity. Second, at the very outset of her brothers' extended exhortation, the Cardinal says, "We are to part from you: and your own discretion / Must now be your director" (1. 2. 213–214). In the lines that follow, both Ferdinand and the Cardinal suggest not that they rely upon the Duchess's discretion, but that they want to shape its terms. In puta-tively attempting to rouse her, then, they limn for the Duchess a field of operations and a desired identity, one akin to that she neatly describes as a "figure cut in alabaster / Kneel[ing] at my husband's tomb" (1. 2. 370–371). Such an identity would not only fix her forever as widow, it would also require that she act as if entirely devoid of desire, like a statue. Her brothers attempt to define for the Duchess her future actions, much as Richard Mulcaster's subject strives to do by exhorting Queen Elizabeth to "Remember old King Henry VIII!"[19] However, while Elizabeth only smiles in apparent approval, the Duchess's "winking and choosing" con-stitutes the crafting of her subjectivity out of the refusal of an identity that her brothers disingenuously claim already exists in the form of her "discretion."

## II

That the world "without this circumference" must encroach upon and destroy Antonio and the Duchess is inevitable in Webster's tragedy. This encroachment is emblematized in a scene alluded to above, in which Ferdinand penetrates the Duchess's bedroom (3. 2. 62–141). In the Duchess's first exchange with her brothers, Ferdinand refers to the role of conscience in the exercise of divine judgment when he says to the Duchess, "Your darkest actions: nay, your privat'st thoughts, / Will come to light" (1. 2. 235–236). The record of her actions and thoughts is what God (through conscience, which is frequently described as a light cast on our sins) will use to judge her. What also needs to be stressed, however, is that Ferdinand conflates conscience and surveillance, for he intends that the Duchess's private thoughts will be revealed to *him* through the assistance of Bosola.[20] The site of conscience-rousing is also one of both surveillance and coercion, and "conscience," like "discretion," becomes a term used to urge the Duchess to internalize imperatives voiced by her brothers. What Ferdinand claims as divine scrutiny is actually his watchful gaze, and he uses the rhetoric of conscience to mask his own examination of the Duchess. It is in the context of this examination that another conception of sleep comes to the fore.

In his first appearance on stage, Ferdinand mockingly argues for a traditional conception of martial honor. Speaking with put on "gravity" (1. 2. 13), he responds thusly to Castruchio's suggestion that, for a prince in wartime, deputization is the better part of valor: "Why should he [i.e., that prince] not as well sleep, or eat, by a deputy?" (1. 2. 19–20). In fact, many of Ferdinand's actions are performed by one deputy in particular, Bosola. Moreover, the conjunction of sleep and deputization becomes important seventy-five lines later. In his description of Ferdinand to Delio, Antonio says,

> He speaks with others' tongues, and hears men's suits
> With others' ears: will seem to sleep o'th' bench
> Only to entrap offenders in their answers;
> Dooms men to death by information,
> Rewards, by hearsay.
>
> (1. 2. 95–99)

The first and third sentences of this description stress how Ferdinand operates by proxy; he is cast here as a judge (though what is presumably at issue are his broader capabilities as Duke of Calabria) who not only depends upon others to hear and speak for him, but who also exercises judgment based on knowledge accumulated by those others: he dooms and rewards by information and hearsay. Read on its own, the second sentence is straightforward enough: Ferdinand plays at being inattentive until those he judges, lulled into a false sense of security, incriminate themselves, at which point he entraps them. (Antonio's characterization here is prophetic of the scene in which Ferdinand sneaks into the bedroom of the happily unaware Duchess.[21])

While the broad contours of this characterization are clearly rendered, what is puzzling is the way in which the false sleep of the second sentence links up with Ferdinand's status as one who hears with others' ears and speaks with others' tongues. What does sleep have to do with his dependence upon others? One answer is that that dependence helps Ferdinand convince those under judgment that he offers no threat to them. His sleep masks intense activity performed not by him but by those in his employ. (I follow Antonio in referring to "others" here, but the play focuses on one agent. Bosola is made Ferdinand's "intelligencer" in the Duchess's household moments before the brothers catechize her [1. 2. 179–183].) The general sense is that others collect information Ferdinand can use at the moment he rouses himself from his false sleep. But that is not what Antonio says. That Ferdinand hears through others' ears and speaks with others' tongues describes a decentering of the subject – Ferdinand is dispersed across multiple bodies – that is a necessary characteristic of Ferdinand's dependence upon those who collect information for him. In this context, it is worth reminding ourselves of what sleep is: as Robert Burton's appropriation of Scaliger has it, "*Sleepe is a rest or binding of all the outward senses, and of the common sense, for the preservation of body and soule.*"[22] The senses of a sleeping Ferdinand, then, would be bound, unable to perform their functions. According to Antonio, however, Ferdinand's sleep is false and his senses are operational; evidence of this is revealed through the ears of others. His seeming sleep masks the fact that Ferdinand is awake, but his wakingness is constituted through and across the bodies of those who provide him with information.

Antonio's depiction of Ferdinand introduces a complicated model of agency and identity that can be construed in terms of what Katherine Rowe has defined as "The problem of how to contain and regulate the relation between principal and agent, of how to know whose will is performed in any given act."[23] The confusion and conflation of Ferdinand and his agents – of body parts and senses – attests to the problem of the relation between principal and agent, will and act. Moreover, sleep plays an important role in this relation. Again, we turn to an example in which sleep is associated with Ferdinand. After discovering that the Duchess is pregnant, Ferdinand grows enraged and indulges in the voyeuristic fantasy of cross-class coupling that Frank Whigham has seen as central to Ferdinand's incestuous desire for his sister.[24] His imagination leads him

> To see her in the shameful act of sin,
> . . .with some strong thigh'd bargeman;
> Or one o' th' wood-yard, that can quoit the sledge
> Or toss the bar, or else some lovely squire
> That carries coals up to her privy lodgings.
>
> (2. 5. 41–46)

Finally, in response to his brother's repeated admonitions that he regulate his behavior – "You fly beyond your reason" the Cardinal asserts (2. 5. 47) – Ferdinand grudgingly relents: "Nay, I have done; /. . . In, in, I'll go sleep: / Till I know who leaps my sister, I'll not stir" (2. 5. 74–78).[25] As in Antonio's characterization of Ferdinand, sleep and the accumulation of knowledge are not incompatible. Again, it is through an agent, Bosola, that that knowledge is to be acquired. Important here is the relationship between sleep and voyeurism. It is a critical commonplace to see Ferdinand as a voyeur, but it is striking how much of the play he spends far from the primary site of his prurient interest. While he does creep unseen into the Duchess's bedroom (narrowly missing catching her engaged with Antonio and Cariola in what Judith Haber has identified as a verbal version of an eroticized "chafing"[26]), this is unusual; for most of the play Ferdinand is conspicuously absent from the Malfian court, relying on others to feed his voyeurism. It is in his imagination that he witnesses the Duchess engaged in "shameful act[s] of sin," and the information that Bosola brings helps to fuel that imagination. In other words, that Ferdinand will "not stir" – or that he is, as Antonio later says of him, "so quiet, that he seems to sleep / The tempest out, as dormice do in winter" (3. 1. 21–22)[27] – is not incompatible with a voyeurism predicated on his reliance upon *another's* senses.

It is worth pausing over the scene in which Ferdinand does spy upon the Duchess. As mentioned above, this scene begins playfully, and the affectionate relations between the Duchess, Cariola and Antonio are represented in a moving way. Ferdinand appears at a crucial moment. Believing that she is talking to Antonio, the Duchess states, "You have cause to love me, I ent'red you into my heart. / Before you would vouchsafe to call for the keys" (3. 2. 61–62). These lines underscore the fact that Antonio is in the position that Ferdinand seems to covet, that of having access to her bedroom, if not her heart. (Ferdinand attains the bedchamber only briefly, thanks to the "false key" supplied by Bosola [3. 1. 80].) However, in the exchange that follows Ferdinand's desires become more opaque. Ferdinand asserts that the knowledge he has attained by entering the Duchess's bedchamber is repulsive to him: "I would not for ten millions / I had beheld thee." Of and to the eavesdropping Antonio he exclaims, "use all means / I never may have knowledge of thy name" (3. 2. 96–98). He also urges the Duchess to create a new secret space for her assignations, one presumably free from his own surveillance: "I would have thee build / Such a room for him, as our anchorites / To holier use inhabit" (102–104). Moreover, before leaving, he asserts twice that he will never see the Duchess again (137–141). Obviously, all of these lines express Ferdinand's revulsion at discovering more about the Duchess's marriage and sexual life, but such revulsion is the obverse of Ferdinand's desire, and these lines also mark the extension of the voyeurism that has been conducted not by Ferdinand himself, but by Bosola. That is, in asserting that he wants the lovers to inhabit a secret cell, or that Antonio should take steps to keep his identity a mystery, Ferdinand is suggesting not that he will no longer seek out information, but that he most assuredly will – only from afar and through another. Shortly after leaving the bedchamber, Ferdinand, who in his strong emotion is "tane up in a whirlwind," rides to Rome (3. 2. 161–162); once again, his voyeurism requires the actions – and the senses – of his agent, Bosola.

If sleep represents a binding of the senses, Ferdinand's sleeps, false or real, describe a form of dispersed agency in which he operates, and even receives sensory information, through others. This is a clever variation on a recognizable dramatic relationship, as Elizabethan and Jacobean tragedies are filled with villains who depend upon those who act in their service. However, Webster thematizes this service relation in a novel way, and sleep becomes the term for the combination of deferred activity and mediated voyeurism that dominates Ferdinand's relationship to his sister. Of course, it is only the activity of Ferdinand himself that is deferred, as his sleep also encompasses and depends upon the constant exertions of those who are in his employ.

Can we connect the Duchess and Ferdinand as sleepers? In both cases, sleep represents the non-self-identical nature of the subject; it describes either self-division or self-dispersal. As noted above, the Duchess appropriates the category of sleep, first deployed in the attempt to shape the terms of her discretion, in such a way that she is able to craft out of her brothers' opprobrium both a desiring self and the space within which to execute her desires. At the same time, sleep as her brothers describe it represents a subject divided from knowledge of self and God. From this perspective, the Duchess's willful self marks a kind of self-alienation. In the case of Ferdinand, however, sleep takes the form of self-dispersal, the extension of the self across the bodies of those who perform actions for him. In each case, sleep connotes and enables sexual desire, admittedly of different sorts: the surrogate voyeurism of Ferdinand and the willful sexual congress of the Duchess. Ferdinand's behavior finally becomes untenable in this play, however; the form of selfhood that it grounds dissolves with the Duchess's death. Moreover, the end of his self-dispersal reveals that sleep for Ferdinand connotes an attempt to inoculate himself from the implications of actions performed through his surrogate.

The problem of "how to contain and regulate the relation between principal and agent" reaches a climax in Ferdinand's accusation that Bosola should have acted independently of his master's orders and not killed the Duchess (see 4. 2. 251–329). Before this, Ferdinand has toyed with his oath never to see the Duchess again; he visits her, but only in her darkened prison cell, and in a manner mediated by his intelligencer, Bosola.[28] Now, in this crucial exchange, Bosola casts himself as a tool of Ferdinand, while Ferdinand claims that Bosola acted as an independent agent. At one point Ferdinand acknowledges that he was the force behind the murder, and he hates Bosola for performing the action that he had urged him to: "for my sake, [I] say thou hast done much ill, well" (4. 2. 285). When Bosola stresses that the authority underwriting the crime was Ferdinand's, Ferdinand replies,

> Mine? Was I her judge?
> Did any ceremonial form of law
> Doom her to not-being? did a complete jury
> Deliver her conviction up i'th' court?
> Where shalt thou find this judgment register'd
> Unless in hell? See: like a bloody fool
> Th' hast forfeited thy life, and thou shalt die for't.
>
> (293–299)

The man known for operating by information and hearsay now pleads due process, and the judgment he goes on to offer is death. It is, of course, a corrupt judgment, predicated upon the notion that Bosola is the only one responsible; a few lines earlier, Ferdinand had already advanced this view, stating that he wished Bosola had taken pity on the Duchess (267–269) when he himself had obviously failed to do so. The point is not that Ferdinand has proven yet again that he is a hypocrite. Instead, it is that this scene marks for him the final disruption of that relation between principal and agent that has gone under the name of sleep.[29] In his grief and guilt, Ferdinand insists that one whose tongue and ears he had earlier put to his own use should now be understood as an independent agent. Of course, this insistence is made in a last ditch effort to inoculate himself from blame by modifying the logic of sleep. Self-dispersal across his agents gives way to his absolute separation from them – the ascription of authority to Bosola and the concomitant denial of his own authority. However, that Ferdinand is unsuccessful in maintaining this position – he leaves the stage "much distracted" (330), well on his way to the madness that consumes him in the final scenes – makes plain that for him the regime of sleep has come to an end.

As a marker of specific relations between principal and agent, sleep is also integral to the Cardinal's demise. As part of his plan to dispose of Julia's body, the Cardinal enjoins members of his entourage not to respond to cries that they might hear from Ferdinand's cell:

> It may be to make trial of your promise
> When he's asleep, myself will rise, and feign
> Some of his mad tricks, and cry out for help,
> And feign myself in danger.
>
> (5. 4. 13–16)

The Cardinal unwittingly parodies the logic of sleep that we have been discussing, a logic that confounds a transparent identification of the relationship between action and identity. "When he's asleep, myself will rise": Bosola might once have uttered these words to describe his relationship to Ferdinand, but as we have seen the actions literally performed by Bosola reveal Ferdinand's agency – they even extend Ferdinand's selfhood across the body of his agent. Here the Cardinal attempts to perform actions of his own – he will be his own agent – but under the shelter of his brother's sleep. At the same time, though, the Cardinal claims that some of those actions in fact issue from his brother ("some of his mad tricks") and would only be mimicked by him. Significantly, the Cardinal's deployment of the logic of sleep culminates in his own demise, as Bosola, Ferdinand's former agent, kills his new master during the putative sleep of his old one. Shortly thereafter he also kills Ferdinand, claiming that "the last part of my life / Hath done me best service" (5. 5. 63–64).

## III

We have seen thus far that sleep in this play bespeaks both "lustful pleasures" and a kind of self-alienation or self-dispersal; in this regard it functions much as self-forgetting does, to constitute a subject in terms of the disruption of his or her identity. That being said, a simple question remains: *why* does sleep signify in this way? One answer lies in the connections to (self-)forgetting stressed in the first chapter, but one can also read the play's emphasis on sleep in terms of conscience as described in casuistical texts that proliferated in the late sixteenth and seventeenth centuries. Webster's play is saturated with references to conscience, and as we will see Ferdinand's madness marks not only the end of his sleep but the rousing of his dormant conscience. Before turning to what the casuists refer to as the "sleepy conscience," we must consider how conscience is conceptualized in the early modern period, with attention paid to its connections to memory and forgetting.

An inevitable product of the Reformation emphasis on individuality over community, casuistical literature stresses the necessity of the godly Protestant exercising his or her conscience in order to manage moral and ethical dilemmas. The most influential of the casuists, William Perkins, generated a number of texts that provided examples of "practical divinity" or "case divinity," in which specific moral quandries are solved through an appeal to conscience mediated by scripture, experience and the very casuistical literature that represents these dilemmas. Many writers followed Perkins's lead, and there was an explosion of casuistical literature in the early portions of the seventeenth century. While the production of this literature was dominated by Puritans, Camille Wells Slights has observed that "English Protestants across the religious spectrum, despite radical disagreements about doctrine, liturgy, and church government, conceived of the conscience as a verbally constructed self and regularly examined their consciences as a religious duty."[30] Thus, for Protestants of all stripes, this literature spoke to crucial issues of morality, ethics and self-conceptualization.

Perkins understands conscience as having two functions, to witness and to judge. He describes the operations of conscience-as-witness as follows:

First it observes and takes notice of all things that we doe: secondly, it doth inwardly and secretly within the heart, tell us of them all. In this respect it may fitly be compared to a notarie, or a register that hath alwaies the penne in his hand, to note and record whatsoever is saide or done: who also because he keepes the rolles and records of the court, can tell what hath bin said and done many hundred yeares past.[31]

We have seen memory described as a "Gardian and Register"; or as the place where "those things that are done and spoken with the senses" are "registred and kept."[32] Memory and conscience, then, are metaphorized in almost exactly the same way. That is not where the connections end, however. Another casuist named Immanuel Bourne, in the service of an argument that sees conscience as located in all of the faculties of the soul at once, asserts that conscience-as-witness is to be found "In the *memory* [as] a *Register*, to witnesse what is done, or what is not done."[33] Richard Bernard makes much the same argument: conscience mobilizes understanding, will and memory; in the memory "it is as a Register, and as a privie Witnesse of our past thoughts, words and deeds."[34] In these two cases, conscience harnesses the faculty of memory in service of its operations. What is most striking, however, is that while memory is fallible, conscience-as-register is infallible: what is recorded there is permanently inscribed and must eventually be retrieved, by God if not man.

The infallibility of conscience-as-witness can be attributed to the fact that conscience is understood as both human and divine in nature; in John Abernethy's words, conscience

> hath *a witnesse in the heaven*, with whom we are said to *conscire*: and hence it is called *conscience*: as a private knowledge with another, then our selves: and this other, is only God . . . God hath deputed it, to give sentence before him, and with him; with us, or against us: for the furthering of his owne ones to be converted, and the wicked to be left convinced.[35]

Much the same argument is made by Perkins, who develops the significance of conscience's etymological roots in "conscire":

> *Scire*, to know, is of one man alone by himselfe: and *conscire* is, when two at the least know some one secret thing; either of them knowing it togither with the other . . . conscience, is that thing that combines two togither, and makes them partners in the knowledge of one and the same secret. Now man and man, or man and Angel can not be combined; because they can not know the secret of any man unlesse it be revealed to them: it remaines therefore that this combination is onely betweene man and God. God knowes perfectly all the doings of man, though they be never so hid and concealed. and man by a gift giv[en] him of God, knows togither with God, the same things of himselfe: and this gift is named Conscience.[36]

Even when conscience depends upon memory, the working assumption is that the records conscience keeps are more permanent than those normally maintained in memory. Conscience, "that thing that combines two togither," both partakes of the memory of man and, as a faculty both human and divine, outstrips it. In its permanence, it represents a form of immortality in which one's actions are recorded forever: "when a man dies, conscience dieth not; when the bodie is rotting in the grave, conscience liveth and is safe and sound: and when we shall rise againe, conscience shall come with us to the barre of Gods judgement, either to accuse or excuse us before God."[37]

The casuists recognize that in our lifetimes our consciences do not always impede us from performing immoral actions. As a witness, conscience is a tireless scribe who takes note of all that we do, but as a judge conscience is sometimes both passive and silent. It is in this context that sleep emerges as an important category. In asserting that heavy sleeps precede damnation, Ferdinand is also suggesting that the Duchess's conscience is asleep. Were it awake, her conscience would alert her not only to her sins, but also to the dark fate to which she is tending; it would prompt her to generate the self-knowledge that comes from focusing on her inevitable end.

Sleepiness is only one of the maladies from which the dysfunctional conscience is said to suffer; it can also be "seared" or "cauterized." However, distinctions between these terms are not absolute; definitions of each routinely overlap. Indeed, John Abernethy attests to the primacy of sleep to the seared conscience:

When hee seemeth to sleepe and take his rest, he is inwardly full of trouble: neither shall hee ever want his secret terrours when hee looketh least for them: As *Nero* (after he slew his mother) confessed how hee was tormented. The seared conscience may lie still quiet a space, and bee calme-like: but like a wilde beast, while it sleepeth, seemeth tame and gentle; but when it is awaked, flyeth in a mans face to devoure him: So it being awaked, and the senselesse slumber falling off, or pulled off, by the severe hand of God; sheweth his fierce eyes, and becommeth like the furies, pursuing him with firebrands.[38]

Similarly, the definitions offered by William Ames of "benummed" and "stupid" consciences emphasize, respectively, "a kind of spiritual *sleepe*" and "*Lethargie* or *Drowsinesse*."[39] That being said, allusions to a conscience identified as sleeping are also common. Immanuel Bourne describes such a conscience as "*secure* and *carelesse*, so over-busied with the entizing pleasures or profits of this world; or lulled asleepe in that bewitching cradle of sinnes darke impurity, that such a man can finde no leasure, no not to dreame of *Heaven*; or if he doe, hee soone forgets his dreame, and falleth toward *Hell* before hee bee aware."[40] Like the seared or stupid conscience, the sleeping conscience does not confront the sinner with evidence either of his or her own transgressions or of the impending inevitability of his or her death and judgment. Both conscience and sinner have succumbed to enticing pleasures that have "lulled [them] asleepe" in sin.

Given that conscience's records are inviolable, one might think there is no role in conscience discourse for forgetting. This is not the case. As the conscience can be said to sleep (thereby not rehearsing that which has been recorded), so can the subject forget that which the conscience has earlier dictated. Strictly speaking, this is a problem of recollection. Consider Richard Bernard's discussion of the forgetting of what conscience teaches us:

Conscience takes information from the Understanding, but yet by the aide of Memorie, which reteineth that, which the Understanding by reasoning hath concluded; which conclusion the Memorie holdeth; and so the Understanding by it carrieth it and propounds it to Conscience. If Memorie faile, our Knowledge is therein so farre lost: for what wee remember not, wee know not; and so no Conscience of that.

Therefore to have Conscience, let us labour to keepe in Memorie what duties we doe know. Forgetfulnesse of that which is taught, is one maine reason why so many make so little Conscience of that which is dailie taught unto them.[41]

In his first two references to memory Bernard is describing the *storage and maintenance* of the memory trace (as is made plain by his use of the verbs "retain" and "hold"). When Bernard next uses the word memory, its meaning has changed. What he calls a failure of memory is best understood as a failure of *recollection*: "what wee remember not" is that which we cannot or will not retrieve from memory. In this case, the contents of conscience are not lost. Instead, forgetfulness of "that which is taught" describes the inability or refusal to deploy lessons that remain firmly engraved in the conscience. Why does the subject not deploy these lessons? Like Faustus, the subject might act against knowledge and conscience in the pursuit of his desires. In addition, as we saw in chapter 1, the forgetful body is an undisciplined and indolent one. Performing such acts of recollection, as well as the spiritual operations to which they are central, is a constant and arduous endeavor: thus the reference to *laboring* to keep duties "in Memorie," which means not only to recollect them but also to perform regularly the behaviors they prescribe. Remembering describes the constitution (or perpetual re-constitution) of a self through the laborious reiteration of duties that makes that self what it is, whereas forgetfulness is (the form of selfhood that emerges out of) the breakdown of this iterative practice.

This kind of forgetfulness, suggestive as it is of indolence and the failure to perform one's duty, resembles the dormant conscience; as Bernard puts it, the sleepy conscience is "the conscience of every drowsie and lazie Christian, who takes no paines for Religion, but is like a sleepie natured fellow." That conscience "soone ceaseth . . . worke, is hardly roused, worketh but weakely, soone giving over, and a sleep againe, and cannot be kept on working, but by hearing of threats, and beholding, but especially feeling the judgements of God."[42] Sleep and forgetfulness each describe a mode of behavior in which the subject performs actions against the knowledge contained in conscience.[43] In addition, excess sleep and forgetfulness are connected through the conceptual linkages elucidated in the first chapter of this book; each evokes an early modern fantasy of an indolent and sinful body. That the conscience is asleep means that it does not function either as judge of or as witness against the forgetful subject who experiences the deep sleep of hedonism; at the same time, "feeling the judgements of God" represents the (sometimes only intermittently) roused conscience awakening that subject from his slumber.

We have seen that Ferdinand refers to the operations of conscience when he says to the Duchess, "Your darkest actions: nay, your privat'st thoughts, / Will come to light" (1. 2. 235–236). Here, the Duchess is described as one of those who Richard Carpenter says "worke[s] in darkenesse." Such people attempt "to contrive in secret those things, which afterward being brought to light, cast shame in their faces, a burthen on their consciences, a blot on their name; and without repentance, everlasting confusion upon body and soule." Moreover, their contrivances are understood by Carpenter in terms of a category that, as we have seen in previous chapters, is associated with both sleep and forgetfulness: these sinners suffer from a "Lethargy and deadly sickenesse," the only cure for which is to be "ever awaked with the remembrance of Gods presence."[44] Being alerted via memory to "Gods presence" entails being awakened to one's conscience, "that thing that combines two [i.e., man and God] togither." This process of awakening not only renders unacceptable the actions performed while sleeping, it marks the end of an alienation from God that is also a self-alienation; it makes it possible "to know God, & our selves." Conscience is an important faculty here, as it represents God-in-man; to know the contents of one's conscience is both to know oneself and to act in accordance with God's law (the two being understood as inseparable). From this perspective, then, knowledge of one's self would seem precisely identical to knowledge of God's law.

However, the situation is not so simple. As Camille Wells Slights has argued, conscience needs to be understood as "at once an authoritative moral norm controlling social relationships and as self-reflexivity," as both "a private inner voice and the obligatory force of moral law."[45] Slights insists that we understand conscience's operations not in terms of the frictionless adoption of moral norms by the subject; subjectivity (or self-reflexivity) marks a relationship between moral law and an inner voice not identical to that law.[46] Sleep stands as one such relationship; it describes the situation when one's "private inner voice" ignores the claims of moral law. Sleep, then, defines a subjectivity at odds with moral law, self-knowledge and knowledge of God. Not merely the cauterizing of conscience, sleep is a mode of being from which, the casuists suggest, one needs to be awakened (via "the remembrance of Gods presence") in order to return to and become oneself.

We have seen that the Duchess's brothers have attempted to use the categories of conscience and discretion to shape her thoughts and actions. They have represented a coercive vision of conscience not as an inviolable internal faculty, but as the tool of a form of subjection. The Duchess, on the other hand, confirms Slights's point that subjectivity or "self-reflexivity" emerges out of a relationship between the subject and "the obligatory force of moral law." As the image of the charmed circle suggests, the Duchess's willfulness is always constituted in relation to but not compliance with "obligatory force."[47] If conscience is both "authoritative moral norm" and "self-reflexivity," Ferdinand and the Cardinal attempt to render the latter identical to (their version of) the former. In embracing sleep, however, the Duchess is simultaneously revealed as self-alienated (in conscience's terms) and as constituted in terms of her desires.

What I have been suggesting, then, is that the Duchess is one who both answers to and retools the casuists' account of the sleeping conscience. Put differently, the Duchess's subjectivity emerges out of her resistance to the identity that her brothers attempt to craft for and impose on her, the identity of a "figure cut in alabaster / Kneel[ing] at [her] husband's tomb." Sleep, then, limns the space of her subjectivity, as it does, in a very different way, the space of Ferdinand's. At the same time, and as I have stressed throughout this book, subjectivity is frequently experienced by a particular character as a crisis of identity, one that often goes by the name of self-forgetting. In Antony's case, subjectivity represents alienation from an idealized Romanness, while for Bertram it connotes the forgetting of his familial identity. For the Duchess, sleep simultaneously marks both resistance to coercion and a passionate worldliness. However, Webster comes to stage the Duchess's self-abnegation, her renunciation of "violent passions" in the service of preparing for death. That is, the Duchess finally remembers both herself and her "end." Intriguingly, this process paves the way for the emergence of another form of sleep – that of the conscience quiet in the face of death.

## IV

As we have seen, critical opinion is divided on the moral nature and significance of the Duchess's pursuit of her "violent passions," but what seems undeniable is that she undergoes a transformation as a result of her wrongful imprisonment and torture. On one level, the Duchess is like Marlowe's Edward II or Shakespeare's Richard II in that she reveals greatest nobility of spirit once the trappings of her noble birth and rule have been stripped from her. (Moreover, even the most strident opponent of the Duchess's behavior would have to admit that her failings neither warrant nor equal in opprobrium the heinous conduct of her brothers.[48]) At the same time, that nobility of spirit, which is revealed partly through the interventions of Bosola, is inseparable from her misery and confrontation with death. As many critics have noted, Bosola in his guise as tomb maker prepares the Duchess for her demise; in his own words, he takes on the role "to bring [the Duchess] / By degrees to mortification" (4. 2. 173–174). Here as elsewhere, we should be careful not to accept any single (or simple) motivation for Bosola's actions, but it is undeniable that he serves to help her "remember her end."[49] Indeed, one can understand his exchange with the Duchess as expanding upon the Cardinal and Ferdinand's early attempt to mortify her, with that scene's dark comedy turned here into prelude to tragedy.[50] Moreover, the hedonism of which her brothers earlier accused her has been supplanted by the kind of resignation that the *ars moriendi* tradition espouses.[51] From the perspective of this resignation, the question of whether or not the play sees her willful desire as positive or negative is irrelevant; in either case the Duchess is one whose worldliness gives way to preparations for death. That is, we can read the Duchess as one who needs to remember her end without necessarily acceding to the harsh view of her sexuality articulated by her brothers. What is most important is that through the course of her mortification, the Duchess's "will" is represented in a new light.

The Duchess's nobility of spirit manifests itself, among other ways, in her touching concern for and emphasis on her family and household. In her final words to Cariola, the Duchess's "will" has strikingly different connotations from those we encountered in the wooing scene:

> In my last will I have not much to give;
> A[s] many hungry guests have fed upon me,
> Thine will be a poor reversion. . .
> I pray thee look thou giv'st my little boy
> Some syrup for his cold, and let the girl
> Say her prayers, ere she sleep.
>
> (4. 2. 197–202)

Here sleep refers ostensibly to the normal "binding of the senses," but the more significant connotation is that of death. (The same connotation is prominent the next two times the word is used [4. 2. 231, 235].) It is through his efforts at mortification that Bosola has prepared the Duchess for the same sleep that her daughter will shortly experience.

Of course, the Duchess's mortification takes place through torture and is prelude to murder – another reason not to take Bosola's virtuous motives at face value. One way or the other, though, the terms of this mortification are significant. Ferdinand's earlier presentation of the (supposedly) dead bodies of Antonio and her children was part of an attempt to drive the Duchess to despair (4. 1. 115).[52] Bosola, on the other hand, has as tomb maker generated in the Duchess a readiness to embrace the somnolence of death without urging her to suicide.[53] At the same time, he also associates the Duchess's mortality with a fitful sleep: as a result of her supposed riotous lifestyle, she "sleep'st worse, than if a mouse should be forc'd to take up her lodging in a cat's ear" (4. 2. 135–136). Then, when a few lines later the Duchess makes her famous assertion "I am Duchess of Malfi still," Bosola / the tomb maker responds by saying, "That makes thy sleeps so broken" (139 140). These may be general comments motivated by Bosola's keen awareness of the thousand natural shocks that flesh is heir to; if so, the mere fact of death (which will "Serve for mandragora to make [the Duchess] sleep" [4. 2. 231]) promises the Duchess eternal rest, while both mortality and the maintenance of her identity have been equated with an uneasy slumber. However, from the viewpoint of mortification, a peaceful death also attests to the state of the Duchess's soul after her repentance. Immanuel Bourne refers to the evil conscience as "a *Bed*, that when a man should sleepe, it giveth him torments, feares and terrors in stead of quietnesse."[54] The quietness of soul that the Duchess evinces is manifest in the peaceful sleep offered by her virtuous death. Most importantly, we see in this instance that the meaning of sleep has in the Duchess's case undergone a transformation. Instead of connoting hedonistic self-forgetting, sleep suggests a still conscience and the acceptance of death. That is, this form of sleep reveals "integrity of life," the production of self-identicality through an encounter with death; it bespeaks that form of self-knowledge that emerges from, in Sutton's phrase, "acknowledg[ing] our mortall being."

If this is so with the Duchess, something else entirely transpires in the cases of Ferdinand, Bosola and the Cardinal. As we have seen, in conscience discourse sleep often describes a form of self-alienation achieved through the disarming of the proper functions of conscience. The end of self-alienation comes for Bosola when, prompted by the Duchess's death, he refers to the "black register" of his conscience:

> a guilty conscience
> Is a black register, wherein is writ
> All our good deeds and bad; a perspective
> That shows us hell.

(4. 2. 350–353)[55]

These lines are uttered immediately after his discussion of the Duchess's "sacred innocence, that sweetly sleeps / On turtles' feathers" (4. 2. 349–350). Bosola's metaphoric transformation of the black register into "a perspective / That shows us hell" – a lens through which Bosola discovers his fate – is ingenious, linking both the witnessing and judging functions of conscience (seeing the record of his sins reveals to Bosola God's judgment: he will be sent to hell). Most important, though, is the fact that Bosola's conscience is awakened by the spectacle of the Duchess dying. Less than twenty lines earlier, and referring to his assertion that he has only been spurned by Ferdinand for acting as his agent, he states that "I stand like one / That long hath tane a sweet and golden dream. / I am angry with myself, now that I wake" (317–319). Typically sardonic in tone, Bosola's second sentence can be read in two contradictory ways – as suggesting either that he is angry for the actions he has performed while he (along with his conscience) was asleep, or that he is angry because that sleep, with its promise of gold and advancement, has come to an end. Arguably both meanings are prominent in Bosola's thoughts; even plagued by conscience he remains wed to the golden dreams that have corrupted him, as is made plain by the fact that his chastisement of Ferdinand goes hand in hand with a plea for payment (4. 2. 286–329). It is worth noting that Antonio initially described Bosola in similarly mixed terms, as one of promise who, despite his valor, might be corrupted – a process defined in terms of an "immoderate sleep" that acts as an "inward rust unto the soul" (1. 1. 77–78).[56]

The rousing of Ferdinand's conscience is manifest in his madness.[57] This marks the end of the self-dispersal achieved through master-servant relations; his sleep, which worked to inoculate him from the consequences of his own actions, gives way to a madness that is linked to conscience. Consider the celebrated moment at which Ferdinand leaps upon his shadow, shortly after saying, "Stay it; let it not haunt me" (5. 2. 36).[58] As Bourne explains, "Conscience [is] of a divine nature, being placed in the middest, as an Ambassador betweene God and man, and given by God unto him for a perpetuall companion: It is like thy shadow, *Nec fugere, nec fugare poteris*, thou canst neither flie from it, nor make it flie from thee."[59] Like his shadow, Ferdinand's conscience both emanates and is at a remove from him. Conscience is an inward state that seems simultaneously outward. It is in this way that conscience troubles us: as a sign from the self that is external to the self.[60] The operation of conscience, then, is a form of self-chastisement that is inseparable from divine judgment.

The Cardinal's newly roused conscience is construed in terms similar to those used in depicting Ferdinand's shadow. The Cardinal opens the final scene of the play "puzzl'd in a question about hell," then goes on to assert,

> How tedious is a guilty conscience!
> When I look into the fishponds, in my garden,
> Methinks I see a thing arm'd with a rake
> That seems to strike at me.

> (5. 5. 1–7)

Critics have offered ingenious explanations for the precise significance of the "thing arm'd with a rake,"[61] but what is clear is that we encounter another figure for conscience that confounds the relationship between internal and external. Peering into a pond, the Cardinal sees his own reflection; he too is haunted by a force that seems to emanate from outside himself while being actually native to him, his "perpetuall companion." In his case, it is not the influence of the Duchess's death alone that has awakened his conscience – his murder of Julia also contributes to this (5. 4. 25–27) – but through her death the Duchess has served as a crucial catalyst for awakening the consciences of both her brothers and their primary agent, Bosola. While in an early scene a hypocritical attempt is made to rouse the Duchess's supposedly sleeping conscience, in these late scenes the Duchess is the vehicle by which her accusers' own consciences are awakened.

It is worth observing that the portrayal of conscience as a reflection of the self is prevalent in casuistical discourse. As Bernard puts it, *"Conscience thus reflect[s] upon a Man, to make him see himself."*[62] That this formulation also speaks to conscience's doubleness is made plain in Perkins: conscience is

*a reflecting* or doubling of [what a man thinks], whereby a man conceives and thinkes with himselfe what he thinks...The minde thinks a thought, now conscience goes beyond the minde, and knowes what the minde thinks; so as if a man would go about to hide his sinnefull thoughts from God, his conscience as an other person within him, shall discover all. By meanes of this ... action conscience may beare witnes even of thoughts.[63]

Again conscience is a kind of doppelganger, the force "whereby a man conceives and *thinkes with himselfe* what he thinks." Both reflection and record, conscience appears in Webster's play as the means by which the subject truly sees himself and is seen by God. Whereas sleep connotes self-division, the doubleness of conscience suggests the magnification rather than the dispersal of the self.

## V

Insofar as the play both represents the operations of conscience and asks us to evaluate the actions of its characters, it bears some affinity to "practical" or "case divinity." That is, *The Duchess of Malfi* not only deploys casuistical discourse, it can be seen as offering an occasion for the moral evaluations central to casuistry.[64] However, such evaluations are not always easy to make, because while the play may adopt casuistry's terms, it does not entirely accept its emphases. The play's representation of sleep has been structured around a simple irony: while her brothers attempt to rouse the Duchess's conscience, they are the ones who are "drowsie and lazie Christian[s]"; while her death is described as a peaceful sleep suggestive of her mortification, it also awakens the slumbering consciences of those who catechized her at the outset of the play. And yet, to accept this view of sleep is never to move beyond casuistry's imperatives. Although one can see the play as fundamentally invested in rousing the consciences of its characters, not all behaviors performed while sleeping are the same: much of what is compelling and affecting about the Duchess goes under the name of sleep. If the Duchess's mortification and death earn her "integrity of life," they also erase the subjectivity constituted out of her "winking and choosing." While casuistical discourse connects sleep to the disabling of conscience, *The Duchess of Malfi* appropriates sleep to describe modes of behavior and forms of subjectivity that, in the Duchess's case, do not easily lend themselves to a simplistic moral or ethical valuation. (Consider again the divided response of critics to her actions.) Of course, the sleep that the Duchess attains with death is slightly different, suggesting peace of mind achieved through her renunciation of all things worldly. However, the idea of renunciation is to the point: if this is what the *ars moriendi* dictates, it is not necessarily (or only) what Webster prescribes. Webster's theatrical energies are directed at least as much to the compelling rendering of sleep as they are to its repudiation, as much toward life as toward death. In all their equivocality, Bosola's lines aptly describe Webster's relation to sleep: "I stand like one / That long hath tane a sweet and golden dream. / I am angry with myself, now that I wake."

As we have seen, there are points of contact between sleep and self-forgetting. Especially in the case of dramatic representation, each is generative, productive of specific subjectivities and the actions concomitant with them. As both this chapter and the one preceding it have suggested, self-identicality is antithetical to sleep and self-forgetting. In this play, sleep finds its opposite as much in "integrity of life" as it does in the notion of the Duchess as a funerary "figure cut in alabaster" – both construe her from the perspective of death, both evacuate her of subjectivity in the name of a lifeless monumentality.[65] With that in mind, we will conclude by returning to where we began. "Integrity of life is fame's best friend, / Which nobly, beyond death, shall crown the end": Delio utters these words shortly after having asserted of Bosola, Ferdinand and the Cardinal that

> These wretched eminent things
> Leave no more fame behind 'em, than should one

Fall in a frost, and leave his print in snow,
As soon as the sun shines, it ever melts
Both form and matter.

(5. 5. 112–116)[66]

In his role as tragic witness, Delio is left to tell the audience who will be remembered and who will be forgotten. However, this operation is part of a specific task that he embarks upon at the very close of the play. "Let us make noble use / Of this great ruin" (109–110), Delio says in reference to the catastrophes of *The Duchess of Malfi*, and he "makes use" by working toward initiating the rule of the unnamed son of Antonio and the Duchess. That son will reign "In's mother's right" (112), a state of affairs perhaps inaugurated by Delio in tribute to his "lov'd and best friend," Antonio (5. 1. 76; the phrase is Antonio's). (It is worth noting that the Duchess's son by her first husband would presumably have a legitimate claim to rule.) With this in mind, we can see that the Duchess's integrity of life is adduced in the service of a male homosocial bond, to underwrite "ANTONIO's son" (5. 5. 107 s.d.) as ruler. More broadly, the act of commemorating some while consigning others to oblivion is part of a pattern of "making use," of bending historical events to one's desires and in the service of the future. The ascription of self-identicality to the Duchess, then, is part of a broader effort to generate a specific future, one in which the actions of the past will be remembered (or forgotten) in certain ways.[67] Fame, then, is something of a sham, the projection of one's desires onto a necessarily unknown future. Perhaps it is for this reason that Webster is drawn to sleep, a category antithetical to fame.[68] Certainly Webster offers a vision of life lived from the viewpoint of both fame and conscience – that is, from the viewpoint of death – but it is finally his fascination with sleep and the forms of behavior that it describes that drives his representation of (in particular) the Duchess and Ferdinand, both of whom are riveting in their non-self-identicality. More than the rousing of their consciences in awareness of the "mischief" that is to come, it is their "heavy sleeps" that are central to Webster's conception of tragic subjectivity.

# 6     Coda: "Wrought with things forgotten"

> The promise of an historical event is always more than what was actually realised. There is more in the past than what happened. And so we have to find the *future of the past*, the unfulfilled potential of the past.[1]

Not long after the witches have informed him that he will one day become king, Macbeth meditates upon his prophesied future and what might be necessary for him to bring that future into being. The thought that he could be required to become a regicide "[S]hakes so [his] single state of man, / That function is smother'd in surmise, / And nothing is, but what is not."[2] Shortly after considering that his coronation might occur without his taking any murderous action ("If Chance will have me King, why, Chance may crown me / Without my stir" [1. 3. 144–145]), Macbeth is interrupted in his musings, and he quickly apologizes for his preoccupation:

> Give me your favour: my dull brain was wrought
> With things forgotten. Kind gentlemen, your pains
> Are register'd where every day I turn
> The leaf to read them.
>
> (150–153)

In the second half of this statement, Macbeth pledges that he will always remember the services performed for him by Angus, Rosse and Banquo; the register described here is the book of his memory, and Macbeth claims that he will daily turn its pages. However, he first tells us that he has been dwelling upon "things forgotten." Kenneth Muir glosses this as Macbeth saying that he has been unsuccessfully trying to remember something, but one can read the line more literally, as suggesting that Macbeth's "dull brain" has been given over to, if not shaped in terms of ("wrought with"), "things forgotten." What the playgoer knows, moreover, is that these "things forgotten" include Macbeth's thoughts regarding the various possible means of attaining a prophesied future.

    This moment encapsulates Macbeth's position at this point in the play; what he will soon show himself to have forgotten in the name of his future is necessary loyalty to Duncan (which partly undercuts his claim that he will always remember the actions of those loyal to him). Put in terms that are familiar to us by now, Macbeth can be seen as someone who has forgotten himself, and this is associated with his self-division, his shaken "single state of man." Worth pausing over is the connection between forgetting and the future. Instead of being preoccupied with things he has failed to remember, Macbeth focuses on that which is to come; indeed, he voices an ontology constituted in terms of the future ("nothing is, but what is not [yet]"). What Macbeth describes as "things forgotten" are indeed both the kingship that has been foretold for him and, to a much greater degree, the different kinds of actions he might take to attain that kingship. His musings are coincident with an obliviousness to his environment – "Look, how our partner's rapt" (143) – that emerges out of his reflection upon that which is to come.

If "things forgotten" stand for both a projected future and the deeds to be performed in the name of it, focusing on these "things" also works to delineate interiority; they bespeak a disjunction between the role of loyal thane that Macbeth should be performing and the thoughts that engross him. Here, Macbeth's *obliviousness* suggests inwardness, his failure to attend to his surroundings suggesting a form of self-forgetting-as-subjectivity. (A similar moment occurs during the banquet scene, in which Macbeth forgets his duties as royal host because of the appearance of Banquo's ghost, symbol of Macbeth's guilty preoccupation with the murder [3. 4, esp. 82–83].) Indeed, dwelling on "things forgotten" is the expression of his self-division, the non-singleness of his unsettled masculinity. Self-forgetting connotes here both the subject's dis-integration from the present and a subjectivity shaped in relation to a projected future.

Of course, Macbeth acts viciously in order to attain the kingship. But it is worth taking seriously his recognition that the crown could be attained without ruthless action on his part. After all, it is not Macbeth's achievement of the kingship that makes him a villain; it is the operations he performs to seize and secure the crown that do so. The "things forgotten" which Macbeth considers include not only taking bloodthirsty actions, but also behaving more passively ("without my stir"). If self-forgetting troubles Macbeth's "single state of man," it also accommodates his consideration of possibilities both ruthless and benign. Certainly the prophesied future remains fixed in Macbeth's mind, but the variable means by which that future might be achieved ("not stirring" versus committing regicide) are also part of the contents of those "things forgotten." In this regard, "things forgotten" gesture towards possible future actions both benign and vicious.

Preoccupied as it has been with things forgotten (more broadly construed than in the above lines), this book has worked to trace connections
between forgetting and dramatic subjectivity. It has also argued that
forgetting, far from suggesting only the erasure of memory and the
concomitant loss of its plenitude, has a content – indeed, different contents in different discursive contexts. In closing, I want also to stress that
forgetting, like commemoration, can be associated with conceptions of
the future: we saw this in Delio's ascription of oblivion to some and fame
to others. Such a future is never the one that actually comes to pass (if we
can say that there is a *single* thing called "the future"); it instead represents a possibility, something not yet realized – and presumably not
realizable – in the present. For Delio, memory and forgetting are the
means by which a desired future is gestured toward. In the case of
Macbeth, we encounter something slightly different. While Macbeth's
actions are in a broad sense pre-inscribed, both by genre and the historical
record, "things forgotten" include that which cannot easily be captured
by a sense of dramatic telos – most importantly, the thought process by
which Macbeth begins to come to terms with his predestined kingship;
and, relatedly, his recognition that he need not stir to achieve his
ambitions.

It is worth thinking more about the pre-inscribed nature of Macbeth's
nefarious actions. This is most vividly suggested earlier in this scene, when
Macbeth is first dressed in the "borrow'd" robes of the dead Thane of
Cawdor, whose treachery Macbeth takes on along with his clothing and
title (1. 3. 109). These robes are similar to Bertram's family ring in that
they incorporate Macbeth into a particular (dramatic) identity – in this
case, that of the traitor. The robes are literally a form of memory – one
that is not predicated upon Macbeth's subjective experience.[3] Given this,
Macbeth's "obliviousness" becomes all the more important. It marks the
play's interrogation of the terms of memory as represented by the traitor's
robes. For the period of time that Macbeth is "wrought with things
forgotten," he exists at a remove from the claims of memory that those
robes make upon him. Obliviousness, then, both reveals Macbeth's briefly
maintained distance from a pre-inscribed role and encapsulates his uneasy
transition from loyal retainer to ruthless villain.

What is true of Macbeth's obliviousness has often been true of forgetting as it has been discussed throughout this book: it marks the distance
between, in Linda Charnes's terms, subjectivity and identity. The traitor's
robes, as a form of memory, interpellate Macbeth into a specific identity.
Forgetting, on the other hand, entails the disarticulation of the subject in
relation to various cultural or social – and, in Macbeth's case, generic –
imperatives. In early modern drama, subjectivity often emerges in the

space of that disarticulation, the space of forgetting. For Macbeth, the possibility of being something other than the traitor that memory (in the form of the "borrowed robes") makes him is only sustained for as long as he forgets; the end of his obliviousness is roughly coincident with the beginning of his murderous adherence to the traitor's role (although he obviously does not remain equally committed to that role at all times). Forgetting, then, connotes for Macbeth not only subjectivity, but also the promise of future actions different from the ones that, through the claims of memory, he is destined to pursue. Forgetting represents possibility, a potential alternative to that future which Macbeth puts on with the traitor's robes. Of course, Macbeth also considers regicide while he is "wrought with things forgotten." But it is the fact of that action being *considered* that matters, suggesting as it does that Macbeth does not yet fully inhabit the role that memory calls upon him to adopt.

From the perspective of a future that Shakespeare could not have imagined – the future represented by and in twenty-first century America – this view of forgetting probably seems strange. Especially in academic culture, memory is greatly valorized, and we are at the same time all keenly aware of the burden and anguish forgetting imposes on both those who suffer from Alzheimer's disease and those who care about them. As one text devoted to Alzheimer's has it, that disease constitutes *The Loss of Self*.[4] Early modern culture has no apparent analogue to Alzheimer's (perhaps because of comparatively early mortality[5]), although the association of forgetfulness with old age is a commonplace one. But neither does that culture routinely celebrate forgetting, which, as we have seen, was often associated with both vice and disease. What does seem to be true, though, is that forgetting both intrigues a wide variety of early modern writers and presents certain writers with a specific kind of opportunity – the opportunity to experiment with and explore the relationship between identity and subjectivity.

What might also trouble the modern reader is the notion that memory in this scene from *Macbeth* is at odds with subjectivity. Or, more precisely, that it is forgetting and not memory that has a subjective content. In one way, the reason for memory's subjective impoverishment is simple: the "borrowed robes" exist at a distance from the cognitive operations of recollection. But there is another way of considering this. While in the modern era we tend to assume the primacy of subjective memory to conceptions of the individual – you are what you remember – such a linkage cannot hold in the same way in the Renaissance, precisely because that individual does not exist as such. Memory understood in the form of Macbeth's robes or Bertram's family ring speaks to an early modern conception of identity as constituted relationally and in terms of material objects – a conception discussed in the introduction. What this means, then, is that it is forgetting, with its strong connection to subjectivity, that offers some of the raw materials out of which the modern notion of the individual was to be built. In more narrowly dramatic terms, the representation of forgetting intersects in this period with a developing interest in "personation."[6] That is, and as in the example of Macbeth, certain elements of forgetting are linked to the delineation of, in the anachronistic and dramatic senses of the term, "character."

Forgetting also enables dramatists to imagine possible futures for their characters – futures not absolutely identical to what social position or genre or chronicle history in the end demand of them. In the example we have been focusing on, another word for such an imagined future is interiority – the thought process which signals Macbeth's (momentary) non-identicality to the role he is called upon to play by memory. Insofar as this is so, both forgetting and the future are figures for possibility and for thought, and it is with possibility in mind – understood as the unrealized and unrealizable, the ever-becoming – that this book will end. Linked as they are to notions of the future, possibility and forgetting also speak to the non-self-identicality of the present. They are examples of what Nietzsche calls "the untimely," that which runs counter to the present and acts on it as such, in the service of both "life" and the possible – in the service of the future.[7] This future is not a determinate one. For instance, while forgetting provides some of the cultural materials from out of which the individual is born, it is not toward that birth that forgetting inexorably tends. (Nor, presumably, would the individual recognize any debt owed to early modern conceptions of forgetting.) Forgetting's importance to dramatists lies in the representational possibilities that it affords, possibilities whose interest resides largely in the degree to which they do *not* tend toward a determinate end.[8]

This book has attempted to historicize forgetting – to suggest how it appears in a distinctly early modern context that would change significantly with the Cartesian revolution. What it has tried to show is that forgetting is generative of certain subjective possibilities within its own time, of alternatives to claims made by memory. Put somewhat differently, this book has sought to consider how and why a range of early modern writers have "planted oblivion." Its aim has been not only to identify a few of the places where forgetting grows – always alongside and entangled with memory – but also to begin to account for oblivion's strange, untimely harvest.

# Notes

INTRODUCTION: PLANTING OBLIVION

1. William Shakespeare, "Venus and Adonis," *The Riverside Shakespeare*, ed. G. Blakemore Evans, *et al.* (Boston: Houghton Mifflin, 1974), lines 556–558. All references to Shakespeare in this chapter are drawn from this text unless otherwise specified.
2. Gail Kern Paster, *The Body Embarrassed: Drama and the Disciplines of Shame in Early Modern England* (Ithaca: Cornell University Press, 1993).
3. One could see these lines as describing the operations of the poem as a whole, for in Shakespeare's epyllion Venus's strong desire is given more than enough space to flourish. At the same time, this is something of a joke: in this poem, has Venus *ever* acted in accordance with the imperatives of shame and honor? The ascendance of oblivion that the poet describes here has arguably been achieved long before.
4. A recent collection that also makes this claim is *Forgetting in Early Modern English Literature and Culture. Lethe's Legacies*, ed. Christopher Ivic and Grant Williams (New York: Routledge, 2004). As Williams and Ivic state, "Forgetting. . .must circulate within culture, possessing its own discourses and practices; it can no longer remain the negative space of an obsolete model of memory" ("Introduction: Sites of Forgetting in Early Modern English Literature and Culture," 1–17, esp. 2).
5. See, for examples, David Cressy, *Bonfires and Bells: National Memory and the Protestant Calendar in Elizabethan and Stuart England* (Berkeley: University of California Press, 1989); Eamon Duffy, *The Stripping of the Altars: Traditional Religion in England, c. 1400 – c.1580* (New Haven: Yale University Press, 1992); Nigel Llewellyn, "The Royal Body: Monuments to the Dead, For the Living," *Renaissance Bodies: The Human Figure in English Culture, c. 1540–1660*, ed. Lucy Gent and Nigel Llewellyn (London: Reaktion Books, 1990): 218–240; Peter Marshall, *Beliefs and the Dead in Reformation England* (Oxford: Oxford University Press, 2002). On memory and religious visual images, see Huston Diehl, "'To Put Us in Remembrance': The Protestant Transformation of Images of Judgment," *Homo, Memento Finis: The Iconography of Just Judgment in Medieval Art and Drama*, ed. David Bevington, *et al.* (Kalamazoo: Medieval Institute Publications, Western Michigan University, 1985): 179–208.

6. Huston Diehl, *Staging Reform, Reforming the Stage: Protestantism and Popular Theater in Early Modern England* (Ithaca: Cornell University Press, 1997), esp. 94–124. See also Anthony Low, "*Hamlet* and the Ghost of Purgatory: Intimations of Killing the Father," *ELR* 29:3 (Autumn 1999): 443–467; Stephen Greenblatt, *Hamlet in Purgatory* (Princeton: Princeton University Press, 2001); Michael Neill, *Issues of Death: Mortality and Identity in English Renaissance Tragedy* (Oxford: Clarendon Press, 1997). For more work on (cultural) memory and drama, see Jonathan Baldo, "Wars of Memory in *Henry V*," *Shakespeare Quarterly* 47 (1996): 132–159; Anthony B. Dawson, "The Arithmetic of Memory: Shakespeare's Theatre and the National Past," *Shakespeare Survey* 52 (1999): 54–67; Robert C. Jones, *These Valiant Dead: Renewing the Past in Shakespeare's Histories* (Iowa City: University of Iowa Press, 1991). For an essay that focuses on remembering and forgetting in Shakespeare, see Jonathan Baldo, "Exporting Oblivion in *The Tempest*," *Modern Language Quarterly* 56 (1995): 111–144.

7. For more on this commonplace, see chapters 1 and 4.

8. George Puttenham, *The Arte of English Poesie* (1589) (Kent State: Kent State University Press, 1970), 54. This quotation appears in a chapter devoted to "historicall Poesie" (54).

9. Lina Bolzoni, "The Play of Images. The Art of Memory from Its Origins to the Seventeenth Century," *The Enchanted Loom: Chapters in the History of Neuroscience*, ed. Pietro Corsi (New York: Oxford University Press, 1991), 16–65, esp. 20. See also Lina Bolzoni, *The Gallery of Memory: Literary and Iconographic Models in the Age of the Printing Press*, trans. Jeremy Parzen (Toronto: University of Toronto Press, 2001).

10. Alison Wright, "The Memory of Faces: Representational Choices in Fifteenth-Century Florentine Portraiture," *Art, Memory and Family in Renaissance Florence*, ed. Giovanni Ciappelli and Patricia Lee Rubin (Cambridge: Cambridge University Press, 2000): 86–113, esp. 87. For a full account of the nature of remembering the dead in late medieval English culture, see Marshall, *Beliefs*, esp. 18–45.

11. J. S. W. Helt, "Women, Memory and Will-Making in Elizabethan England," *The Place of the Dead: Death and Remembrance in Late Medieval and Early Modern Europe*, ed. Bruce Gordon and Peter Marshall (Cambridge: Cambridge University Press, 2000): 188–205, esp. 194.

12. On Petrus Ramus's influential sixteenth-century revision of this tradition, in which memory is separated from rhetoric and relocated in dialectic or logic, see Paolo Rossi, *Logic and the Art of Memory: The Quest for a Universal Language*, trans. Stephen Clucas (Chicago: University of Chicago Press, 2000), 97–102. On classical conceptions of memory, see Janet Coleman, *Ancient and Medieval Memories: Studies in the Reconstruction of the Past* (Cambridge: Cambridge University Press, 1992).

13. Bolzoni, "Play of Images," 20; Rossi, *Logic*.

14. Edward Reynoldes, *A Treatise of the Passions and Faculties of the Soule of Man* (London: R. H[earne] and John Norton for Robert Bostock, 1640), 13.

15. On the art(s) of memory, see Bolzoni, "Play of Images" and *Gallery of Memory*; Rossi, *Logic*; Frances Yates, *The Art of Memory* (Chicago: University of Chicago Press, 1966); Mary Carruthers, *The Book of Memory*

(Cambridge: Cambridge University Press, 1990); and *The Craft of Thought: Meditation, Rhetoric, and the Making of Images, 400–1200* (Cambridge: Cambridge University Press, 1998); William E. Engel, *Mapping Mortality: The Persistence of Memory and Melancholy in Early Modern England* (Amherst: University of Massachusetts Press, 1995); and *Death and Drama in Renaissance England: Shades of Memory* (Oxford: Oxford University Press, 2002). It must be noted both that Carruthers's focus is pre-modern and that the art of memory is often said to be either moribund or marginalized by the end of the sixteenth century (see, for instance, Jonathan D. Spence, *The Memory Palace of Matteo Ricci* [London and Boston: Faber and Faber, 1988], 12–13), thanks to the gradually felt effects of print, the fact that the art was often associated with mystical or cabalistic practice, and, somewhat contradictorily, the growing perception that, in any case, its uses were often trivial: as one not unsympathetic writer disparagingly points out, the art was helpful when it came to "the remembrance of all such pleasant tales and histories as shall passe in table talke, from conceipted wits" (Hugh Platt, *The Jewell House of Art and Nature* [1594], facs. edn. [Amsterdam and Norwood, NJ: Theatrum Orbis Terrarum and Walter J. Johnson, Inc., 1979], 85; see also Henrie Cornelius Agrippa, *Of the Vanitie and Uncertaintie of Artes and Sciences*, trans. James Sanford [London: Henry Wykes, 1569], 24v–25r). That being said, the influence of this memory tradition extends well into the seventeenth century – the Donne sermon discussed in chapter 3 makes this plain, as does Rossi's study – even if its contents are also modified (see Engel, *Death and Drama*).

16. Carruthers, *The Book of Memory*, 7.
17. Carruthers has recently drawn our attention to the medieval art of oblivion. This is an art to which the "rigid, easily reconstructable order" associated with the art of memory is also crucial:

> To treat text [by which Carruthers means any memory system, including the architectural mnemonic familiar from Frances Yates's work]. . .as a habitually retained "foundation" for other material, is to use it like a set of mnemonic places, or backgrounds. A text can only serve in this way when its customary context is "forgotten," at least for this occasion, by a deliberate act of the author's will. . .It is this willed forgetting that actually enables creative mental "play," the recombinatory engineering of meditative *memoria*. (*The Craft of Thought*, 30)

Thus, as Carruthers would be the first to acknowledge, the art of oblivion is understood as a subset of that of memory. "To have forgotten things is seen by us as a failure of knowledge and a reason for distrusting memory altogether; to have forgotten some things was seen in Augustine's culture as a necessary condition for remembering others" (29). See also Bolzoni: "With great precision (and often with great tedium), the manuals of memory written during the fifteenth, sixteenth, and seventeenth centuries pass on sound advice on how to remove from the memory those images that are no longer useful" (*The Gallery of Memory*, 142). These contributions notwithstanding, forgetting has remained underexamined and undertheorized, especially outside the arts of memory.

18. For an analysis that discusses drama and the memory arts, see Engel, *Death and Drama.*

19. Jonas Barish, "Remembering and Forgetting in Shakespeare," *Elizabethan Theater: Essays in Honor of S. Schoenbaum,* ed. R. B. Parker and S. P. Zitner (Newark: University of Delaware Press, 1996): 214–221, esp. 219–220. I would only disagree with Barish's assumption that *all* early modern arts of memory had an occult component, and that Shakespeare had *no* interest in memory as "a separable psychological datum"; references to memory as such appear in both *Love's Labour's Lost* and *The Two Gentlemen of Verona.*

20. See *The First Part of Henry IV,* ed. A. R. Humphreys (London: Methuen, 1960), 1. 3. 236, 239–244; *Hamlet,* ed. Harold Jenkins (London: Methuen, 1982), 2. 1. 50–52. (Future references to *Hamlet* are to this edition.) *Antony and Cleopatra,* ed. John Wilders (London: Routledge, 1995), 1. 3. 88–93. On moments such as these, see Amanda Watson, "Off the Subject: Early Modern Poets on Rhyme, Distraction, and Forgetfulness," *Forgetting in Early Modern English Literature and Culture,* ed. Ivic and Williams, 83–95, esp. 90.

21. William E. Engel, *Death and Drama*; see also Baldo, "Wars of Memory," and Dawson, "Arithmetic of Memory." Marvin Carlson has argued, in a discussion of theatrical representation in general, that the theatre functions as a "memory machine." "All theatrical cultures have recognized, in some form or another, this ghostly quality, this sense of something coming back in the theatre, and so the relationships between theatre and cultural memory are deep and complex" (Marvin Carlson, *The Haunted Stage: The Theatre as Memory Machine* [Ann Arbor: University of Michigan Press, 2001], 2). See also Joseph Roach, *Cities of the Dead* (New York: Columbia University Press, 1996); Greenblatt, *Hamlet in Purgatory.*

22. Thomas Heywood, *An Apology for Actors* (London: Nicholas Okes, 1612), F3V.

23. The connection between subjective and collective memories is often simply assumed, and the precise nature of that connection remains undertheorized. See Kerwin Lee Klein, "On the Emergence of *Memory* in Historical Discourse," *Representations* 69 (Winter 2000): 127–150.

24. Aristotle, "On Memory," trans. J. I. Beare, *The Complete Works of Aristotle: The Revised Oxford Translation,* 2 vols., ed. Jonathan Barnes (Princeton: Princeton University Press, 1984), I: 714–720; see also Coleman, *Ancient and Medieval Memories,* 15–38. This distinction informs Spenser's depiction of memory in the House of Alma. The old man Eumnestes ("good memory") is assisted by the boy Anamnestes ("the reminder"; anamnesis means "recollection"); the former represents memory and the latter recollection ("And oft when things were lost, or laid amis, / That boy them sought, and vnto him [Eumnestes] did lend" [Bk. II, Canto IX, 58. 6–7]). Edmund Spenser, *The Faerie Queene,* ed. Thomas P. Roche, Jr., assisted by C. Patrick O'Donnell, Jr. (Harmondsworth: Penguin, 1978). On memory in this episode, see Alan Stewart and Garrett A. Sullivan, Jr., "'Worme-eaten, and full of canker holes': Materializing Memory in *The Faerie Queene* and *Lingua,*" *Spenser Studies* 17 (2003): 215–238.

25. Patrick J. Geary describes Augustine's model of memory as follows: "With memory one moves through a three-step process of knowledge: first, what is external and known by the senses; second, what is internal and known by introspection; and, finally, what is beyond man and can be known through participation. The process of thought involves gathering together (*colligere*) the data stored in the vast chambers of the memory. But beyond the knowledge of the world, memory is the fundamental means by which one knows oneself" (*Phantoms of Remembrance: Memory and Oblivion at the End of the First Millennium* [Princeton: Princeton University Press, 1994], 17). On the significance of the Augustinian model for the historical development of inwardness, see Charles Taylor, *Sources of the Self: The Making of the Modern Identity* (Cambridge, Mass.: Harvard University Press, 1989), 127–142.

26. "[C]*ognitive* entails an assumption shared with pre-Cartesian psychology of the early modern period, the assumption that the mind is inextricably part of the material body" (Mary Thomas Crane, "Male Pregnancy and Cognitive Permeability in *Measure for Measure*," *Shakespeare Quarterly* 49 (1998): 269–292, esp. 271).

27. Andy Clark, *Being There: Putting Brain, Body, and World Together Again* (Cambridge, Mass.: MIT Press, 1997), 201. Arguing against the Cartesian separation between mind and body, Clark's account of developments in cognitive science offers "a vision that puts explicit data storage and logical manipulation in its place as, at most, a secondary adjunct to the kinds of dynamics and complex response loops that couple real brains, bodies, and environments" (1–2).

28. See John Sutton's *Philosophy and Memory Traces: Descartes to Connectionism* (Cambridge: Cambridge University Press, 1998) for a book on early modern memory that draws connections to cognitive science, especially in its discussion of the function of animal spirits in relation to the notion of distributed cognition.

29. Andy Clark and David J. Chalmers, "The Extended Mind," *Analysis* 58 (1998): 10–23, esp. 10.

30. John Willis prefigures Clark's discussion of "offloading" memory when he refers to a commonplace book as that in which "you will keep in mind things worthy remembrance, better, safer, sooner, more certainly, profitably, and delightfully, then by that monstrous repetition, prescribed by some Authors in this Art of Memory" (John Willis *Mnemonica; or, the Art of Memory* [London: Leonard Sowersby, 1661], 11–12). As in Clark, the book here is a form of memory, one that helps one "keep *in mind*" what one wants to recollect. Chapter 1 talks of the relationship between strengthening memory and the living of an orderly life, a relationship that gestures toward an awareness of the relationship between memory and both somatic action and environment.

31. On this topic, see Mary Floyd-Wilson, *English Ethnicity and Race in Early Modern Drama* (Cambridge: Cambridge University Press, 2003).

32. Katherine Rowe, "'Remember me': Technologies of Memory in Michael Almereyda's *Hamlet*," *Shakespeare the Movie, Pt. 2*, ed. Richard Burt and Lynda Boose (London: Routledge, 2003): 37–55, esp. 42; see also Katherine

Rowe, "Memory and Revision in Chapman's *Bussy* Plays," *Renaissance Drama* n.s. 31 (2002): 125–152. Insofar as recollection is tied to practice and place, the memory arts seek to generate both a place (the memory theatre) and a practice (the orderly passage from one memory locus to another) that regularizes the operations of recollection.

33. "[T]he cognitive concept of an embodied mind seems closer to early modern humoral physiology than the radically dualistic post-Cartesian paradigm" (Mary Thomas Crane, *Shakespeare's Brain: Reading with Cognitive Theory* [Princeton: Princeton University Press, 2001], 14). In alluding to a Cartesian mind-body split, I am referring less to Descartes's work itself than to its legacy. As John Sutton (*Philosophy and Memory Traces*) has recently reminded us, the role of the animal spirits in Descartes's formulation of memory complicates any simple distinction between mind and body.

34. Compare my distinction between "memory" and "remembering" with the two sets of meanings identified by Leo Salingar: "The words *memory* and *remember* have varied senses in Shakespeare's language, but they fall broadly into two divisions. There is the mental faculty, private and personal. And there is the public knowledge of past people or events or of enduring custom. *The second carries a strong bias towards obligation or action, even where there may be no question of mentally bridging a gap of time – as, for example, in the biblical commandment, 'Remember the sabbath day, to keep it holy'*" ("Memory in Shakespeare," *Cahiers Élisabéthains* 45 [April 1994], 59–64, esp. 59, emphasis in last sentence mine).

35. [Richard Mulcaster,] "The Passage of our most dread Sovereign Lady, Queen Elizabeth," *Tudor Tracts 1532–1588*, ed. A.F. Pollard (New York: Copper Square, 1964), 367–395, esp. 393.

36. While emulation represents a signal form of remembering, not all forms of remembering are necessarily emulative.

37. Of course, the call to remember also offers Elizabeth an opportunity to stage her queenship within certain conditions. Elizabeth here, as elsewhere in her royal entry (and, indeed, throughout her reign), shrewdly manipulates her own image through and in response to claims like the one this unidentified subject makes of her. Moreover, the specific conditions under which this act of remembering emerges are hardly those that will obtain as Elizabeth exercises her authority over the course of her queenship.

38. Comparing Elizabeth's royal entry with Mary's five years earlier is instructive here. Whereas this pageant emphasized Elizabeth's connection with her father, Mary's downplayed her relationship to Henry VIII in favor of both her and Philip's genealogical links to the house of Lancaster, in part to deemphasize the reforms associated both with her father and her half-brother. See David Starkey, *Elizabeth: Apprenticeship* (London: Vintage, 2001), 171–172.

39. During her entry, Elizabeth's "remembering" would presumably be signaled by her deportment, the way in which her body language telegraphs the nature of her response to the citizen's request.

40. Linda Charnes, *Notorious Identity: Materializing the Subject in Shakespeare* (Cambridge, Mass.: Harvard University Press, 1993), 8, 9.

41. Thomas Kyd, *The Spanish Tragedy*, in *The First Part of Hieronimo and The Spanish Tragedy*, ed. Andrew S. Cairncross (Lincoln: University of Nebraska Press, 1967), 1. 2. 95–120.

42. In this regard, the inwardness that Katharine Eisaman Maus (*Inwardness and Theater in the English Renaissance* [Chicago: University of Chicago Press, 1995]) has reclaimed for the Renaissance is, in tragedy, often a representation of disrupted identity.

43. Consider also Katharine Maus's assertion that "'Subjectivity' is often treated casually as a unified or coherent concept when, in fact, it is a loose and varied collection of assumptions, intuitions, and practices that do not all logically entail one another and need not appear together at the same cultural moment" (*Inwardness*, 29).

44. Recent accounts of the meaning of this potent phrase are offered by (among others) Greenblatt, *Hamlet in Purgatory*, who considers it in relation to the competing claims of revenge and intercessory remembrance, and Richard Kearney: "'Remember me' says King Hamlet to his son. Tell my story. Carry my memory, my legacy, my legitimacy, into the next generation, to my people, to my children and grandchildren" ("Narrative and the Ethics of Remembrance," *Questioning Ethics: Contemporary Debates in Philosophy*, ed. Kearney and Mark Dooley (London and New York: Routledge, 1999), 18–32, esp. 18). See also Marshall, *Beliefs*, 270.

45. Greenblatt offers an interesting account of what it means to remember in this play, and even notes that "it seems faintly ludicrous to imagine that Hamlet would or could ever forget the Ghost" (*Hamlet in Purgatory*, 207).

46. It is worth considering what this example has in common with the one drawn from Mulcaster: both represent, paradoxically enough, the subjection of princes, to either the popular will or the imperatives of the patriarch (if not both – remember Henry VIII, the citizen exclaimed!). They also represent princes at liminal stages in their lives, stages in which the rhetorical appeal to and of remembering is particularly strong.

47. This is actually the most relevant of four definitions of the term, the other three of which are as follows: to omit care for oneself; to lose one's way; to lose consciousness. This book does not aspire to account for every possible form of (self-)forgetting isolable in the period; certainly more could be done to explore moments like this one, in which *Julius Caesar*'s Cassius says to Brutus, "You forget yourself / To hedge me in. I am a soldier, I, / Older in practice, abler than yourself / To make conditions" (4. 3. 29–32).

48. James Turner, *The Politics of Landscape: Rural Scenery and Society in English Poetry 1630–1660* (Cambridge, Mass.: Harvard University Press, 1979), 5. For more on property and propriety, see Garrett A. Sullivan, Jr., *The Drama of Landscape: Land, Property and Social Relations on the Early Modern Stage* (Stanford: Stanford University Press, 1998), esp. 159–193.

49. On the "individual," see Peter Stallybrass, "Shakespeare, the Individual, and the Text," *Cultural Studies*, ed. Lawrence Grossberg, *et al.* (New York: Routledge, 1992): 593–610; Raymond Williams, "Individual," *Keywords: A Vocabulary of Culture and Society*, rev. edn. (New York: Oxford University Press, 1985), 161–165.

50. A neat definition of self-forgetting is offered (but not explicitly as such) in John Donne's "The First Anniversarie" (*The Complete Poetry of John Donne*, ed. John T. Shawcross [Garden City, New York: Doubleday and Co., 1967]): "Prince, Subject, Father, Sonne, are things forgot, / For every man alone thinkes he hath got / To be a Phoenix, and that there can bee / None of that kinde, of which he is, but hee" (215–218). The "man alone" is the self-forgetting subject who has dislodged himself from the social relations constitutive of identity. Here the self-forgetter is represented as proud, imagining that he has become the phoenix and thus *sui generis*. A good example of erotic self-forgetting is to be found in Dorastus's self-description in Robert Greene's *Pandosto* (1588; New Rochelle, NY: Elston Press, 1902): "Ah Dorastus, wilt thou so forget thy selfe as to suffer affection to suppresse wisedome, and Love to violate thine honour? How sower will thy choice be to thy Father, sorrowful to thy Subjects, to thy friends a griefe, most gladsome to thy foes!" (32).

51. Margreta de Grazia, "The Ideology of Superfluous Things: *King Lear* as Period Piece," *Subject and Object in Renaissance Culture*, ed. Margreta de Grazia, Maureen Quilligan and Peter Stallybrass (Cambridge: Cambridge University Press, 1996): 17–42; also, "Weeping for Hecuba," *Historicism, Psychoanalysis and Early Modern Culture*, ed. Carla Mazzio and Douglas Trevor (New York: Routledge, 2000): 350–375.

52. De Grazia, "Weeping," 364, 365.

53. Barish, "Remembering and Forgetting," 218.

54. In the Norton facsimile of *The First Folio of Shakespeare, 1623* (1968; New York: Applause Books, 1995) the speech prefixes underscore this identity, as Sly's utterances are prefixed with "Beg." for "Begger." The stage directions preceding his transformation into a Lord describe him as "the drunkard" (208, 209).

55. Christopher Marlowe, *Tamburlaine the Great, Parts 1 and 2*, ed. John D. Jump (Lincoln: University of Nebraska Press, 1967), *Pt. 1*, 5. 1. 500. Henceforth cited in the text.

56. This final point is confirmed by Tamburlaine's plan, articulated in response to Zenocrate's request that he raise the siege, to name "the provinces, cities, and towns / After my name and thine, Zenocrate" (4. 4. 77–78). This act of naming actually entails the renaming of already existing "provinces, cities, and towns," and in a way clearly designed to erase Zenocrate's allegiance to her own country.

57. See especially chapter 1 for more on this topic.

58. Valerie Traub, *The Renaissance of Lesbianism in Early Modern England* (Cambridge: Cambridge University Press, 2002), 23.

59. Both *All's Well* and *Tamburlaine, Pt. 1* offer comic endings, although admittedly complex and surprising ones.

60. William Rankins, *A Mirrour of Monsters* (London: I. C. for T. H., 1587), C3r.

61. Steven Mullaney, *The Place of the Stage* (Chicago: University of Chicago Press, 1988).

62. There is (at least) one form of self-forgetting that is not taken up in this book, and it has a valence strikingly different from the other forms discussed here. It is what might be called ascetic self-forgetting, which is most clearly

exemplified by medieval religious practice through which monks entirely "forget themselves" in their service to God. This is self-forgetting understood in terms of self-abnegation, the renunciation of the world, the mortification of the body and complete devotion to God. We catch a glimpse of this model in this exhortation of Pierre de la Primaudaye's: "Let us not propound to our selves this ende, to seeke after that which is expedient for us according to the flesh. Let us forget our selves as much as may be, and all things that are about us" (*The French Academie*, trans. T. B. [London: Edmund Bollifant for G. Bishop and Ralph Newbery, 1586], 797; see also Samuel K. Cohn, Jr., "Collective Amnesia. Family, Memory, and the Mendicants: A Comment," *Art, Memory, and Family in Renaissance Florence*, ed. Giovanni Ciappelli and Patricia Lee Rubin [Cambridge: Cambridge University Press, 2000]: 275–283, esp. 278). However, this is one of very few early modern texts that I have seen in which we encounter ascetic self-forgetting (although I have admittedly not examined works focusing on monasticism). Most importantly, this is a form of self-forgetting that does not interest the playwrights taken up in this book.

63. One version of this insight is evident in Lacan's discussion of the mirror stage and the formation of a self-alienated identity: "*The mirror stage* is a drama whose internal thrust is precipitated from insufficiency to anticipation – and which manufactures for the subject, caught up in the lure of spatial identification, the succession of phantasies that extends from a fragmented body-image to a form of its totality that I shall call orthopaedic – and, lastly, to the assumption of the armour of an alienating identity, which will mark with its rigid structure the subject's entire development" (Jacques Lacan, "The Mirror Stage as Formative of the Function of the I as Revealed in Psychoanalytic Experience," *Écrits: A Selection*, trans. Alan Sheridan [New York: W.W. Norton & Co, 1977]: 1–7, esp. 4). Both Freud's and Lacan's belief that the subject is alienated from itself – caught between an "orthopaedic" idealization of the self and "the turbulent movements that the subject feels are animating him" (Lacan, "The Mirror Stage," 2) – has been enabling for this study, even if the *forms* of self-alienation examined here do not resemble the ones posited by psychoanalysis.

64. See, for example, Regina Schwartz with Valeria Finucci, "Introduction: Worlds Within and Without," *Desire in the Renaissance: Psychoanalysis and Literature*, ed. Valeria Finucci and Regina Schwartz (Princeton: Princeton University Press, 1994): 3–15; Mazzio and Trevor, eds., *Historicism, Psychoanalysis, and Early Modern Culture*; and Heather Hirschfeld, "Hamlet's 'first corse': Repetition, Trauma, and the Displacement of Redemptive Typology," *Shakespeare Quarterly* 54 (2003): 424–448.

65. On *Hamlet*, memory and revenge, see Neill, *Issues of Death*; Richard Helgerson, "What Hamlet Remembers," *Shakespeare Studies* 10 (1977): 67–97; Robert N. Watson, "Giving up the Ghost in a World of Decay: *Hamlet*, Revenge, and Denial," *Renaissance Drama* n.s. 21 (1990): 199–223; John Kerrigan, "Hieronimo, Hamlet and Remembrance," *Essays in Criticism* 31 (1981): 105–126; Marjorie Garber, "'Remember Me': *Memento Mori* Figures in Shakespeare's Plays," *Renaissance Drama* n.s. 12 (1981): 3–25; Greenblatt, *Hamlet in Purgatory*. For a compelling reading of *Hamlet*, Nietzsche, and

forgetting, see Marjorie Garber, *Shakespeare's Ghost Writers* (New York: Methuen, 1987), 124–176; see also Peter Holbrook, "Nietzsche's *Hamlet*," *Shakespeare Survey* 50 (1997): 171–186.

66. St. Augustine, *The Confessions of the Incomparable Doctovr S. Augustine, Translated into English*, trans. Sir Tobias Matthew (St. Omer, 1620), 482, 479.

67. For example, while it situates a number of individual plays in relation to conceptions of forgetting drawn from a range of discourses, the book cannot do justice to either the full complexity of these discourses or the numerous ways in which they overlap and inflect one another.

I    EMBODYING OBLIVION

1. William Shakespeare, *As You Like It*, ed. Agnes Latham (1975; London: Routledge, 1989), 2. 7. 163–166.

2. Michael C. Schoenfeldt, *Bodies and Selves in Early Modern England: Physiology and Inwardness in Spenser, Shakespeare, Herbert and Milton* (Cambridge: Cambridge University Press, 1999). Physiological description is always already shot through by religious and ethical discourses. The language of lethargy, forgetting and excess sleep offers an example of what Lori Schroeder Haslem calls the "ethicomedical" attitude to disease (or, more precisely here, physiological function) in the period ("'Troubled with the Mother': Longings, Purgings, and the Maternal Body in *Bartholomew Fair* and *The Duchess of Malfi*," *Modern Philology* 92: 4 [1995]: 438–459, esp. 440).

3. Early modern definitions of oblivion routinely list the word "forgetfulness" as a synonym. See, for instance, John Bullokar, *An English Expositor 1616* (Menston: Scolar Press, 1967). Randle Cotgrave (*A Dictionarie of the French and English Tongues* [1611; Amsterdam and New York: Theatrvm Orbis Terrarvm and De Capo Press, 1971]) translates the French "Oblivion" into "*Oblivion, forgetfulnesse; unmindfulnesse.*" As unmindfulness, oblivion functions as the sustained failure to attend to something one should attend to.

4. The term antitheatrical is used advisedly, as some of the texts discussed below do not limit themselves to critiques of the theatre.

5. Thomas Vicary, *A Profitable Treatise of the Anatomie of Mans Body* (London: Henry Bamforde, 1577), D3R. In this account of the place of memory in the body, I am simplifying somewhat a complex topic. For instance, early modern accounts of the faculties often distinguished between not only the intellective and the sensitive souls but also the memories proper to each; the former contained memory of concepts, the latter memories of sense. See Katharine Park, "The Organic Soul," *The Cambridge History of Renaissance Philosophy*, ed. Charles B. Schmitt, *et al.* (Cambridge: Cambridge University Press, 1988): 464–484, esp. 467.

6. Pierre de la Primaudaye, *The Second Part of the French Academie* (London: George Bishop, 1605), 146–147.

7. Pierre Charron, *Of Wisdome*, trans. Samson Lennard (London: Edward Blount and Witt Aspley, 1608), 46.

8. The number of ventricles in the brain was the subject of debate, especially between the Aristotelian and Galenic traditions. More importantly, the idea that memory was located in a specific ventricle was also not always taken as a

given; see Helkiah Crooke, *Microcosmographia. A Description of the Body of Man* (London: J. Jaggard, 1615), 506.

9. M. Andreas Laurentius, *A Discourse of the Preservation of the Sight*, trans. Richard Surphlet (London: Felix Kingston for Ralph Jacson, 1599), 77.

10. It is worth considering the references both to "running streams" and "rich treasury." Arguably, the former gestures toward the functions of the animal spirits in the brain (discussed below), while the latter suggests memory as a storehouse (a common period metaphor). John Sutton (*Philosophy and Memory Traces: Descartes to Connectionism* [Cambridge: Cambridge University Press, 1998]) notes that "Thinking of spirits and fluids made memories seem like motions: but thinking of memory as a collection of stored items, analogous to the images placed in artificial memory loci in the arts of memory, made memories seem like individual bodies. . .Memories 'stored' in a fluid medium characterised by incessant motion could not easily be thought of as located in a single place. Spirits theories of memory are unlikely to be literalist storehouse models, in which static items are piled up in a place called 'the memory'. . .Indeed, an intuition of memory as motions is implicit in general spirits theory, for animal spirits are always bearers of history in the body, their condition and flow already marked by the past as well as by present context" (48–49).

11. Ben Jonson, "The Minde of The Front," Sir Walter Ralegh, *The History of the World* (London: Walter Burre, 1614).

12. From Richard Day, *The Booke of Christian Prayers* (London, 1608), quoted in William E. Engel, *Mapping Mortality: The Persistence of Memory and Melancholy in Early Modern England* (Amherst: University of Massachusetts Press, 1995), 2.

13. The alignment of history with memory is made explicit in the column furthest to the right. Marked as "vita memoria," this column represents the last of four functions in terms of which, according to the poem, history is known: "Times witnesse, Herald of Antiquitie, / The light of Truth, and life of Memorie." The image quotes Cicero's *De Oratore*: "Historia vero testis temporum, lux veritatis, vita memoriae, magistra vitae" ("History is the witness of the times, the light of truth, the life of memory, the mistress of life"). At the same time, the representation of good and evil fame is arguably a recasting of the Virgilian conception of fame as discussed by Leo Braudy in relation to Book 4 of *The Aeneid*: "At one extreme is the *Fama* that runs around the world to spread gossip with a thousand tongues about what Aeneas and Dido are doing in the cave; at the other is *fama* that warriors properly seek, the *fama* validated and approved by the gods " (*The Frenzy of Renown: Fame and Its History* [New York: Oxford University Press, 1986], 125).

14. James P. Bednarz, "The Collaborator as Thief: Ralegh's (Re)Vision of *The Faerie Queene*," *ELH* 63 : 2 (1996): 279–307, esp. 290.

15. In a discussion of various forms of the sleeping disease, Christopher Wirtzung [or Christof Wirsung] distinguishes between *Lethargus* and *Congelatio* (or numbness) by suggesting that "in *Lethargo* the eies be shut; and in the numnesse they remain open" (*Praxis Medicinae universalis; Or A generall Practise of Physicke*, trans. Jacob Mosan [London: George Bishop, 1598],

135). However, Wirtzung is unusual in differentiating so carefully between various diseases usually lumped together under the category of lethargy; what he calls "numbness" can be read as a variant form of lethargy (as is suggested by Wirtzung's own references to lethargy as *the* sleeping disease [e.g., 118]).

16. La Primaudaye, *The Second Part*, 166.

17. John Bullokar, *An English Expositor 1616*, facs. edn. (Menston: Scolar Press, 1967). The connection between lethargy and an excess of phlegm is typical. See, for instance, Gulielmus Gratarolus Bergomatis, *The Castel of Memorie*, trans. Willyam Fulwod (London: Rouland Hall, 1562), C1v.

18. Stephen Batman, *Batman Uppon Bartholome* (London: Thomas East, 1582), 89r.

19. Andrew Boorde on lethargy: "In englyshe it is named obliviousnes or forgetfulnes. . .This impediment dothe come thorowe colde reume the whiche doth obnebulate a mannes memory, and doth lye in the hinder part of a mannes heed within the skull or brayne panne" (*The Breviary of Helthe* (1547), facs. edn. [Amsterdam and New York: Da Capo Press and Theatrvm Orbis Terrarvm, 1971], lxxxv r).

20. In that Bullokar refers to both reason and the senses, it is clear that he sees both the intellective and sensitive souls as being impeded by lethargy.

21. "[T]he Braine is the Pallace of the Rationall Soule, which soule using for her instrument the temper & confirmation of the braine, according to the diversity of her functions bringeth forth mixt actions by the mediation of the animall spirit. These very actions, produced according to the variety of the temperament and *medium*, into divers acts of Ratiocination Imagination and Memory as the soule is best pleased to worke, we call Faculties" (Crooke, *Microcosmographia*, 432).

22. This is suggested by Batman, who just before taking up lethargy talks of a related disability called stupor, which is often caused by "superfluitie of humours, that stoppeth [and] letteth [the] wayes of the spirits in the braine" (Batman, *Batman Uppon Bartholome*, 89r). John Abernethy states that lethargy "oppres[ses] the animall spirits" (*A Christian and Heavenly Treatise. Containing Physicke for the Soule* [London: Feliz Kyngston for John Budge, 1622], 91).

23. An *OED* example of postume, drawn from Boorde's *Breviary of Health* (1547), defines it as "no other thynge but a collection or a runnynge of evyll humours."

24. Of course, one's ability to remember varies depending upon one's complexion.

25. Thomas Eliot, *Bibliotheca Eliotae: Eliotes Dictionarie, by Thomas Cooper the Third Tyme Corrected* (London: T. Bertheleti, 1559), "*Letargia*, or *Lethargus*." See also Batman: "Sometime loosing of speach commeth by loosing of wit, as in phrensie and *Litargi*" (46r).

26. See Bergomatis, *Castel of Memorie*, B6v–B7r.

27. Desiderius Erasmus, *The Prayse of Follie*, trans. Sir Thomas Chaloner (London: Thomas Dawson and Thomas Gardiner, 1577), B6v (italics added).

28. Walter Bruel [Gualtherus Bruele], *Praxis Medicinae, Or, The Physicians Practise*, 2nd edn. (London: John Norton for William Sheares, 1639), 88.

29. A similar depiction of lethargy is offered in John Donne's "The First Anniversarie" (*The Complete Poetry of John Donne*, ed. John T. Shawcross [Garden City, New York: Doubleday and Co., 1967]), in which the "sicke world" is suffering from a lethargy that has led to its having "lost [its] sense and memory"; it has "speechlesse growne" and has "forgot [its] name" (23–31).

30. In the latter case, not only effeminization but also infantilization is at issue; these men enter their second childhoods as their bodies become like the moist bodies of infants. Thanks to Gail Kern Paster for pointing this out to me.

31. Batman asserts that "forgetting is [a] token of moisture. . . " (38v), a view compatible with what I have been arguing. In particular, if the hindmost ventricle of the brain, devoted to memory, is too moist – coldness and dryness being the ideal Batman attributes to Aristotle – then problems with recollection occur. (This is because memory inscriptions cannot fix themselves in the brain under these circumstances.) At the same time, early modern anatomists asserted that the brain as a whole is by definition cold and moist (although this was subject to debate in the period). The well-functioning memory, then, is drier than the rest of the brain.

32. This paragraph owes a debt to Gail Kern Paster's "The Unbearable Coldness of Female Being: Women's Imperfection and the Humoral Economy," *ELR* 28 (1998): 416–440. The link between coldness and the effeminization of the male subject can be identified at the level of physiological function. In contradiction to the view held by writers such as Batman, Pierre Charron states that "there are but three principall temperatures, which serve and cause the reasonable *Soule* to worke, and distinguish the spirits, that is to say, Heat, Driness, Moisture: Colde is not active, nor serveth to any purpose, but to hinder all the motions and functions of the Soule" (*Of Wisdome*, 49). Here, coldness only disrupts the operations of a reasonable soul traditionally gendered male. The same point is made by Juan Huarte (*Examen de Ingenios. The Examination of Mens Wits* [London: Adam Islip for Richard Watkins, 1594], 56) – who also claims that phlegm interferes with the workings of "the reasonable facultie" (60).

33. William Shakespeare, *Hamlet*, ed. Harold Jenkins (London and New York: Methuen, 1982), 1. 5. 29–34. Henceforth cited in the text.

34. That History is gendered female speaks to the limits of a physiologically determinative reading of forgetting. Here, the classical trope of History as female collides with the physiologically informed representation of an effeminized male Oblivion.

35. John Ford, *'Tis Pity She's A Whore*, ed. Brian Morris (1968; London: A. & C. Black, 1990), 5. 1. 28–29.

36. John Willis, *Mnemonica, or, The Art of Memory* (London: Leonard Sowersby, 1661), 140. Willis lists various ways of sleeping that are deleterious of memory – in the sun, during the day, on one's back or belly – but only after he mentions "overmuch" sleep (140).

37. *Ibid.*, 141.

38. Thomas Cogan, *The Haven of Health* (London: Melch. Bradwood for John Norton, 1605), 231.

39. *Ibid.*, 237. As William Vaughn puts it, "Immoderate sleepe maketh the braine giddie, ingendereth rheume and impostumes, causeth the pasie [palsy?], bringeth oblivion, and troubleth the spirits" (*Approved Directions for Health, both Naturall and Artificiall*, 4th edn. [London: T. S. for Roger Jackson, 1612], 58). As for how much is too much, Vaughn states "Seaven houres sleepe, is sufficient for sanguine and cholerick men; and nine houres for flegmatick, and melancholick men" (58).

40. Too much sleep is also linked to the related transgressions of idleness or sloth, the latter of which is familiar as one of the seven deadly sins.

41. Here sleep is linked with concupiscible passions that hold undue influence over the body, as in Galen: "Suppose it were to happen that a man laid down the principle of doing good to men because doing good to people is a true end. If he then neglects to do good either because of sleep, or laziness, or love of pleasure, or some such reason, he has erred because of passion" ("The Diagnosis and Cure of the Soul's Errors," *Galen on the Passions and Errors of the Soul*, trans. Paul W. Harkins [Columbus: Ohio State University Press, 1963]: 27–107, esp. 87–88).

42. Cogan's reference to "the horse and mule in whom there is no understanding" is scriptural – see Psalm 32. 9 – but a telling cognate example appears in an early seventeenth-century translation of Augustine's *Confessions*. In book 10, just before the inception of his discussion of memory, Augustine distinguishes between rational man and "the Horse, and Mule which have no understanding" (St. Augustine, *The Confessions of the Incomparable Doctovr S. Augustine, Translated into English,* trans. Sir Tobias Matthew [St. Omer, 1620], 476).

43. Paster, "Unbearable Coldness," 419.

44. W[illiam] W[illymat], *Physicke, to Cure the Most Dangerous Disease of Desperation* (London: Robert Boulton, 1605), 50–51.

45. Similarly, such sleep derails the operations of conscience, which both mediates between God and man and offers a record of man's actions. For more on sleep and conscience, see chapter 5.

46. Compare Plato's notion that incarnation itself constitutes a form of forgetting that is *foundational* of human identity. Abraham Fraunce (*The Third Part of the Countesse of Pembroke's Yvychurch* [London: Printed for T. Woodcocke, 1592]) rather fancifully describes this idea as follows:

> The *Platonists* call the body a Hell, in respect of the minde, which being thither thrust downe, first, forgetteth all celestiall conceipts, drinketh of *Lethe*, and then passeth over *Acheron*: for, being bereaft of celestiall ornaments, it soroweth and greevth, and therefore compast with Stygian waves, displeaseth itselfe, hateth and abhorreth his owne acts, howles, and makes pitifull lamentation; and that is *Cocytus* . . .to howle and crie out, as *Plato* expoundeth it. (28r)

Human suffering, then, is bred of the loss of celestial knowledge, and, as Plato has it, any knowledge one acquires is only knowledge recalled from before the time of the soul's incarnation. In Plato's pre-Christian schema, forgetting "celestiall conceipts" obviously does not constitute a sin, and forgetting is a component of corporeality.

47. It is worth considering literary characters such as Verdant in Spenser's *The Faerie Queene* in these terms. Associated four times in five stanzas with sleep, Verdant lets down his guard and gives himself over to pleasure: his "warlike armes" are "hong vpon a tree" (*The Faerie Queene*, ed. Thomas P. Roche, Jr., assisted by C. Patrick O'Donnell, Jr. [Harmondsworth: Penguin, 1978], 2. 12. 80. 1–2) while he sleeps with his head in Acrasia's lap (2. 12. 76. 8–9). He is a figure who "in lewd loues, and wastfull luxuree, / His dayes, his goods, his bodie he did spend" (2. 12. 80. 7–8). On the significance of sleep and security for the Sidney circle's Protestant ambitions, see Blair Worden, *The Sound of Virtue: Philip Sidney's "Arcadia" and Elizabethan Politics* (New Haven: Yale University Press, 1996), e.g., 60 65.

48. Benjamin Austin, *The Presumptuous Mans Mirrour: Or A Watch-bell to rouze up a secure Sinner out of his sleep of security* (London: G. M. for George Edwards, 1641), 30–31. The linkage between sleep and security is a common one. See, e.g., Thomas Nash, *Christ's Tears Over Jerusalem* (1593), facs. edn [Menston: Scolar Press, 1970], 86v. At the same time, Calvin draws an important distinction between two kinds of security: "Paul is dissuading Christians, not from all security [in their election], but from supine, unguarded, carnal security, which is attended with pride, arrogance, and contempt of others, extinguishes humility and reverence of God, and produces forgetfulness of favours received" (John Calvin, *Institutes of the Christian Religion*, 2 vols., trans. John Allen [Philadelphia: Presbyterian Board of Christian Education, 1936], II: 227).

49. Grant Williams and Christopher Ivic, "Introduction: Sites of Forgetting in Early Modern English literature and culture," *Forgetting in Early Modern English Literature and Culture: Lethe's Legacies*, ed. Christopher Ivic and Grant Williams (New York: Routledge, 2004): 1 17, esp. 15.

50. On conscience and memory, see chapter 5.

51. William Shakespeare, *Macbeth*, ed. Kenneth Muir (1951; London: Routledge, 1988), 1. 7. 62–71.

52. See chapter 4 for more on wine, fumes and forgetting.

53. This failure of service is later presented by Macbeth as evidence of their status not as loyal retainers but as professional killers who perform their trade for money: "there [lie] the murtherers, / Steep'd in the colours of their trade" (2. 3. 112–113).

54. John Webster, *The Duchess of Malfi*, ed. Elizabeth M. Brennan (1983; London: A. & C. Black, 1987), 1. 2. 244–247.

55. Norman M. Klein, *The History of Forgetting: Los Angeles and the Erasure of Memory* (New York: Verso, 1997), 302.

56. The significance to the training of memory of both order and repetition is recognized in the Ciceronian and Aristotelian traditions. For a brief, clear account of the influence of these traditions through the seventeenth century, see Paolo Rossi, *Logic and the Art of Memory: The Quest for a Universal Language*, trans. Stephen Clucas (Chicago: University of Chicago Press, 2000), esp. 6–28.

57. In her most recent study of pre-modern memory, Carruthers states that "The great vice of *memoria* is not forgetting but disorder" (*The Craft of Thought: Meditation, Rhetoric, and the Making of Images, 400–1200* [Cambridge:

Cambridge University Press, 1998], 82). In this context, *curiositas* functions as a form of disorder that has deleterious effects on memory. "In terms of mnemotechnic, curiosity constitutes both image 'crowding' – a mnemotechnical vice, because crowding images together blurs them, blocks them, and thus dissipates their effectiveness for orienting and cueing – and randomness, or making backgrounds that have no pattern to them." Crucially, "Mnemotechnical *curiositas* results from sloth, laziness, a mind that neglects to pay attention to thinking as a process of *building*" (82, 84).

58. Bergomatis, *Castel of Memorie*, D8r.
59. Juan Luis Vives, *Introduction to Wisedom*, trans. Sir R. Morison (London: Thomas East for Abraham Veale, 1575), E1r–E1v, E6v.
60. Bergomatis, *Castel of Memorie*, B6v–B7r; C1r–C1v.
61. Willis, *Mnemonica*, 145–155. Willis's notion of a "prescript order of life" characterized in part by regulated sleep owes a debt to the Galenic notion of sleep and waking as one of the six "non-naturals." As Vivian Nutton puts it, "Without proper attention to these non-naturals [listed by Nutton as 'food and drink; sleep and waking; air; evacuation and repletion; motion and rest; and the passions or emotions'], the body's natural state would turn to the contra-natural state of illness as a result of changes in its humoral balance. Similarly, by regulating the non-naturals one could protect the body in advance of predictable changes" ("Medicine in Medieval Western Europe, 1000–1500," *The Western Medical Tradition, 800 BC to AD 1800*, ed. Lawrence I. Conrad, *et al.* [Cambridge: Cambridge University Press, 1995]: 139–205, esp. 141). Excess sleep, then, would affect the humoral balance of the body, while discipline constituted a form of preventive medicine. As Andrew Wear ("Medicine in Early Modern Europe, 1500–1700," Conrad *et al.*, eds., *Western Medical Tradition*: 215–361) points out, "Regimen, the way to lead a healthy life, continued to be structured well into the eighteenth century in terms of the traditional 'six non-naturals'" (360).
62. The point is fully made by Levinius Lemnius (*The Touchstone of Complexions*, trans. Thomas Newton [London: Thomas Marsh, 1576]): "A good stedfast and fyrme Memory therefore is to be referred unto the disposition and temperature of the Brayne: & this power of the minde, is ascribed to the benefite of Nature: but yet so, that it may be holp*ed* and maynteyned in his perfect state by Arte, and if perhaps it decay or take harme, yet through care & industry, it may againe be restored. And therfore special care must be employed, and great diligence taken, that the bodye may in perfect health and sound constitution be preserved: that moderati*on* both in life and diet be used: alwayes within the compasse of tempera*un*ce and frugality" (120v–121r).
63. Richard Halpern, *The Poetics of Primitive Accumulation* (Ithaca: Cornell University Press, 1991), 19–60. The relationship between memory and the production of the ideal subject is articulated by Edward Reynolds (*A Treatise of the Passions and Faculties of the Soule of Man* [London: R. H. for Robert Bostock, 1640]), who argues that memory aids (and shapes) the subject by "affording speciall assistance for the direction and discreet managing of our actions, conforming them either unto Precepts and Rules in Moralitie, or unto Principles of Wisdome and publike Prudence, gathered from Historicall

observations; while the Minde, by the helpe of Memorie, being as it were conversant with Ages past, and furnished with Examples or any service and imployment, doth by mature application, weighing particulars, comparing times, circumstances, and passages of affaires together, enable it selfe with the more hope and resolution, to passe successefully through any enterprise or difficultie" (14–15).

64. For an argument that overlaps with the following, see Zackariah Long, "'Unless you could teach me to forget': Spectatorship, Self-forgetting, and Subversion in Antitheatrical Literature and *As You Like It*," *Forgetting in Early Modern English Literature and Culture*, ed. Ivic and Williams: 151–164.

65. John Northbrooke, *A Treatise wherein Dicing, Dauncing, Vaine Playes or Enterluds. . .are Reproved* (London: H. Bynneman for George Byshop, 1577), 25.

66. William Rankins, *A Mirrour of Monsters* (London: I. C. for T. H., 1587), C3r.

67. *Ibid.*

68. *Ibid.*, D2r; C4r–C4v. See also William Prynne, *Histrio-mastix* (London: E. A. and W. I. for Michael Sparke, 1633), 505.

69. Thomas Heywood, who argues that the theatre schools its audiences in virtue, depicts the shaping function of theatre in ways that interestingly intersect with and deviate from Rankins's account of theatre as an agent of self-forgetting: "so bewitching a thing is lively and well spirited action, that it hath power to new mold the harts of the spectators and fashion them to the shape of any noble and notable attempt" (*An Apology for Actors* [London: Nicholas Okes, 1612], B4r).

70. Stephen Gosson, *Playes Confuted in five Actions* (London: Thomas Gosson, 1582), C7v–C8r.

71. Stephen Gosson, *The School of Abuse* (1579) (London: Shakespeare Society, 1841), 14–15. See also p. 32: "This have I set downe of the abuses of poets, pipers and players, which bring us to pleasure, slouth, sleepe, sinne, and without repentaunce to death and the devill."

72. Thomas Nashe offers a counter-argument to Rankins and others, one that sees the theatre as offering an antidote to forgetting. Plays educate the audience in virtue; "the subject of them, (for the most part) it is borrowed out of our English chronicles, wherein our forefathers' valiant acts (that have lain long buried in rusty brass and worm-eaten books) are revived, and they themselves raised from the grave of oblivion, and brought to plead their aged honors in open presence. . .How would it have joyed brave Talbot, the terror of the French, to think that after he had lain two hundred years in his tomb, he should triumph again on the stage" (*Pierce Penniless, His Supplication to the Devil* [1592], *Renaissance England: Poetry and Prose from the Reformation to the Restoration*, ed. Roy Lamson and Hallett Smith [New York: W. W. Norton & Co., 1956], 451). Theatrical representation entails the performance of forgotten valiant acts that are central to British history.

73. In a crucial source for Shakespeare's play, Amleth (the precursor to Hamlet) feigns lethargy in order to evade the scrutiny of Feng (Claudius) and others; see the excerpt from Saxo Grammaticus, *Historiae Danicae*, trans. Oliver

Elton (1894), *Narrative and Dramatic Sources of Shakespeare*, 7 vols., ed. Geoffrey Bullough (London and Henley: Routledge and Kegan Paul; New York: Columbia University Press, 1973), VII: 60–79, esp. 62.

2    "BE THIS SWEET HELEN'S KNELL, AND NOW FORGET HER":
FORGETTING AND DESIRE IN ALL'S WELL THAT ENDS WELL

1. Henry Green, *Back* (1946; New York: New Directions, 1981), 188.
2. William Shakespeare, *All's Well That Ends Well*, *The Riverside Shakespeare*, ed. G. Blakemore Evans, *et al.* (Boston: Houghton Mifflin, 1974), 1. 1. 79–85. All references in this chapter to Shakespearean texts are from the *Riverside* and will be cited in the body of the chapter.
3. Assumed here is a relational conception of identity that arises out of and is constructed by social and familial networks; see the introduction for more on identity and subjectivity.
4. The term "psychologist" is of course anachronistic. The work of "Renaissance psychologists" has ethical and theological elements, as will be discussed below.
5. La Primaudaye is not typical, however, in alluding to the operations of forgetting. For more on the work of "Renaissance psychologists," see Herschel Baker, *The Image of Man* (1947; New York: Harper & Brothers, 1961); Ruth Leila Anderson, *Elizabethan Psychology and Shakespeare's Plays* (Iowa City: University of Iowa Studies, 1927); J. B. Bamborough, *The Little World of Man* (London: Longmans, Green and Co., 1952); and Ruth E. Harvey, *The Inward Wits: Psychological Theory in the Middle Ages and the Renaissance* (London: Warburg Institute, 1975).
6. Pierre de la Primaudaye, *The Second Part of the French Academie* (London: George Bishop, 1605), 160.
7. Mary Carruthers, *The Book of Memory: A Study of Memory in Medieval Culture* (Cambridge: Cambridge University Press, 1990), 33.
8. Pierre Charron, *Of Wisdome: Three Books*, trans. Samson Lennard (London: Edward Blount and Witt Aspley, c. 1608), 46; M. Andreas Laurentius, *A Discourse of the Preservation of the Sight*, trans. Richard Surphlet (London: Felix Kingston for Ralph Jacson, 1599), 77. On "treasurie," see also Thomas Vicary, *A Profitable Treatise of the Anatomie of Mans Body* (London: Henry Bamforde, 1577), D3R.
9. What is perhaps gestured toward here is a notion of writing as repetition or reiteration, what cognitive scientists refer to as the "elaborative encoding" that helps ensure that a certain fact or idea will be remembered.
10. Michel de Montaigne, *The Essayes of Montaigne*, trans. John Florio (New York: Modern Library, 1933), 24. It should be pointed out that Montaigne repeatedly refers in the *Essayes* to his faulty memory. At the same time, as William E. Engel has shown, there are striking affinities between artificial memory systems and the design of both Montaigne's book (especially in Florio's translation) and his library. Thus, the sites of Montaigne's protestations of forgetfulness – book and study – are constructed in accordance with the logic of memory, provocatively suggesting the interanimation of memory and forgetting. See Engel, *Mapping Mortality:*

*The Persistence of Memory and Melancholy in Early Modern England* (Amherst: University of Massachusetts Press, 1995), esp. 95–128.

11. Montaigne, *Essayes*, 25.

12. Jonathan Dollimore's account of Montaigne's conception of "custom" as ideology intersects with my discussion of "other mens traces." See *Radical Tragedy: Religion, Ideology and Power in the Drama of Shakespeare and his Contemporaries*, 2nd edn. (Durham: Duke University Press, 1993), esp. 3–28.

13. It is worth noting that Montaigne does not discuss here the recollection of judgments made earlier by the subject; all remembered matter is "forren" here.

14. While I am not arguing that any expression of desire is necessarily antithetical to rational self-control, it is worth noting that some commentators on the passions (of which desire is one) have argued that they are intrinsically unruly and disruptive. In the words of Susan James ("The Passions in Metaphysics and the Theory of Action," *The Cambridge History of Seventeenth-Century Philosophy*, vol. I [of 2] [Cambridge: Cambridge University Press, 1998]: 913–949), "It was thus generally taken for granted that our passions drive us to respond to the external world, to manipulate the material objects we encounter in ways that go beyond our most basic needs, and to relate to other people. Without them, as many writers pointed out, we should be condemned to narrow and isolated lives. However, the view that the passions are in these respects functional was counterbalanced by an equally deep-seated conviction that they are simultaneously dysfunctional – they are treacherous and wayward, and drive us to harm, frustration and misery" (914). This final view was often associated with stoical self-abnegation and disdain for the passions; see, e.g., Thomas Rogers, *A Philosophicall Discourse, Entituled, The Anatomie of the Minde* (London: J[ohn] C[harlewood] for Andrew Maunsell, 1576), 1r–1v. See also Susan James, *Passion and Action: The Emotions in Seventeenth-Century Philosophy* (Oxford: Clarendon Press, 1997).

15. A version of the ideal, in which self-knowledge, reason and moderation are all imbricated, is given in one sentence by Phillipe de Mornay: "The knowledge of a mans owne selfe, availeth, not onely for preservation of the bodies health, but likewise to moderate the vehemencie of inordinate affections, which hinder and impeach the health of judgement" (*The True Knowledge of a Mans Owne Selfe*, trans. An. Mundy [London: J. R[oberts] for William Leake, 1602], 2).

16. Thomas Wright, *The Passions of the Minde* (London: V. S. for W. B., 1601), 12–14. Nicholas Coeffeteau defines passion similarly, as "a motion of the sensitive appetite, caused by the apprehension or imagination of good or evill, the which is followed with a change or alteration in the body" (*A Table of Humane Passions. With their Causes and Effects* [London: Nicholas Okes, 1621], 2).

17. Steven Mullaney, "Mourning and Misogyny: *Hamlet, The Revenger's Tragedy*, and the Final Progress of Elizabeth I, 1600–1607," *Shakespeare Quarterly* 45 (1994): 139–162, esp. 144.

18. These three examples suggest points of contact between male self-forgetting and Renaissance depictions of what Mark Breitenberg has called "anxious

masculinity": "Masculine subjectivity constructed and sustained by a patriarchal culture. . . inevitably engenders varying degrees of anxiety in its male members." One area of anxiety is sexual desire, since in this period "sexuality is by definition an anarchic force constantly besieging the gates of collective order and individual self-control" (*Anxious Masculinity in Early Modern England* [Cambridge: Cambridge University Press, 1996], 1). Of course self-forgetting represents a crucial figuration of a subjectivity produced by the loss of individual self-control.

19. Alexander Leggatt, "*All's Well That Ends Well*: The Testing of Romance," *Modern Language Quarterly* 32 (1971): 21–41, esp. 23–24.

20. David S. Berkeley and Donald Keesee ("Bertram's Blood-Consciousness in *All's Well That Ends Well*," *Studies in English Literature, 1500–1900* 31 [1991]: 247–258) argue that "In [rejecting Helena] Bertram is realistic; the King, the Countess, and Lord Lafew romantic: blood-consciousness was. . . a realistic approach to fruitful marriage; marrying upwards under virtually impossible conditions was (and still is) 'romance,' an eloquent but improbable lie" (248). Moreover, "Helena is not simply (and naively) an atomistic individual but the present representative of many generations of her base family" (254).

21. Above Breitenberg defines sexuality as an "anarchic force" potentially corrosive of order. Whereas tragedy tends to foreground this potential, comedy is more likely to manage both elements of the paradox Mary Beth Rose pithily articulates here: "Sexuality therefore presents itself as a paradox: the human need for sexual relationships could lead to the mindless disruption of society, but without fulfillment of this need, there would be no ordered society at all" (*The Expense of Spirit: Love and Sexuality in English Renaissance Drama* [Ithaca: Cornell University Press, 1988], 37).

22. We should also note the absence in this formulation of Helena's biological mother. One has the sense that Helena's father's two "offspring" – his daughter and his "receipt" – issued directly and unaided from him. While her father may be both forgotten and remembered, Helena's mother is simply absent.

23. Helena's acts of simultaneously forgetting and remembering – of being at once desiring agent and good daughter – can be mapped onto Susan Snyder's astute observations that "Helena's career strangely mixes aggressive initiative and passivity," and that the play "enact[s]. . . the difficulties and conflicts of imagining a woman as active, desiring subject" ("*All's Well That Ends Well* and Shakespeare's Helena: Text and Subtext, Subject and Object," *ELR* 18 [1988]: 66–77, esp. 66, 77) .

24. Rose, *Expense of Spirit*, 27. Rose is developing ideas advanced in Northrop Frye's *A Natural Perspective* (New York: Columbia University Press, 1965), some others of which she summarizes as follows: "Frye shows that the sense of vitality underlying comedy often takes the form of a drive toward identity that, in romantic comedy, is always erotic. The harsh and irrational laws impeding the fulfillment of the sexual drive of the hero and heroine must be overcome in order to bring about the freedom and self-knowledge that will form the basis of the new society symbolized in the festive conclusion. Romantic comedy, then, dramatizes the longing for a happy ending which is a

wish-fulfillment fantasy of attaining all of one's desires without social, emotional, or moral cost" (27).

25. Vivian Thomas, *The Moral Universe of Shakespeare's Problem Plays* (London: Croom Helm, 1987), 140.

26. Margaret Loftus Ranald, "'As Marriage Binds, and Blood Breaks': English Marriage and Shakespeare," *SQ* 30 (1979): 68–81, esp. 79–80. For more information on wardship, a topic underdeveloped in *All's Well* criticism, see Joel Hurstfield, *The Queen's Wards: Wardship and Marriage under Elizabeth I* (London: Longmans, Green and Co., 1958).

27. Berkeley and Keesee, "Bertram's Blood-consciousness," 250.

28. Richard P. Wheeler, *Shakespeare's Development and the Problem Comedies: Turn and Counter-Turn* (Berkeley: University of California Press, 1981), 34.

29. Baker, *The Image of Man,* 290, 291, 292. See also Bamborough, *The Little World,* esp. 47; and Anderson, *Elizabethan Psychology,* esp. 23–24. La Primaudaye defines will as "that facultie and vertue of the soule, whereby we desire that which is good, and eschew evill by the direction and guiding of reason" (*Second Part,* 204).

30. On the relationship between testamentary gift-giving and memory, see J. S. W. Helt, "Women, Memory and Will-Making in Elizabethan England," *The Place of the Dead: Death and Remembrance in Late Medieval and Early Modern Europe,* ed. Bruce Gordon and Peter Marshall (Cambridge: Cambridge University Press, 2000): 188–205.

31. Michael D. Friedman, "'Service is no heritage': Bertram and the Ideology of Procreation," *Studies in Philology* 92 (1995): 80–101, esp. 85.

32. Charron, *Of Wisdome,* 136–137, italics added.

33. The character from Shakespearean comedy who most resembles Bertram in his inconstancy is *The Two Gentlemen of Verona's* Proteus, who disparagingly gestures toward his own changeability when at play's end he states that "were man / But constant, he were perfect" (5. 4. 110–111). Like *All's Well,* this play concerns itself with forgetting in numerous ways, especially in its explorations, first, of the intersection of (self–) forgetting and sexual desire (e.g., 2. 4. 192–214; 2. 6); and, second, of forgetting as a precondition for the generation of a new set of social relations (5. 4. 142–147).

34. Michael D. Friedman, "Male Bonds and Marriage in *All's Well* and *Much Ado,*" *SEL* 35 (1995): 231–249, esp. 238.

35. Wheeler, *Shakespeare's Development,* 56.

36. David Scott Kastan, "*All's Well That Ends Well* and the Limits of Comedy," *ELH* 52 (1985): 575–589, esp. 584.

37. "In a typically festive conclusion all previous conflicts are forgiven and forgotten . . . If we are to accept the reconciliation of Claudio and Hero, of Angelo and Mariana, of Imogen and Posthumus, [and, I would add, of Bertram and Helena,] we have to think of them also as awakenings, where it is possible to forget as well as forgive what has happened" (Frye, *A Natural Perspective,* 128–129).

38. Barbara Hardy, "Shakespeare's Narrative: Acts of Memory," *Essays in Criticism* 39 (1989): 93–115, esp 100.

39. Cynthia Marshall, *The Shattering of the Self: Violence, Subjectivity, and Early Modern Texts* (Baltimore: Johns Hopkins University Press, 2002), 4.

3  "IF HE CAN REMEMBER": SPIRITUAL SELF-FORGETTING AND
DR. FAUSTUS

1. Christopher Marlowe, *Doctor Faustus: A and B Texts*, ed. David Bevington
   and Eric Rasmussen (Manchester: Manchester University Press, 1992), 1. 1.
   1–2, 35. This chapter's analysis is based on the B-text of *Doctor Faustus*,
   published in 1616, as it offers a fuller articulation of the significance of (self-)
   forgetting and remembering than does the earlier printed version. Future
   citations will appear in the body of the chapter.
2. Judith Weil, *Christopher Marlowe: Merlin's Prophet* (Cambridge: Cambridge
   University Press, 1977), 55. See also A. N. Okerlund, "The Intellectual Folly
   of Dr. Faustus," *Studies in Philology* 74 (1977): 258–278.
3. Weil, *Christopher Marlowe*, 57.
4. In stressing the link between the visual and theatrical here, I do not mean to
   suggest that theatre was a narrowly visual medium. I take Mephistopheles'
   leading of Faustus's eye to emblematize Mephistopheles' seduction of
   Faustus through *all* of his senses.
5. Richard Waswo, "Damnation, Protestant Style: Macbeth, Faustus, and
   Christian Tragedy," *Journal of Medieval and Renaissance Studies* 4
   (1974): 63–99, esp 79. On Marlowe's incomplete recollection of the passage
   as a sign of his despair, see Matthew N. Proser, *The Gift of Fire: Aggression
   and the Plays of Christopher Marlowe* (New York: Peter Lang, 1995), esp.
   147.
6. Paul Bayne[s], *A Caveat for Cold Christians* (London: Felix Kyngston for
   Nathanael Newbery, 1618), 15–16.
7. W[illiam] W[illymat], *Physicke, to Cure the Most Dangerous Disease of
   Desperation* (London: Robert Boulton, 1605), 55. Self-recollection should be
   contextualized in terms of the attainment of self-knowledge, an attainment
   that in turn has implied divine knowledge since at least Plotinus' discussion of
   intellectual beauty in *The Enneads*.
8. Also worth consulting are the sermons of the Arminian preacher Lancelot
   Andrewes. In "A Sermon Preached before Queene Elizabeth, at Hampton
   Court, on Wednesday, being the 6th of March, AD 1594" (*XCVI. Sermons*
   [London: George Miller for Richard Badger, 1629], 299–308), Andrewes
   states that "Nothing is so farr from our minds, as we our selves. For,
   naturally (as saith the *Apostle* [in Heb. 2.1 (?)]) we do . . . *leake*, and *runne
   out*; and when we have looked *in the glasse*, we streight *forgett our fashion
   againe*. Therefore we have in charge to put men in minde of many things, and
   to call upon them with diverse *Memento's*" (301). Significantly, self-forgetting
   does not bear a narrowly doctrinal provenance, as examples from the
   Arminian Andrewes and the Puritan Baynes (as well as the lapsed Catholic,
   possibly Laudian Donne) have suggested.
9. John Donne, "Sermon Number 2. Preached at Lincolns Inne [1618]," *The
   Sermons of John Donne*, ed. G. R. Potter and E. M. Simpson, vol. II
   (Berkeley: University of California Press, 1953–1962): 72–94, esp. 73.
   Donne's sermons are filled with the language of memory and forgetting; on
   this, see Robert L. Hickey, "Donne's Art of Memory," *Tennessee Studies in
   Literature* 3 (1958): 29–36. Forgetting and memory are also significant for

Donne's poetry, as in his representation of the world as lethargic and forgetful in "The First Anniversarie."

10. Mary Carruthers draws a distinction between the art of memory and other forms of memory training: "The art of memory is specifically an aid for speakers, not for learners, for composers, not for readers. This distinguishes it most clearly from the elementary rules of memory training" (*The Book of Memory: A Study of Memory in Medieval Culture* [Cambridge: Cambridge University Press, 1990], 155).

11. *Ibid.*, 7. The best-known memory structure is that of the "memory theatre," which Carruthers shows is only one kind of artificial memory structure.

12. *Ibid.*, 34.

13. *Ibid.*, 25–26.

14. Cicero's *De Oratare* is the locus classicus here. He defines the role of memory for the rhetor as follows: "*Invention* is the excogitation of true things (*res*), or things similar to truth to render one's cause plausible; *disposition* is the arrangement in order of the things thus discovered; *elocution* is the accommodation of suitable words to the invented (things); *memory* is the firm perception in the soul of things and words; *pronunciation* is the moderating of the voice and body to suit the dignity of the things and words" (quoted in Frances Yates, *The Art of Memory* [Chicago: University of Chicago Press, 1966], 8–9).

15. Carruthers, *Book of Memory*, 16.

16. The art of memory was also recognized as useful for the production of sermons themselves; see Lina Bolzoni, *The Gallery of Memory: Literary and Iconographic Models in the Age of the Printing Press*, trans. Jeremy Parzen (Toronto: University of Toronto Press, 2001), esp. 76–82.

17. Donne, *Sermons*, 72.

18. *Ibid.*, 74–75.

19. *Ibid.*, 94.

20. *The Doctrine of the Bible: Or, Rules of Discipline* (London: Richard Braddocke for Thomas Pavier, 1606), G3r. See also Andrewes, who states that "In which office of *Preaching*, we are imployed as much about *Recognosce*, as about *cognosce*; as much in calling to their mindes the things they know and have forgott, as in teaching them the things they know not, or never learnt" ("A Sermon Preached," 301).

21. "For the Mind seemes seated in the highest part, the HEAD, as God in the Heavens; but when it is in some Meditation, or deeper thoughts, to retire into the Brest, and as it were to goe aside into some secret Closet, or darker Studie, that it might bring forth Counsaile as out of a hidden Treasurie: and this causeth us, when wee are in thoughtfull contemplation, neither to heare nor see the objects of the Eyes and Eares before us" (Samuel Purchas, *Purchas his Pilgrim* [London: W[illiam] S[tansby] for Henry Fetherstone, 1619], 58–59). Recollection (or bringing forth counsel from the "Treasurie") here obviously entails retrieving what we know "by heart."

22. The link between meditation and remembering one's end is apparent in Christopher Sutton's *Disce Mori. Learne to Die* (London: John Wolfe, 1601). In a chapter that argues that every Christian should "meditate of his ende," Sutton advocates the kind of "remembraunce [that], if it did sincke

into the hart . . . [would] worke better effectes in the worlde, then commonly it is wont" (37, 39). On meditation and memory in the medieval period, see Mary Carruthers, *The Craft of Thought: Meditation, Rhetoric, and the Making of Images, 400–1200* (Cambridge: Cambridge University Press, 1998).

23. Donne, *Sermons*, 74.

24. Mircea Eliade, *Myth and Reality*, trans. Willard R. Trask (New York: Harper and Row, 1963), 125. See also Robert Burton's discussion of Plato's idea of the soul, which "was from God at first, & knew all, but being inclosed in the Body, it forgets, and learnes anew, which he calls *reminiscentia*, or *recalling*" (*The Anatomy of Melancholy*, ed. Thomas C. Faulkner, Nicolas K. Kiessling and Rhonda L. Blair, 3 vols. [Oxford: Clarendon Press, 1989–1994], III: 156). Plato's (or Burton's) *reminiscentia* is a precursor to Donne's self-remembering, the accessing of matter forgotten under the demands of the fleshly. The important point is that in this formulation forgetting is a condition of embodiment; in remembering itself, the soul recalls that which preceded its incarnation.

25. Donne is also recognizably indebted to the syncretic philosophy of St. Augustine, who devotes the tenth book of his *Confessions* to a fascinating account of the relationship between memory and the divine. On Plato, Augustine and Donne, see A. M. Guite, "The Art of Memory and the Art of Salvation: The Centrality of Memory in the Sermons of John Donne and Lancelot Andrewes," *The Seventeenth Century* 4: 1 (1989): 1–17. For more on Donne's conception of memory, see also Dennis Quinn, "Donne's Christian Eloquence," *ELH* 27 (1960): 276–297; and Hickey, "Donne's Art of Memory."

26. Donne, *Sermons*, 74. Relevant here is Romans 2: 14–16, which argues for conscience (or the Law) as innate to man: "For when the Gentiles which have not the law do by nature the things contained in the law, these, having not the law are a law unto themselves. Which shew the work of the law written in their hearts, their conscience also bearing witness and their thoughts the meanwhile accusing or else excusing one another. In the day when God shall judge the secrets of men, by Jesus Christ, according to my Gospel."

27. Guite, "Art of Memory," 11–12.

28. In a broader sense, biblical narratives function as examples of what Peter Burke describes as "memory schema": "In early modern Europe, many people had read the Bible so often that it had become part of them and its stories organized their perceptions and their memories" ("History as Social Memory," *Memory: History, Culture and the Mind*, ed. Thomas Butler [Oxford: Basil Blackwell, 1989]: 97–113, esp. 103).

29. It is in this way that "the textual apparatus is transformed into a 'libidinal apparatus,' a machinery for ideological investment" (Frederic Jameson, *The Political Unconscious: Narrative as a Socially Symbolic Act* [Ithaca: Cornell University Press, 1981], 30).

30. Judith Butler, "Imitation and Gender Insubordination," *The Lesbian and Gay Studies Reader*, ed. Henry Abelove, Michele Aina Barale and David M. Halperin (New York: Routledge, 1993): 307–320, esp. 313 (italics in original).

31. *Memento mori* function as examples of what William E. Engel defines as monitory memory: they are images or objects that admonish the readers or viewers to remember their future—that is, their inevitable death and salvation or damnation. See *Mapping Mortality: The Persistence of Memory and Melancholy in Early Modern England* (Amherst: University of Massachusetts Press, 1995), esp. 57.

32. Similar arguments about this monologue have been advanced by Waswo, who sees it as representing a sin against the Holy Ghost, and Paul R. Sellin ("The Hidden God: Reformation Awe in Renaissance English Literature," *The Darker Vision of the Renaissance: Beyond the Fields of Reason*, ed. Robert S. Kinsman [Berkeley: University of California Press, 1974]: 147–196), for whom it reveals Faustus's status as a reprobate.

33. Baynes, *Caveat*, 16. Wittingly or not, Baynes echoes the commonplace insistence of writers of memory treatises that building the memory requires discipline and constant repetition.

34. Stephen Greenblatt has said of the Marlovian character that he "repeats himself in order to continue to be that same character on the stage. Identity is a theatrical invention that must be reiterated if it is to endure" (*Renaissance Self-Fashioning* [Chicago: University of Chicago Press, 1980], 201). This obtains in the case of Faustus, who repeatedly "backslides" only subsequently to reinforce his commitment to Lucifer.

35. On Faustus as one who seeks to remember or emulate Satan, see Pompa Banerjee, "I, Mephastophilis: Self, Other, and Demonic Parody in Marlowe's *Doctor Faustus*," *Christianity and Literature* 42: 2 (1993): 221–241.

36. This point is also made by Clare Harraway (*Re-citing Marlowe: Approaches to the Drama* [Aldershot: Ashgate, 2000]), who refers here to both the A- and B-texts: "When Lucifer appears in place of Christ, the Devil deflects Faustus's attention away from his thwarted salvation towards the pageant of the Seven Deadly Sins. This process of theatrical distraction continues throughout the plays as Faustus becomes increasingly forgetful of why he sold his soul" (45–46).

37. In addition, for Faustus to forget God is for him to forget that spark or image of the divine that exists within him.

38. Quoted in Joseph T. McMullen, "Dr. Faustus and Renaissance Learning," *Modern Language Review* 51 (1956): 6–16, esp. 8.

39. If sloth is not incompatible with activity, it is contrary to the continual (self-) recollection advocated above by Baynes. Baynes's depiction of repeated acts of remembering harnesses the logic of self-discipline, which is antithetical to sloth, to the representation of "remember[ing] your wayes, sinnes, declinings."

40. On Actaeon, see James Knowles, "'Infinite Riches in a Little Room': Marlowe and the Aesthetics of the Closet," *Renaissance Configurations: Voices/Bodies/Spaces, 1580–1690*, ed. Gordon McMullan (Houndmills: Macmillan, 1998): 3–29, esp. 21–22; Christopher Wessman, "'I'll Play Diana': Christopher Marlowe's *Doctor Faustus* and the 'Actaeon Complex,'" *English Studies* 82 (2001): 401–419.

41. Geffrey Whitney, *A Choice of Emblemes* (1586, facs. edn.; ed. Henry Green [New York: Benjamin Blom, 1967]), 15.

42. Alan Bray, *Homosexuality in Renaissance England* (New York: Columbia University Press, 1995), 21–23. Bray notes that the sodomite was often described as the offspring of a diabolical union.

43. *Ibid.*, 25, 26.

44. Alan Shepard argues that "Faustus is unambiguously thrilled by the virtual Helen that Mephistopheles cheerfully creates. Her presence seems to him to hold out the prospect of a radical metamorphosis of his own identity" *(Marlowe's Soldiers: Rhetorics of Masculinity in the Age of the Armada* [Aldershot: Ashgate, 2002], 186).

45. On limits and transgression in this play, see Jonathan Dollimore, *Radical Tragedy: Religion, Ideology and Power in the Drama of Shakespeare and his Contemporaries*, 2nd edn. (Durham: Duke University Press, 1993), 110–116.

46. For analysis of this scene that overlaps with the above, see Graham Hammill, "Faustus's Fortunes: Commodification, Exchange, and the Form of Literary Subjectivity," *ELH* 63 (1996): 309–336, esp. 328–329.

47. See also 2. 1. 74–91.

48. This scene reworks and expands upon the exchange between Faustus and the Knight in the A-text, in which Faustus asserts, "Are you remembered how you crossed me in my conference with the Emperor?" (4. 1. 85–86). While Faustus here has called upon the Knight to pay the reckoning for his actions, in the above B-text scene (absent from A), it is Faustus whose debt is stressed.

49. The language of debt-paying continues to the end of the scene, with the Duke and Duchess acknowledging themselves beholden to Faustus and pledging to "recompense" him "With all the love and kindness that we may" (4. 6. 122–124).

50. Henrie Swinburn, *A Briefe Treatise of Testaments and Last Willes* (London: John Windet, 1591), G1r.

51. Alan Sinfield, *Faultlines: Cultural Materialism and the Politics of Dissident Reading* (Berkeley: University of California Press, 1992), 234, 235. On doctrinal differences between the A- and B-texts, see Leah Marcus, *Unediting the Renaissance: Shakespeare, Marlowe, Milton* (New York: Routledge, 1996), esp. 38–67.

52. Friedrich Nietzsche, "On the Uses and Disadvantages of History for Life," *Untimely Meditations*, ed. Daniel Breazeale, trans. R. J. Hollingdale (Cambridge: Cambridge University Press, 1997): 59–123, esp. 60–61. W. L. Godshalk echoes Nietzsche (and, more immediately, Hamlet) when he notes that in these lines "Faustus desires the oblivion of bestiality" (*The Marlovian World Picture* [The Hague: Mouton, 1974], 195), an oblivion that for Godshalk is of a piece with the beast-like sensuality evinced by Faustus throughout.

53. Henry King, "Lent 1" (1625), *The Sermons of Henry King (1592–1669), Bishop of Chichester*, ed. Mary Hobbs (Rutherford: Fairleigh Dickinson University Press, 1992): 115–125, esp. 116.

54. "Knowe thy selfe, and thou shalt not offend: forget thy self, and what wilt thou not do? . . . At one worde art thou a man? forget thy selfe, and what art thou but a beast? And such a beast, as surpasseth all beasts in beastlinesse"

(Thomas Rogers, "The Preface to the Friendly Reader," *A Philosophicall Discourse, Entituled, The Anatomie of the Minde* [London: J[ohn] C[harlewood] for Andrew Maunsell, 1576], n.p.).

55. "Lifetimes are brief, and not to be regained, / For all mankind. But by their deeds to make / Their fame last: that is the labor for the brave" (Virgil, *The Aeneid*, trans. Robert Fitzgerald [New York: Random House, 1983], 310).

56. See Leo Braudy (*The Frenzy of Renown: Fame and Its History* [Oxford: Oxford University Press, 1986]) for a discussion of different models of fame in the classical tradition and its transmutation into Christian conceptions of immortality or glory. Conversations with Patrick Cheney have helped me think about fame as a memory category. In relation to Faustus's wish to "make men to live eternally" (1. 1. 22), Cheney argues that "Marlowe filters Christian glory back through classical fame to produce a new and striking version of the concept: *eternal life within time*" (*Marlowe's Counterfeit Profession: Ovid, Spenser, Counter-Nationhood*[Toronto: University of Toronto Press, 1997], 206).

57. Both the sinner's desire to forget his or her fate and the inexorability of that fate are routinely referred to in early modern texts designed to reform the sinful. An example: "All must come, and the houre may be neere, but it cannot be farre off; and howsoever wee forget it, it will bee sure to remember us" (Henry Thompson, *The Soules Alarum-bell* [London: Jo[hn] Beale, 1618], 30).

58. On the failure of exemplarity in this scene, see Katharine Eisaman Maus, *Inwardness and Theater in the English Renaissance* (Chicago: University of Chicago Press, 1995), 89.

59. For a related argument, see Susan Snyder, "Marlowe's *Doctor Faustus* as an Inverted Saint's Life," *Studies in Philology* 63 (1966): 565–577. Many critics have traced connections between Marlowe's play and the morality tradition. Most noteworthy is David Bevington, *From Mankind to Marlowe* (Cambridge, Mass.: Harvard University Press, 1962).

60. Huston Diehl, "'Infinite Space': Representation and Reformation in *Measure for Measure*," *Shakespeare Quarterly* 49 (1998): 393–410, esp. 407. The quoted passage is from "The Content of a Book of Articles devised by the King [Henry VIII, 1538]," *The Actes and Monuments of John Foxe*, ed. Stephen Reed Cattley, 8 vols. (London: R. B. Seeley and W. Burnside, 1937–1941), V: 163. In this passage, the distinction is drawn less between *kinds* of works of art than between appropriate and inappropriate *uses* of specific works. That is, to idolize an image is wrong, while to use it as a prompt for self-recollection is sanctioned.

61. In both of these instances, recollection entails and prompts a complex interpretive task, requiring recognition of the text, the context from out of which it emerges, and the way in which Faustus is perverting the biblical message. This task underscores Carruthers's point, articulated above, that recollection is always interpretive.

62. Michael Goldman, "Marlowe and the Histrionics of Ravishment," *Two Renaissance Mythmakers: Christopher Marlowe and Ben Jonson* (Baltimore: Johns Hopkins University Press, 1977): 22–40.

63. Greenblatt, *Renaissance Self-Fashioning*, 199.

64. Harry Levin, *The Overreacher: A Study of Christopher Marlowe* (Cambridge, Mass.: Harvard University Press, 1952).
65. Of course the play can be seen as harnessing such desires so as to condemn them; as in Aristotelian conceptions of tragedy, the members of the audience empathize with the hero's *hamartia* in order finally to be purged of the same fault.
66. Phillip Stubbes, *The Anatomie of Abuses* (London: Richard Jones, 1583), 90v. See also John Northbrooke, *A Treatise wherein Dicing, Dauncing, Vaine Playes or Enterluds . . . are Reproved* (London: H. Bynnenian for George Byshop, 1577), 64. The opposition between church and theatre is complicated by Henry King's identification of auditors who act at church much as Stubbes's playgoers do: "There are many now adaies who never thinke they have preaching enough, but as exquisite gluttons lay all markets for fare, so doe they lay all Churches where there is any suspicion of a Sermon . . . to glut their eares" ("A Sermon Preached at Pauls Crosse, the 25. of November. 1621," *The Sermons*, 63–82, esp. 65). King here contributes to the debate about the efficacy and primacy of the sermon that Lancelot Andrewes was famously involved in; see Peter Lake, "Lancelot Andrewes, John Buckeridge, and Avant-Garde Conformity at the Court of James I," *The Mental World of the Jacobean Court*, ed. Linda Levy Peck (Cambridge: Cambridge University Press, 1991): 113–133.
67. Jeffrey Knapp (*Shakespeare's Tribe: Church, Nation, and Theater in Renaissance England* [Chicago: University of Chicago Press, 2002], esp. 114–140) has recently argued that the theatre could serve not as the church's enemy but as an alternative source of religious instruction.
68. *Edward II*, ed. W. Moelwyn Merchant (1967; New York: W. W. Norton, 1989), 1. 1. 50–54. This sodomitically charged use of theatricality echoes the spectacle of Charles's self-forgetting.

4    "MY OBLIVION IS A VERY ANTONY"

1. John Frow, *Time and Commodity Culture: Essays in Cultural Theory and Postmodernity* (Oxford: Clarendon Press, 1997), 229.
2. Linda Charnes, *Notorious Identity: Materializing the Subject in Shakespeare* (Cambridge, Mass.: Harvard University Press, 1993), 113 (italics added). Nancy A. Cluck puts the standard view plainly: "The contrast between the former Antony – strong, honorable, heroic – and the present Antony – lackey of Cleopatra – is striking" ("Shakespearean Studies in Shame," *Shakespeare Quarterly* 36 [1985]: 141–151, esp. 148).
3. Mary Hamer, "Reading *Antony and Cleopatra* through Irigaray's *Speculum*," *Antony and Cleopatra*, ed. Nigel Wood (Buckingham: Open University Press, 1996): 66–91, esp. 70.
4. Cynthia Marshall is an exception to this; she asserts that "The play presents from its opening moments an Antony whose identity is already fragmented, despite its gestures toward a time when Antony 'knew himself' through his supposedly intact Roman identity. Unless we wish to submit to a nostalgic vision of heroism lost, we can only assume that the Antony present in the play *is* Antony – a character constituted by his internal displacements" ("Man of

Steel Done Got the Blues: Melancholic Subversion of Presence in *Antony and Cleopatra*," *Shakespeare Quarterly* 44 [1993]: 385–408, esp. 397).

5. A partial exception is Andrew Hiscock's "'Here is my Space': the Politics of Appropriation in Shakespeare's *Antony and Cleopatra*," *English* 47 (1998): 187–212, esp. 199.

6. For a reading of the play that is sensitive to the implications of climate differences to identity and cross-cultural encounter, see Mary Floyd-Wilson, "Transmigrations: Crossing Regional and Gender Boundaries in *Antony and Cleopatra*," *Enacting Gender on the English Renaissance Stage*, ed. Viviana Comensoli and Anne Russell (Urbana: University of Illinois Press, 1999): 73–96.

7. C. C. Barfoot, "News of the Roman Empire: Hearsay, Soothsay, Myth and History in *Antony and Cleopatra*," *Reclamations of Shakespeare*, ed. A. J. Hoenselaars (Amsterdam: Rodopi, 1994): 105–128; Janet Adelman, *The Common Liar* (New Haven: Yale University Press, 1973).

8. Samuel Daniel, "A Letter from Octavia to Marcus Antonius," *The Poeticall Essayes of Sam. Danyel* (London: P. Short for Simon Waterson, 1599), B1v.

9. As Carol Cook puts it, "Roman identity is that abstraction of the will and that concentration of energies that consolidates the empire and the self in the service of power" ("The Fatal Cleopatra," *Shakespearean Tragedy and Gender*, ed. Shirley Nelson Garner and Madelon Sprengnether [Bloomington: Indiana University Press, 1996]: 241–267, esp. 247).

10. All references to the play are drawn from William Shakespeare, *Antony and Cleopatra*, ed. John Wilders (London: Routledge, 1995).

11. See, for example, Francis Bacon, *The Advancement of Learning and New Atlantis*, ed. Arthur Johnston (Oxford: Clarendon Press, 1974), 117–118.

12. This self-characterization of Antony's comes as he is trying to patch up his alliance with Caesar, a process that engenders a few lines later these words from Maecenas, uttered in reference to the past grievances of Caesar and Antony: "to forget them quite / Were to remember that the present need / Speaks to atone you" (2. 2. 106–108). Here we have an example of what we encountered in *All's Well*, forgetting as a precondition for the formulation of a new social alliance. The doomed nature of this attempt is made plain by Enobarbus's reference to it as no more than a strategic and short-lived allegiance, followed by his statement that "That truth should be silent, I had almost forgot" (114–115). While asserting that he had *almost* forgotten, Enobarbus has nevertheless spoken a truth that functions as an accurate prediction of the eventual failure of Antony and Caesar's attempt to forget "The griefs between" them (106).

13. Antony's references to being "bound up" from his own knowledge and Pompey's description of him as "tied up" via Cleopatra's witchcraft emerge out of the Circean legacy. While in neither Homer nor Ovid does Circe bind her captives, her early modern descendant, Armida (in Tasso's *Gerusalemme Liberata*), "fram'd a soft, but surely holding chaine" of flowers, "Wherewith she bound [Rinaldo's] necke, his hands, and feete" (Torquato Tasso, *Godfrey of Bulloigne*, trans. Edward Fairfax [1600], ed. Kathleen M. Lea and T. M. Gang [Oxford: Clarendon Press, 1981] 14. 68). Similarly, Spenser's

Acrasia is described as weaving a "More subtile web [than] *Arachne*" to ensnare her captives – most notably Verdant, who resembles Antony in that he, upon Guyon and the Palmer's arrival, "layd a slombering, / In secret shade, after long wanton ioyes" (Edmund Spenser, *The Faerie Queene*, ed. Thomas P. Roche, Jr., assisted by C. Patrick O'Donnell, Jr. [Harmondsworth: Penguin, 1978], 2. 12. 77, 72).

14. Henry King, "A Sermon Preached at Pauls Crosse, the 25. of November. 1621," *The Sermons of Henry King (1592–1669), Bishop of Chichester*, ed. Mary Hobbs (Rutherford: Fairleigh Dickinson University Press, 1992): 63–82, esp. 67.

15. On the relationship between sexual pleasure and forgetting, see Elizabeth D. Harvey, "Pleasure's Oblivion: Displacements of Generation in Spenser's *Faerie Queene*," *Forgetting in Early Modern English Literature and Culture: Lethe's Legacies*, ed. Christopher Ivic and Grant Williams (New York: Routledge, 2004): 53–64.

16. C. C. Sallustius, *The Conspiracie of Cateline, The Two Most Worthy and Notable Histories*, trans. Thomas Heywood (London: John Jaggard, 1609), B2r.

17. For Sallust, fame is greatest when achieved not through valorous action but through learning or artistic production (B1v). Sallust's account of fame differs from a Virgilian model built upon martial activity – a model closer to the one associated with Caesar's view of Romanness.

18. For a discussion of Dr. Faustus's desire for such degeneration, see chapter 3.

19. Sallust, *Conspiracie of Cateline*, B1r.

20. William Shakespeare, *Hamlet*, ed. Harold Jenkins (London: Methuen, 1982), 4. 4. 40, 35. On Sallust and *Hamlet*, see Clifford J. Ronan, "Sallust, Beasts that 'Sleep and Feed,' and *Hamlet*, 5. 2," *Hamlet Studies* 7 (1985): 72–80.

21. For more on sleep, see Tanya Pollard, "'A Thing Like Death': Sleeping Potions and Poisons in *Romeo and Juliet* and *Antony and Cleopatra*," *Renaissance Drama* n.s. 32 (2003): 95–121.

22. Clifford Davidson states that, "The Queen of Egypt is very like the enchantress Circe, who also holds out a cup to visiting kings and other strangers, who thereby are made to lose their rational human stance as they are transformed into beasts" ("*Antony and Cleopatra*: Circe, Venus, and the Whore of Babylon," *Shakespeare: Contemporary Critical Approaches*, ed. Harry R. Garvin [Lewisburg: Bucknell University Press, 1980; Bucknell Review 25]: 31–55, esp. 39). While Davidson is the only critic I know of to discuss the Circe myth in relation to the play in any detail, he is not the first commentator to connect the two. See, for example, George Bernard Shaw, who states that "The very name of Cleopatra suggests at once a tragedy of Circe, with the horrible difference that whereas the ancient myth rightly represents Circe as turning heroes into hogs, the modern romantic convention would represent her as turning hogs into heroes" (quoted in Michael Neill, "Introduction," *The Tragedy of Anthony and Cleopatra*, ed. Michael Neill [Oxford: Clarendon Press, 1994]: 1–130, esp. 69). On the association of Circe with witches, see Gareth Roberts, "The descendants of Circe: witches and Renaissance fictions," *Witchcraft in Early Modern Europe*, ed. Jonathan

Barry, Marianne Hester and Gareth Roberts (Cambridge: Cambridge University Press, 1996): 183–206.

23. Abraham Fraunce, *The Third Part of the Countesse of Pembroke's Yvychurch* (London: Printed for T[homas] Woodcocke, 1592), 48r. Circe is also associated with the triumph of the passions over reason, a process described by Thomas Wright in terms that suggest self-forgetting: "By this alteration which Passions worke in the Witte and the Will, we may understand the admirable Metamorphosis and change of a man from himselfe, when his affectes are pacified, and when they are troubled. *Plutarch* sayde they changed them like *Circes* potions, from men into beastes" (*The Passions of the Minde in Generall* [London: Valentine Simmes for Walter Burre, 1604], 58–59). See also Roger Ascham, *The Schoolmaster*, ed. Lawrence V. Ryan (Charlottesville: University of Virginia Press for the Folger Shakespeare Library, 1967), 63–64, in which pleasure, represented by Circe's turning of men into beasts, is linked with, among other things, "forgetfulness of all good things learned before" (64). That Circe could be read in a more positive light is also made plain in Fraunce; she is associated with generation and "wrought many wonders by inchaunting" (48r). For more on the equivocality of Circe, see Davidson, "*Antony and Cleopatra*"; Merritt Y. Hughes, "Spenser's Acrasia and the Circe of the Renaissance," *Journal of the History of Ideas* 4 (1943): 381–399, esp 397.

24. *Homer's Odysses*, trans. George Chapman (London: Rich. Field for Nathaniell Butter, 1615 [?]), 151.

25. *Homer's Odysses*, 157.

26. *Homer's Odysses*, 155–156.

27. *Homer's Odysses*, 154.

28. The possibility of emasculation through self-forgetting is one that is also associated with a different episode in Homer's text. A few lines after Abraham Fraunce describes Circe, he refers to the fates of other shipmates of Ulysses who "in the region of the *Lothophagi*, by tasting forren fruit, did forget their own countrey." Like those turned into beasts, these were men who "did yet yeeld and give over themselves to pleasure and sensualitie" (Fraunce, *The Third Part*, 48r).

29. In another essay on this play, I argue that Antony's sojourn in Egypt can be seen in relation to romance episodes in epic that include Circe figures, such as Acrasia in *The Faerie Queene*. See Garrett A. Sullivan, Jr., "Sleep, Epic and Romance in *Antony and Cleopatra*," *Antony and Cleopatra: New Critical Essays*, ed. Sara Munson Deats (London: Routledge, 2005), 259–273. On romance, epic and Antony and Cleopatra, see David Quint, *Epic and Empire: Politics and Generic Form from Virgil to Milton* (Princeton: Princeton University Press, 1993), esp. 21–49; Ania Loomba, *Shakespeare, Race, and Colonialism* (Oxford: Oxford University Press, 2002), esp. 117.

30. Catherine Belsey identifies a strain of Renaissance thought that argues that "Suicide re-establishes the sovereign subject" and is "the crowning affirmation of the supremacy of the self, and simultaneously the extinction of finitude . . . In the absolute act of suicide the subject itself is momentarily absolute" (*The Subject of Tragedy: Identity and Difference in Renaissance Drama* [1985; London: Routledge, 1993], 124–125). See also Michael Neill's

description of suicide as connoting "an assertion of integrity in the very act of disintegration" (*Issues of Death: Mortality and Identity in English Renaissance Tragedy* [Oxford: Clarendon Press, 1997], 319).

31. Of course Antony's suicide can also be read as an effort made to reunite with the "dead" Cleopatra; even as he seeks the supposed stability of a Roman death, Antony is also driven by the desire that he has perceived as undermining his Roman identity. For a discussion of the play's association of Antony with the trope of hyperbole and Cleopatra with that of paradox, see Adelman, *The Common Liar*.

32. See also Antony's complaint that Caesar is always "harping on what I am, / Not what he knew I was" (3. 13. 147–148).

33. On emulation, see Coppélia Kahn, *Roman Shakespeare: Warriors, Wounds and Women* (New York: Routledge, 1997).

34. Enobarbus's trajectory mirrors Antony's, although Enobarbus's self-forgetting comes from his abandonment of his master. His repentance of this action is a form of self-recollection that, he fears, does not diminish his status as infamous. His action is one for which "the world [will] rank [him] in register / A master-leaver and a fugitive" (4. 9. 24–25). This "register" is the book of memory, and Enobarbus has shortly before referred to the "hateful memory" he has produced by his actions (4. 9. 11).

35. See, for instance, Ellis Hanson, "Sodomy and Kingcraft in *Urania* and *Antony and Cleopatra*," *Homosexuality in Renaissance and Enlightenment England: Literary Representations in Historical Context*, ed. Claude J. Summers (New York: Haworth Press, 1992): 135–151; Jonathan Gil Harris, "'Narcissus in thy face': Roman Desire and the Difference it Fakes in *Antony and Cleopatra*," *Shakespeare Quarterly* 45 (1994): 408–425. Also relevant here are recent discussions of Cleopatra's Otherness that foreground issues of race. See, among others, Loomba, *Shakespeare, Race, and Colonialism*, esp. 112–134; Kim F. Hall, *Things of Darkness: Economies of Race and Gender in Early Modern England* (Ithaca: Cornell University Press, 1995), esp. 141–160; Arthur L. Little, Jr., *Shakespeare Jungle Fever: National-Imperial Re-Visions of Race, Rape, and Sacrifice* (Stanford: Stanford University Press, 2000), esp. 102–176; Francesca T. Royster, *Becoming Cleopatra: The Shifting Image of an Icon* (New York: Palgrave Macmillan, 2003), esp. 1–57.

36. Janet Adelman suggests how Octavius Caesar's construction of Romanness is different even from his father's, and in ways that serve Octavius's own need to come to terms with the model of masculinity enacted by Julius Caesar. See *Suffocating Mothers: Fantasies of Maternal Origins in Shakespeare's Plays, Hamlet to The Tempest* (New York: Routledge, 1992), esp. 179–182.

37. This view is essentially a "Roman" rather than an "Egyptian" one. As Cynthia Marshall puts it, "One [critical] tradition treats [Antony's] decline in terms of emasculation. Adopting an essentially 'Roman' viewpoint, critics in this camp see Antony as seduced away from his proper self, from the paragon of valor and abstemiousness celebrated by Octavius Caesar. . .Another group of critics, seeking to align themselves with Cleopatra's Egypt, finds positive value in the dissolution Antony suffers." Marshall rightly points out that while the latter group has offered illuminating views of the play, such work

"cloud[s] the fact of Antony's complaint: he feels himself to be coming apart" ("Man of Steel," 392).

38. Adelman, *Suffocating Mothers*, 177.

39. Cynthia Marshall has recently argued both for the non-self-identical nature of many of the central figures in Plutarch's *Lives* and for the significance of Plutarch for Shakespeare's conception of character; see "Shakespeare, Crossing the Rubicon," *Shakespeare Survey* 53 (2000): 73–88.

40. Plutarke, "The Life of Marcus Antonius," *The Lives of the Noble Grecians and Romanes*, trans. Thomas North (London: Richard Field for Thomas Wight, 1595), 969.

41. *Ibid.*, 972. Plutarch draws on Cicero's *Second Phillipic Oration*.

42. *Ibid.*, 973. Surely there is a negative echo of this moment in the unaccompanied journey of Octavia to her brother (3. 6. 43–56). More immediately, given that Cleopatra's theatricality has been a trope of recent criticism of the play, Antony's earlier dalliance with a "plaier" is intriguing. On Cleopatra and theatricality, see especially Jyotsna Singh, "Renaissance Antitheatricality, Antifeminism, and Shakespeare's *Antony and Cleopatra*," *Renaissance Drama* n.s. 20 (1990): 99–121; and Laura Levine, *Men in Women's Clothing: Anti-Theatricality and Effeminization, 1579–1642* (Cambridge: Cambridge University Press, 1994), esp. 44–72.

43. Plutarke, "Life," 976.

44. *Ibid.*, 977.

45. The phrase is Michael Neill's: "In the Roman world identity (and heroic identity above all) requires . . . absolute self-consistency and singleness of being" ("Introduction," 102). Admittedly, Cleopatra is responsible in Plutarch for an escalation in Antony's dissipation – she "did waken and stirre up many vices yet hidden in him, and were never seene to any" (Plutarke, "Life," 979). However, this should not lead the reader to associate that dissipation exclusively with Egypt.

46. Neill, "Introduction," 101. See also Adelman, *The Common Liar*, 131–132; and Floyd-Wilson, "Transmigrations."

47. Mary Carruthers, *The Book of Memory* (Cambridge: Cambridge University Press, 1990), 16.

48. *Ibid.*, 21.

49. Unless otherwise specified, "Romanness" refers to Caesar's conception of Rome and Roman identity.

50. For more on this Shakespearean trope, see the introduction.

51. For a different reading of these lines, see H. W. Fawkner, *Shakespeare's Hyperontology: Antony and Cleopatra* (Rutherford: Fairleigh Dickinson University Press, 1990), 44–45.

52. "[Cleopatra's] allegedly 'female' attributes demand in many instances to be understood as displaced or misrecognized Roman characteristics . . . Cleopatra's 'variety' provides the specular image – is, in many respects, the very effect – of Antony's own" (Harris, "Narcissus," 422).

53. Antony states in the previous scene, "I must from this enchanting queen break off. / Ten thousand harms, more than the ills I know, / My idleness doth hatch" (1. 2. 135–137). Here again Cleopatra evokes Circe, whose

enchanting nature is linked to Antony's idleness and to the prospect of his "los[ing him]self in dotage" (123).

54. Peter Berek ("Doing and Undoing: The Value of Action in *Antony and Cleopatra*," *Shakespeare Quarterly* 32 [1981]: 295–304) argues that Antony and Cleopatra reject Roman martial "doing" in favor of their love (e.g., "The nobleness of life / Is to do thus" [1. 1. 37–38]). Antony wants to believe that idleness is something he has performed in the recent past and now can distance himself from; he does not see it as a form of doing that is (or has been) constitutive of his selfhood.

55. Adelman, *Suffocating Mothers*, 176.

56. *Ibid.*, 177, 183. "Even when [Antony] is on stage . . . his presence is suffused with a sense of absence or loss; except in his triumphant land battle, his heroic grandeur is always constructed retrospectively in his – and its – absence" (177).

57. Brian Cheadle, "'His legs bestrid the ocean' as a 'form of life,'" *Drama in Philosophy*, ed. James Redmond (Cambridge: Cambridge University Press, 1990), 102. Compare Jonathan Dollimore's response to this speech: "His legs bestrid the ocean: in dream, in death, Antony becomes at last larger than life; but in valediction is there not also invoked an image of the commemorative statue, that material embodiment of a discourse which, like Caesar's encomium, skilfully overlays (without ever quite obscuring) obsolescence with respect?" (*Radical Tragedy*, 2nd edn. [Durham: Duke University Press, 1993], 213).

58. John Danby states that in this speech we witness "the past catching fire from the urgent needs of the present, flaring in memory and imagination as it never did in actuality" (*Poets on Fortune's Hill* [London: Faber and Faber, 1952], 147).

59. Adelman, *Suffocating Mothers*, 183.

60. The liberality of Antony that Cleopatra stresses in this speech ("realms and islands were / As plates dropped from his pocket" [5. 2. 90–91]) can also be found in Plutarch, but as a symptom of his dissolution.

61. This deferral of her death intersects interestingly with what Catherine Belsey has described as a pattern of deferrals fundamental to Cleopatra's seductiveness: "It is not. . .Cleopatra's presence which seduces. . .nor simply her absence, but her imagined, promised, deferred presence" ("Cleopatra's Seduction," *Alternative Shakespeares, Volume 2*, ed. John Drakakis [London: Routledge, 1996]: 38–62, esp. 43).

62. Barfoot, "News of the Roman Empire," 111.

63. Relevant here is a line from Samuel Daniel's play, *The Tragedie of Cleopatra*, the events of which all take place after Antony's death. In this text, Cleopatra's love for Antony emerges only after his death; she states that "even affliction makes me truly love thee. / Which *Antony*, I must confesse my fault / I never did sincerely untill now: / Now I protest I do, now am I taught / In death to love, in life that knew not how" (*The Tragedie of Cleopatra, Poeticall Essayes*, C1v–C2r). Interestingly, Daniel's Cleopatra asserts that Antony and Cleopatra have "both made shipwracke of our fame" (C1v), although her suicide will, she later states, "In after ages live in

memory" (I2v). In Shakespeare, there is also a moment at which love is retrospectively – indeed, seemingly posthumously – asserted: "My mistress loved thee, and her fortunes mingled / With thine entirely" (4. 14. 24–25). These lines are Mardian's, spoken to Antony after Cleopatra's supposed suicide.

64. John Gillies says of the Roman triumph that it "acted as a ritual means of domesticating geographic otherness (or barbarism) – of bringing it safely within the orbit of the eternal city, offering it to the tutelary gods, disarming it, subordinating it, and assimilating it" ("Marlowe, the *Timur* Myth, and the Motives of Geography," *Playing the Globe: Genre and Geography in English Renaissance Drama*, ed. John Gillies and Virginia Mason Vaughan [Madison and Teaneck: Fairleigh Dickinson University Press, 1998]: 203–229, esp. 213). On this, see book 8 of the *Aeneid*, as part of the passage describing the shield of Aeneas takes as its topic Augustus Caesar's victory over Cleopatra.

65. "Rather than be part of the trappings of Caesar's monumentalizing ambition. . .she proposes to become her own monument. In the process her death reverses the transformation suffered by the dying Anthony, becoming the act of supreme distinction at which Anthony can only gesture" (Neill, *Issues of Death*, 321). On Cleopatra as monument, see also John M. Bowers, "'I Am Marble-Constant': Cleopatra's Monumental End," *Huntington Library Quarterly* 46 (1983): 283–297.

66. Lorraine Helms argues that "Cleopatra's suicide. . .is an achieved rite of passage through eroticism into marriage" ("'The High Roman Fashion': Sacrifice, Suicide, and the Shakespearean Stage," *PMLA* 107 [1992]: 554–565, esp. 559). See also Cleopatra's metaphoric reference to herself as mother of the nursing asp (5. 2. 308–309).

67. At one point Caesar says to Cleopatra that "we intend so to dispose you as / Yourself shall give us counsel. Feed and sleep" (5. 2. 185–186). Read through Sallust, these final words may attest to Caesar's desire to prevent Cleopatra attaining fame through suicide. However, we have seen that Caesar elsewhere plans to make Cleopatra immortal as his trophy.

68. Enobarbus's death is also misrecognized as sleep (4. 9. 30).

69. What Michael Neill says of sexual desire can be seen to be more generally true of what Caesar would characterize as Antony's pursuit of hedonistic self-forgetting: "For Anthony, sexual appetite is invariably a temptation to self-abandonment – losing oneself in dotage. . . . [D]esire turns out always to have been the desire for annihilation" (Neill, *Issues of Death*, 319).

70. Tasso, *Godfrey of Bulloigne*, 14. 63–64.

71. Indeed, given that early modern descriptions of the mirror have it as not only reflecting back at one but also as providing a model for behavior (e.g., *A Mirror for Magistrates*), Antony's sleep represents a model erosive of Caesar's self-conception. This is only reinforced by the fact that Caesar's "enmity coexisted with . . . intense identification" with Antony (Kahn, *Roman Shakespeare,* 137).

72. On the importance of Rome to Shakespeare, see Kahn, *Roman Shakespeare,* 1–26.

73. Frow, *Time and Commodity Culture,* 229.

74. Kahn, *Roman Shakespeare,* 8.

5  SLEEP, CONSCIENCE AND FAME IN THE DUCHESS OF MALFI

1. Thomas Kyd, *The Spanish Tragedy*, in *The First Part of Hieronimo and The Spanish Tragedy*, ed. Andrew S. Cairncross (Lincoln: University of Nebraska Press, 1967), 3. 15. 24.

2. John Webster, *The Duchess of Malfi*, ed. Elizabeth M. Brennan (New York: W. W. Norton, 1983), 5. 5. 119–120. Henceforth cited in the text. On the Duchess as the subject of these lines, see Michael Neill, *Issues of Death: Mortality and Identity in English Renaissance Tragedy* (Oxford: Clarendon Press, 1997), 332; and Lee Bliss, *The World's Perspective: John Webster and the Jacobean Drama* (New Brunswick: Rutgers University Press, 1983), 166–167.

3. John Willis, *Mnemonica, or, The Art of Memory* (London: Leonard Sowersby, 1661), 140.

4. Two of the three forms of self-forgetting come together in the accusations of the Duchess's brothers: *erotic* self-forgetting in her pursuit of "lustful pleasures," and *spiritual* self-forgetting in her neglect of her inevitable demise. The Duchess's forgetting of her *country* is evident in her abdication of responsibility as ruler through giving herself over to a love affair with her steward.

5. Christopher Sutton, *Disce Mori. Learne to Die* (London: John Wolfe, 1601), 8.

6. John S. Wilks (in *The Idea of Conscience in Renaissance Tragedy* [London: Routledge, 1990]) argues, with particular emphasis paid to this utterance, that the Duchess's and Antonio's "blindness. . . is to some extent a determination not to see, their ignorance a deliberate evasion of conscience." (202). In the primary source for Webster's play, the Duchess articulates her plan of marriage as follows: "I purpose to make [Antonio] my loyall and lawfull husband, meaning therby not to offend God & men togither, & pretend to live without off[en]se of conscience, wherby my soule shall not be hindred for any thing I do" (William Painter, *The Second Tome of the Palace of Pleasure* [London: Henrie Bynneman, for Nicholas England, 1567], 176r). Painter sees this statement as being both self-interested and far from credible.

7. William Shakespeare, *Macbeth*, ed. Kenneth Muir (1951; London: Routledge, 1988), 1. 4. 52.

8. A later reference to winking connotes both closing one's eyes and sleeping (as made plain in the mention of dreaming). Delio states to Antonio upon their reunion in act three, "Let me but wink, / And not behold your face, which to mine eye / Is somewhat leaner: verily I should dream / It were within this half hour" (3. 1. 8–11).

9. See also the Duchess's assertion that she is "going into a wilderness, / Where I shall find nor path, nor friendly clew / To be my guide" (1. 2. 278–280). She is knowingly entering a moral wilderness that is also a labyrinth (as mention of the "clew," referring to Ariadne's thread, suggests).

10. The mixture of autonomy and constraint evinced in the Duchess's actions emerges out of the complexities of her social position, which have been admirably described by Mary Beth Rose (*The Expense of Spirit: Love and Sexuality in English Renaissance Drama* [Ithaca: Cornell University Press, 1988]): "Proud of her royal birth and stature, the widowed Duchess is also in

love with her steward and determined to disobey her brothers, woo Antonio, and marry him. Thus she is caught between classes, between sexes, between tenses: as a young widow, she has a past and seeks a future; as an aristocrat who is also royal, she is independent, politically central, a ruler; but as a woman she is marginal, subordinate, and dependent – a status that her brothers' tyranny makes abundantly clear" (159). Both independent and dependent, central and marginal, the Duchess must always confront the limits placed upon her as she enacts her desires.

11. This is an example of what Emily Bartels has identified as a characteristic strategy of the Duchess, who Bartels discusses in terms of her "self-assertion within circumscription" ("Strategies of Submission: Desdemona, the Duchess, and the Assertion of Desire," *Studies in English Literature, 1500– 1900* 36 [1996]: 417–433, esp. 422–423).

12. Charles R. Forker, *Skull Beneath the Skin: The Achievement of John Webster* (Carbondale: Southern Illinois University Press, 1986), 297. Forker critiques such views as evidence of a "tradition of prim moralism [that] has crept steadily into academic commentaries" (297). Lee Bliss similarly rehearses this view: "[U]nconcerned with her duchy's political health, the Duchess seeks private happiness at the expense of public stability. As a ruler, she can no more be lauded for the example she sets than her brothers" (145). This vision of the Duchess is usually associated with Joyce E. Peterson's *Curs'd Example: The Duchess of Malfi and Commonweal Tragedy* (Columbia: University of Missouri Press, 1978).

13. Martha Ronk, "Embodied Morality," *Sexuality and Politics in Renaissance Drama*, ed. Carole Levin and Karen Robertson (Lewiston: Edwin Mellen Press, 1991), 243–244. Judith Haber has recently valorized sites such as this circle as *loci* of feminine pleasure ("'My Body Bestow upon My Women': The Space of the Feminine in *The Duchess of Malfi*," *Renaissance Drama* n.s. 28 [1997]: 133–159).

14. Painter, *Second Tome*, 185r.

15. *Ibid.*, 173r.

16. Lori Schroeder Haslem, "'Troubled with the Mother': Longings, Purgings, and the Maternal Body in *Bartholomew Fair* and *The Duchess of Malfi*," *Modern Philology* 92:4 (1995): 438–459. See also Dale B. J. Randall, "The Rank and Earthy Background of Certain Physical Symbols in *The Duchess of Malfi*," *Renaissance Drama* n.s. 18 (1987): 171–203.

17. Similar sentiments are expressed by the Duchess elsewhere in the play; see also 3. 2. 158–159 and 3. 5. 17–20.

18. See Gail Kern Paster, "The Unbearable Coldness of Female Being: Women's Imperfection and the Humoral Economy," *ELR* 28 (1998): 416–440, esp. 419; Valerie Traub, *The Renaissance of Lesbianism in Early Modern England* (Cambridge: Cambridge University Press, 2002), 23; see also the introduction and chapter one to this book.

19. On this, see the introduction.

20. The play repeatedly concerns itself with the scrutinizing of that which is "private" or hidden; in just a single scene of the play, the Old Lady anxiously avers that Bosola has become "well acquainted with [her] closet" (2. 1. 36–37); Antonio claims to "understand [Bosola's] inside" (85); and, most

importantly, Bosola cries in relation to the Duchess, "A whirlwind strike off these bawd farthingales, / For, but for that, and the loose-bodied gown, / I should have discover'd apparently / The young springal cutting a caper in her belly" (152–155). The two final utterances both suggest the anatomical penetration of the body, with Bosola's utterance even gesturing toward the processes of unveiling that Patricia Parker has argued are essential to the constitution and discovery of truth in early modern thinking ("Fantasies of 'Race' and 'Gender': Africa, *Othello*, and Bringing to Light,"*Women, "Race," and Writing in the Early Modern Period*, ed. Margo Hendricks and Patricia Parker [London: Routledge, 1994]: 84–100). See also Lisa Hopkins, "With the Skin Side Inside: The Interiors of *The Duchess of Malfi*," *Privacy, Domesticity, and Women in Early Modern England*, ed. Corinne S. Abate (Aldershot: Ashgate, 2003): 21–30.

21. It is worth noting that Ferdinand can be understood as lulling others to sleep. Two sentences into Ferdinand's silent appearance on stage, the Duchess ironically jokes to the now absent Antonio – he has sneaked out of the room with Cariola – that "We shall one day have my brothers take you napping" (3. 2. 63).

22. Robert Burton, *The Anatomy of Melancholy* (Oxford: John Lichfield and James Short, for Henry Cripps, 1621), C2v, italics in original.

23. Katherine Rowe, *Dead Hands: Fictions of Agency, Renaissance to Modern* (Stanford: Stanford University Press, 1999), 14. Rowe pays particular attention to the severed (wax) hand that Ferdinand delivers to the Duchess.

24. Frank Whigham, *Seizures of the Will in Early Modern English Drama* (Cambridge: Cambridge University Press, 1996), esp. 188–224.

25. It is worth noting that the play draws attention to the period of Ferdinand's not stirring; the next scene opens (two lines after Ferdinand's announcement of his plan to sleep) with the revelation that much time has passed, and that the "heavy sleeps" of Antonio and the Duchess have lead to the birth of two more children. It is in this scene (3.1) that Ferdinand, who has arrived with Delio, sneaks into the Duchess's bedchamber, and the revelation of the children's existence follows quickly on the heels of the announcement of Ferdinand's arrival.

26. Haber, "My Body Bestow upon My Women," 138–139.

27. In conversation with Ferdinand, Bosola finishes Ferdinand's interrupted reference to a "politic dormouse" by talking of those who "Feed in a lord's dish, half asleep, not seeming / To listen to any talk" (1. 2. 203–205).

28. The mediated nature of this encounter is emblematized by the fact that the Duchess takes a hand she believes to be Ferdinand's, but which is actually a wax model of Antonio's. See Rowe for an astute discussion of this "dead hand."

29. Of course, master-servant relations remain complex for Bosola, who kills Antonio as ordered to by the Cardinal, but against his own desires; he remains a servant even as he resists the role. It is after he asserts that he will be his own example (5. 4. 81) that he stabs both the Cardinal and Ferdinand, the latter killing which he performs while noting that "the last part of my life / Hath done me best service" (5. 5. 63–64). At the same time, in this same scene he is dealt a death blow by Ferdinand, his former master.

30. Camille Wells Slights, "Notaries, Sponges, and Looking-Glasses: Conscience in Early Modern England," *ELR* 28 (1998): 231–246, esp. 235–236. Dramatic literature repeatedly concerns itself with the topic of conscience; obvious examples include Shakespeare and Fletcher's *Henry VIII* as well as Shakespeare's *Richard III* and *Hamlet*. For more on conscience, casuistry and literature, see also Slights, *The Casuistical Tradition in Shakespeare, Donne, Herbert and Milton* (Princeton: Princeton University Press, 1981); Meg Lota Brown, *Donne and the Politics of Conscience in Early Modern England* (Leiden: E. J. Brill, 1995); Frederick Kiefer, *Writing on the Renaissance Stage* (Newark: University of Delaware Press, 1996), 111–162; Lowell Gallagher, *Medusa's Gaze: Casuistry and Conscience in the Renaissance* (Stanford: Stanford University Press, 1991); Ned Lukacher, *Daemonic Figures: Shakespeare and the Question of Conscience* (Ithaca: Cornell University Press, 1994).

31. William Perkins, *A Discourse of Conscience* (Cambridge: John Legate, 1596), 8.

32. Pierre Charron, *Of Wisdome*, trans. Samson Lennard (London: Edward Blount and Witt Aspley, 1612), 46; Thomas Vicary, *A Profitable Treatise of the Anatomie of Mans Body* (London: Henry Bamforde, 1577), D2V–D3R. Like memory, conscience is routinely compared to a book. Richard Bernard (*Christian, See to Thy Conscience* [London: Felix Kyngston for Edward Blackmore, 1631]) tacitly compares the book of conscience to the Bible: "Conscience is it selfe a Booke, whereof all other Bookes are expositions: It is as the Text, they the interpretation" (A2r).

33. Immanuel Bourne, *The Anatomie of Conscience* (London: G. E[ld] and M. F[lesher] for Nathaniel Butter, 1623), 9.

34. Bernard, *Christian, See to Thy Conscience*, 7.

35. John Abernethy, *A Christian and Heavenly Treatise. Containing Physicke for the Soule* (London: Felix Kyngston for John Budge, 1622), 103.

36. Perkins, *Discourse of Conscience*, 5.

37. *Ibid.*, 8.

38. Abernethy, *Christian and Heavenly Treatise*, 108–109. Jeremiah Dyke (in *Good Conscience* [London: J[ohn] D[awson] for Robert Milbourne, 1624]) has it that the seared conscience is one in which the following does not happen: "If a man be negligent, or careles & drowsie in good duties, it comes to him with that voyce, *Ephes. 5.14. Awake thou that sleepest*" (27–28). Immanuel Bourne describes cauterized consciences as ones that are "full of sin, yet feele it not, they are asleepe and cannot see it" (*Anatomie*, 17).

39. William Ames, *Conscience with the Power and Cases Thereof* (Leiden and London: W. Christiaens, E. Griffin and J. Dawson, 1639), 42, 43.

40. Bourne, *Anatomie*, 23. Operating outside the casuistical tradition, the anonymous author of *The Drousie Disease* describes sinners as sleepers who have "stop[ped] the light of the Word, put out the light of their owne consciences, and forbid even those whose office it is to awake them out of sleepe [i.e., preachers], to awake them till they please" (*The Drousie Disease; Or, An Alarme to Awake Church-Sleepers* [London: J[ohn] D[awson] for Michael Sparke, Jr., 1638], 14). The author speaks both metaphorically and

literally here; he desires to awaken the consciences of all sinners as well as to awaken those who sleep in church.

41. Bernard, *Christian, See to Thy Conscience*, 36–37.

42. *Ibid.*, 148–149.

43. In the interest of rhetorical economy, I am omitting discussion of an important distinction between two parts of conscience. The first is called *synteresis* (or *synderesis*) and it represents the moral principles that exist in the consciences of all of us; it exists as divinely implanted and inviolable moral code. The second form of conscience has to do with the operations of judgment and leads to the production of a register of one's own actions. The results of "case divinity" emerge from the application of *synteresis*'s principles to one's own actions. For a brief account of the history of *synteresis*, see Lukacher, *Daemonic Figures*, 143–144.

44. Richard Carpenter, *The Conscionable Christian* (London: F[elix] K[ingston] for John Bartlet, 1623), 100.

45. Slights, "Notaries, Sponges, and Looking-Glasses," 232.

46. This relationship between law and inner voice is closely analogous to that of *synteresis* and the application of it to our own experience. See the above note on *synteresis*.

47. Relevant here is Judith Butler's distinction between the psyche and the subject: the psyche "is precisely what exceeds the imprisoning effects of the discursive demand to inhabit a coherent identity, to become a coherent subject" (*The Psychic Life of Power: Theories in Subjection* [Stanford: Stanford University Press, 1997], 86).

48. For an expression of this view, see 3. 4. 23–26.

49. Bettie Anne Doebler ("Continuity in the Art of Dying: *The Duchess of Malfi,*" *Comparative Drama* 14:3 [Fall 1980]: 203–215) sees Bosola as first tempting the Duchess to despair, then functioning as a source of comfort for her. Others who have written provocatively on this scene and its connection to the *memento mori* tradition include David M. Bergeron ("The Wax Figures in *The Duchess of Malfi,*" *SEL* 18 [1978]: 331–339) and Neill, *Issues of Death*.

50. The vizarded Bosola even echoes the argument of her brothers when he claims to the Duchess that his role is akin to that of one who sounds a note that "frights the silly birds / Out of the corn" rather than a note that "allure[s] them / To the nets" (3. 5. 99–101). The first note requires that the Duchess eschew the worldly in favor of remembering her end.

51. Glimpses of the Duchess's resignation precede her imprisonment (see, for instance, 3. 5. 7), but the theme is most fully developed in the prison scenes.

52. Ferdinand is already thinking in these terms when he leaves with the Duchess a dagger that she might use to kill herself (3. 2. 149–151).

53. Even earlier, and as himself, Bosola has counselled the Duchess not to succumb to despair by killing herself (4. 1. 69–75), and has encouraged her to pray rather than curse (94–105).

54. Bourne, *Anatomie*, 24.

55. In neither his case nor Ferdinand's does the awakening of conscience promise the reformation of the subject. As the casuists make plain, conscience might function to lead one of the elect to accept divine grace, but for reprobates like

Ferdinand and Bosola it could only offer a preview of the harsh judgment to be meted out later by God. That Calvinist logic notwithstanding, the Catholic context of the play is sometimes foregrounded by Webster. Shortly before referring to the "black register," Bosola imagines the Duchess as a saint or martyr who might lead him from hell to heaven (4. 2. 336–337, 341–343).

56. Here's how this metaphor works: sleep is associated with moisture, and moisture leads to rust. As is regularly stated in early modern natural philosophy, the soul is understood in terms of the operations of the faculties, and key operations of the rational soul – not only reason, but also purposeful recollection – are suspended during sleep. "Immoderate sleep," then, means that reason in particular is never used, and the sleeping subject becomes little different from a beast.

57. Bosola describes this madness as a "fatal judgment" that has "fall'n upon this Ferdinand" (5. 2. 83–84). This madness was foreshadowed in Ferdinand's response to reports of the Duchess's sex life, reports which temporarily "put [Ferdinand] out of his wits" (2. 6. 69).

58. That what prompts this haunting is Ferdinand's guilt over the murder of the Duchess is obvious to the Cardinal, who in offering an explanation for Ferdinand's mad behavior concocts a story of a different but related haunting. In this tale, Ferdinand sees a harbinger of death in the form of the ghost of an old woman who was murdered by her nephews for money (5. 2. 87–100). The Cardinal modifes the story of the murder of the Duchess, an act which we are told late in the play was also motivated by greed (4. 2. 277–280).

59. Bourne, *Anatomie*, 13.

60. This simultaneous inwardness and outwardness speaks to the status of those laws contained in *synteresis*, laws that are both innate and external to man.

61. For example, R. K. R. Thornton has linked the rake with an iconographic tradition of representations of simoniacs ("The Cardinal's Rake in *The Duchess of Malfi*," *Notes and Queries* 214 / n.s. 16 [1969]: 294–295), while Michael Neill reads it as a parody of the Cardinal's pastoral crozier (*Issues of Death*, 345).

62. Bernard, *Christian, See to Thy Conscience*, 29, italics in original; see 22–30. Bernard makes this assertion in the context of a discussion in which forgetting is the reason that some do not reform even after seeing themselves in the mirror of conscience.

63. Perkins, *Discourse of Conscience*, 7.

64. On the theatre as a site for exploring the nature and operations of conscience, see Kevin Sharpe, *Remapping Early Modern England: The Culture of Seventeenth-Century Politics* (Cambridge: Cambridge University Press, 2000), 153–154.

65. Mary Beth Rose describes the transition of the Duchess from one who acts in the service of her desires and of the future to one who has only a passive role as exemplum: "At the end of the play, Webster resolves the conflict [between future and past] by discarding the future and reinscribing the Duchess in the dualistic discourse that idealizes (or degrades) women, thus placing her above and beyond the action, in a position that she, pursuing the future, had specifically resisted and that is unambiguously associated in the play with death and the disappearing past. As Bosola seeks to avenge her murder and

the Cardinal and Ferdinand die, leaving 'no more fame behind 'em than should one / Fall in a frost, and leave his print in snow,' the associations of the past with pathology and corruption also recede, while the dead Duchess's elegiac role assumes greater prominence" (*Expense of Spirit*, 171). As David Bergeron puts it, by the fourth act, "The one who valued life so highly has begun to resemble a ruined monument" ("Wax Figures," 337).

66. I should point out that it is not made entirely clear who "these wretched eminent things" are, just as the Duchess is not explicitly alluded to in Delio's reference as "integrity of life." Nevertheless, there is internal evidence for linking the Duchess to integrity of life and fame. Bosola construes his projected oblivion as a dead wall or grave that "yields no echo" (5. 5. 97), thus making the echo a figure for fame, and it is an echo that emanates from the Duchess's grave in 5. 3.

67. In this light, it is worth noting that the "child's nativity" generated for Antonio has it that their son will die young and in a violent fashion (2. 3. 55–63).

68. See the discussion of Sallust in the previous chapter; also worth considering is Dante's Virgil, who states that "resting upon soft down, or underneath / The blanket's cloth, is not how fame is won" (*The Inferno of Dante*, trans. Robert Pinsky [New York: Farrar, Straus and Giroux, Inc., 1994], Canto XXIV, 48–49). See also Hamlet's discussion of his "let[ting] all sleep" while Fortinbras pursues "trick[s] of fame" (4.4.59–61); Samuel Daniel's "Ulysses and the Siren" (1605), *The Norton Anthology of Poetry*, 3rd shorter edition, ed. Alexander W. Allison, *et al.* (New York: Norton and Co., 1983), 84–85.

## 6    CODA: "WROUGHT WITH THINGS FORGOTTEN"

1. Paul Ricoeur, "Imagination, Testimony and Trust: A Dialogue with Paul Ricoeur," *Questioning Ethics: Contemporary Debates in Philosophy*, ed. Richard Kearney and Mark Dooley (London: Routledge, 1998): 12–17, esp. 14.

2. William Shakespeare, *Macbeth*, ed. Kenneth Muir (1951; London: Routledge, 1988), 1. 3. 140–142. Henceforth cited in the text.

3. Clothes are "the material establishers of identity itself"; "they are bearers of identity, ritual, and social memory" (Ann Rosalind Jones and Peter Stallybrass, *Renaissance Clothing and the Materials of Memory* [Cambridge: Cambridge University Press, 2000], 4, 5). This is true in a heightened sense in the case of Macbeth, given that the robes bear the memory of "The multiplying villainies of nature" that "swarm[ed] upon" the previous Thane of Cawdor (1. 2. 11–12).

4. Donna Cohen, *et al.*, *The Loss of Self: A Family Resource for the Care of Alzheimer's Disease and Related Disorders*, rev. edn. (New York: W.W. Norton & Co., 2002).

5. I am indebted to David Hawkes for this suggestion.

6. Andrew Gurr, *The Shakespearean Stage 1574–1642*, 3rd edn. (Cambridge: Cambridge University Press, 1992), esp. 99–100. Personation is "a relatively

new art of individual characterisation . . . distinct from the orator's display of passions or the academic actor's portrayal of . . . character-types" (99).

7. Friedrich Nietzsche, "On the Uses and Disadvantages of History for Life," *Untimely Meditations*, ed. Daniel Breazeale, trans. R. J. Hollingdale (Cambridge: Cambridge University Press, 1997): 59–123, esp. 60.

8. This analysis overlaps with the discussion of becoming and forgetting in Gilles Deleuze and Felix Guattari, *A Thousand Plateaus*, trans. Brian Massumi (Minneapolis: University of Minnesota Press, 1987), esp. 232–309.

# Index

*Note:* Works subjected to detailed analysis or frequent mention appear at their own main headings; works mentioned only in passing appear as subheadings under the authors' names (where these are known).

*Cambridge Studies in Renaissance Literature and Culture*

*General Editor*
STEPHEN ORGEL
Jackson Eli Reynolds Professor of Humanities, Stanford University